DATE DUE

MAY 2 1 2015

MAY 2 1 2015

PRINTED IN U.S.A.

When Race and Policy Collide is both timely and relevant in terms of national discussions on immigration, particularly given the intricacies of understanding U. S. Supreme Court and other court decisions and the implications for federal, state, and local laws and policies. Brown and Rodriguez explore important topics related to education, language usage, housing, and voting rights, critical areas for protecting immigrant and non-immigrant rights alike, especially for Latina/os in the United States.

Stacey K. Sowards, PhD
Chair, Department of Communication,
The University of Texas at El Paso

When Race
and Policy Collide

When Race and Policy Collide

Contemporary Immigration Debates

Donathan Brown and Amardo Rodriguez

 PRAEGER

AN IMPRINT OF ABC-CLIO, LLC
Santa Barbara, California • Denver, Colorado • Oxford, England

Library of Congress Cataloging-in-Publication Data

Brown, Donathan.
    When race and policy collide : contemporary immigration debates / Donathon Brown and Amardo Rodriguez.
        pages   cm.
    ISBN 978-1-4408-3124-9 (hardback) — ISBN 978-1-4408-3125-6 (ebook)
1. United States—Emigration and immigration—Social aspects. 2. United States—Emigration and immigration—Government policy. 3. United States—Race relations. 4. Immigrants—Government policy—United States. 5. Immigrants—United States—Social conditions. 6. Emigration and immigration law—United States. I. Rodriguez, Amardo. II. Title.
    JV6475.B86 2014
    325.73—dc23   2013042816

ISBN: 978-1-4408-3124-9
EISBN: 978-1-4408-3125-6

18 17 16 15 14   1 2 3 4 5

This book is also available on the World Wide Web as an eBook.
Visit www.abc-clio.com for details.

Praeger
An Imprint of ABC-CLIO, LLC

ABC-CLIO, LLC
130 Cremona Drive, P.O. Box 1911
Santa Barbara, California 93116-1911

This book is printed on acid-free paper ∞
Manufactured in the United States of America

Contents

Introduction:
The Continual Problems
with Race and Public Policy

Race, along with the discursive policy struggles and grievances inherent within this area of politics, is perhaps one of the most controversial and multifaceted social issues in the United States.[1] A look across American political development throughout history informs us of the various transformations of countervailing forces that over time came to include Indian removal,[2] antimiscegenation statutes,[3] nineteenth-century "scientific racism,"[4] and Jim Crow,[5] to unfortunately name only a few.[6] Race and public policy together are an economic issue,[7] inasmuch as they comprise sociological,[8] psychological,[9] political,[10] and cultural issues.[11] For instance, are the descendants of African slaves owed economic redress for the severe exploitation their ancestors suffered, or have African Americans already received past compensation through social policies like welfare, as David Horowitz contends?[12] Questions like this only articulate a small segment of the ongoing debates involving racial controversies seeking political legal remedies.

Race and public policy continue to be controversial inasmuch as no golden arrow exists leading us toward the best course of action. The relationship between race and public policy continues to undergo various shifts, largely influenced by multiple value hierarchies and the perceptions of reality held by lawmakers. Moreover, that relationship is inherently rhetorical because of the very nature of policymaking. For example, if an area of concern is to be addressed through traditional bureaucratic channels, Eugene Bardach contends that there are generally five steps associated with generating and assessing policy solutions, all of which are innately rhetorical. According to Bardach, these steps include: 1) defining the problem; 2) establishing the criteria to evaluate alternatives; 3) generating policy alternatives; 4) evaluating and selecting problems, that is, evaluating problems according to each evaluation criterion; and 5) evaluating adopted policy by assessing effectiveness in light of changing social, political, cultural, and economic conditions.[13] Again, at each step of the process, policy formation and evaluation inevitably become rhetorically framed to better suit each policymaker's orientation. Within the confines of public policy, race not only matters, but it duly plays a pivotal role within American political development regarding who gets what, when, why, and how.

As early as America's "founding," tensions pertaining to race and equal access to resources and representation have been at the forefront of much debate and protest. The "crucible of race," as best described by Joel Williamson,[14] illuminates the many ways in which race permeates the legal and political process/structure, with recurring disparaging results for certain sectors of society. Particularly during times of war, when there are rumors of immigration reform, or when national demographics shift, we see questions of authenticity and belonging surface around defining and articulating national identity. Questions of who is and is not "American" become entrenched talking points, occupying various dimensions within the policy process. Whether these debates and their outcomes are sparked in defense of "national unity"[15] or otherwise, how "American" national identity is defined and debated continues to be anything but neutral.

Historically, race and nationality in relationship to immigration have undergone many controversial policy shifts. The political and legal formation of American immigration policy is filled with questionable actions and executions. Among these manifestations were the Chinese Exclusion Act of 1882, the Immigration Restriction Act of 1921 (known also as the Emergency Quota Act of 1921), and the Immigration Act of 1924. The Chinese Exclusion Act served as a model for later political use by limiting or prohibiting certain demographics from entering the United States. Anti-Chinese sentiment, like that witnessed by the 1876 testimony of H.N. Clement before the California State Senate Committee, provides many such examples. Through Clement's eyes, Chinese immigration was something to be feared; accordingly, he argued, "The Chinese are upon us. How can we get rid of them? The Chinese are coming. How can we stop them?"[16] Such apocalyptic renderings of Chinese immigration only grew stronger with time.

Signed into law by President Chester A. Arthur, the Chinese Exclusion Act created a ten-year moratorium on Chinese labor immigration, making it the first federal law to forbid the entry of an ethnic group on the premise that it endangered the good order of certain localities. The Chinese Exclusion Act was the first act of Congress to prohibit the entry of immigrants based on both race and class, as the law barred Chinese laborers from naturalized citizenship, yet provided exemptions for diplomats, students, teachers, travelers/tourists, and merchants. Congress, in most famously declaring, "The Chinese are peculiar in every aspect" (despite previously enlisting Chinese labor to help construct American railroads), sought to capture a growing movement of disenchantment that surfaced around "cheap" Chinese labor. Perhaps providing a rhetorical parallel to contemporary debates over Latin American immigrants, the Chinese Exclusion Act established and expanded legal boundaries pertaining to race and immigration. It distinguished various classes of people, demarcating them by labels such as "desirable," "undesirable," etc.

As an act of the 47th Congress, the Chinese Exclusion Act affirmed that:

> Whereas, in the opinion of the Government of the United States the coming of Chinese laborers to this country endangers the good order of certain localities within the territory thereof: Therefore, Be it enacted by the Senate and House of Representatives of the United States of America in Congress assembled, That from and after the expiration of ninety days next after the passage of this act, and until the expiration of ten years next after the passage of this act, the coming of Chinese laborers to the United States be, and the same is hereby, suspended; and during such suspension it shall not be lawful for any Chinese laborer to come, or, having so come after the expiration of said ninety days, to remain within the United States.[17]

This act of Congress, notes Erika Lee, "set into motion the government procedures and bureaucratic machinery required to regulate and control both foreigners arriving to and foreigners and citizens residing in the United States."[18] In what was a watershed moment in American immigration history, racial conceptualization became a focal point—efforts to create both racial distinction and peculiarity were founded on the depiction of Chinese immigrants as being in opposition to what defines an "American." Said best by Kitty Calavita, "When Congress passed the first exclusion law in 1882, they did so on the assumption that the Chinese were a distinct race with a biologically determined nature that was reflected in moral behavior, cultural preferences and physiological traits," noting that the race argument was the "single most common thread" found throughout these debates.[19] With race occupying a distinct placeholder within early debates on immigration reform, it should come as no surprise that such language and sentiment continued to guide immigration policy well after the act.

The Emergency Quota Act of 1921 was the next legislative manifestation pertaining to race to occupy Congress after the Chinese Exclusion Act. The Emergency Quota Act chiefly sought to serve one purpose: to "limit the immigration of aliens to the United States." With this sole aim in mind, the Emergency Quota Act of 1921 minced no words in both *how* it sought to accomplish this goal and *who* it sought to target. According to the act:

> The number of aliens of any nationality who may be admitted under the immigration laws to the United States in any fiscal year shall be limited to 3 per centum of the number of foreign born persons of such nationality resident in the United States as determined by the United States census of 1910. This provision shall not apply to the following, and they shall not be counted in reckoning any of the percentage limits provided in this Act: (1) Government officials, their families, attendants, servants, and employees; (2) aliens in continuous transit through the United States; (3) aliens lawfully admitted to the United States who later go in transit from one part of the United States to another through foreign contiguous territory; (4) aliens visiting the United States as tourists or temporarily for business or pleasure; (5) aliens from countries immigration from which is regulated in accordance with treaties or agreements relating solely to immigration; (6) aliens from the so-called Asiatic barred zone, as described in section 3 of the Immigration Act; (7) aliens who have resided continuously for at least one year immediately preceding the time of their admission to the United States in the Dominion of Canada, Newfoundland, the Republic of Cuba, the Republic of Mexico, countries of Central or South America, or adjacent islands; or (8) aliens under the age of eighteen who are children of citizens of the United States.[20]

As seen here, the Emergency Quota Act of 1921 not only applied the same rhetorical momentum of exclusionary and separatist sentiment as the Chinese Exclusion Act, but it further advanced United States sentiment toward articulating "desirable" and "undesirable" peoples. While it did not restrict an entire group of people from entering the United States based on claims of cultural peculiarity, neither did the Emergency Quota Act stray far from such sentiment. Congress capped the number of immigrants coming to the United States based off 3 percent of the number of their respective nationalities residing in the United States, as determined by the 1910 census. This act too represented a critical moment in American immigration policy, as it was the first federal policy to establish both numerical limits on immigration from Europe and the use of a quota system to enforce those limits.

The Emergency Quota Act successfully executed its purpose inasmuch as the law's quota system was concerned. Because the act restricted the number of immigrants admitted from any country annually, it significantly decreased the number of new immigrants admitted from 805,228 in 1920 to 309,556 in 1921–22.[21] With anti-immigrant sentiment on the continual rise—coupled with the growth of the Ku Klux Klan—political pressures caused Congress to revisit immigration reform within just three years, resulting in the Immigration Act of 1924. This measure reduced the annual percentage of immigrants who could be admitted from any country to 2 percent of the number of people from that country who were already living in the United States in 1890, down from the previous 3 percent cap. In effect, these laws largely excluded people of Asian lineage from becoming naturalized citizens. Persistent throughout the 1900s was the presence of a "race-based natavism, which favored the 'Nordics' of northern and western Europe over the 'undesireable races' of eastern and southern Europe," according to Mae Ngai.[22] Ngai argues that, "At one level, the new immigration law differentiated Europeans according to nationality and ranked them in hierarchy of desirability," affecting both who and how many immigrants could become "Americans."[23]

What remained fairly peculiar about early revisions to immigration law in America was the insistence on containing and controlling the "foreign stock" by means of quotas. Similar to what Rodney Hero refers to as "ascriptive hierarchy," early movements on the immigration front ironically mirrored the age-old Great Chain of Being.[24] The Great Chain of Being denotes hierarchy, representing all degrees of perfection from the highest and fullest to the lowest and least: God, angelic beings, humanity, animals, plants, and minerals. Similarly, in immigration policy, a distinct order—here, a racial one—exists. Charles Linnaeus, also known as the "father of taxonomy," provided this linkage.[25] His 1735 book, *In General System of Nature*, provided an outline that defended the racial articulation of societal positioning, linking those of non-European background with lower forms of life. Perhaps most frequently used by eighteenth- and nineteenth-century "racial scientists" and slavery sympathizers, Linnaeus's system divided society into four main categories.[26] In his defense of a hierarchical society, race mattered. For instance, when discussing Native Americans (*Americanus*), Linnaeus referred to them as "stubborn" and "prone to anger"; African Americans (*Africanus*) were "inattentive, and ruled by impulse," therefore occupying the lower rungs of society. On the other hand, those of European background (*Europeaus*) were dubbed "clever" and "governed by laws." From Linnaeus's early configuration, the relationship between race and hierarchy became forged in many early debates over issues pertaining to race and public policy, especially immigration policy.

Today, as in the early 1900s, shifting racial and ethnic demographics have become reinserted as an area of policy concern for some lawmakers. Since a 2003 report by the U.S. Census Bureau indicating that Latinos have overtaken African Americans to become the nation's largest and fastest growing "minority" group, much conversation has taken place. Concerns over the supposed perils that a new Latino majority would inflict upon the nation led to scores of legislative attempts at all levels of government, which in turn resulted in highly questionable political movements aimed at this growing population. The momentum surrounding these initiatives began to invite much inquiry over the absorption of Latinos, regardless of legal status, into the "American mainstream." Recently, campaigns galvanized by "securing our borders" continue to gain traction at the state level, where Republican office holders and office seekers insist that Latin American immigrants who refuse to assimilate by means of language and cultural values and beliefs stifle efforts toward national unity and border security.

A cursory glance across the United States highlights not only how much past immigration reform efforts have contributed to the measures we encounter today, but also just how widespread these calls for reform have become. House Bill 1023, signed into law in 2006 by Colorado Republican Governor Bill Owens, denies most nonemergency state benefits to undocumented immigrants 18 years of age and older, and requires people to prove legal residency in Colorado when applying for benefits or renewing their eligibility. In 2007, Missouri Senate Bill 348 made it illegal to employ "unauthorized aliens" and mandated that every employer in the state must participate in a federal program to verify an employee's work authorization status. It also barred "illegal aliens" from attending all public universities in the state or receiving any type of public assistance or benefit. Furthermore, the act authorized cities, villages, and towns to enact ordinances prohibiting the employment of unauthorized aliens or unlawful workers and denying business licenses to employers who employ unlawful workers. Mississippi Senate Bill 2179 (2010) allows law enforcement officers to inquire about a person's status during the course of enforcing other laws, like a traffic infraction. The law made it a state crime to be caught without immigration papers and allowed law enforcement to arrest, "without warrant," a person "reasonably believed" to be in the country undocumented. Perhaps more publicized in 2010 was Arizona's Senate Bill 1070, which made it a misdemeanor for an undocumented immigrant to be in Arizona without carrying required documents; allowed state law enforcement officers to determine an individual's immigration status during a "lawful stop, detention or arrest" when there is "reasonable suspicion" that the individual is an "illegal" immigrant; prohibited state or local officials or agencies from restricting enforcement of federal immigration laws; and made it a crime to shelter, hire, or transport "illegal" immigrants.

The 2011 passage of laws in South Carolina, Utah, Indiana, Georgia, and Alabama pale in comparison to the overall amount of immigration reform legislation introduced since the first quarter of 2011. During the first quarter of 2011, 1,538 bills were introduced; Montana, Nevada, North Dakota, Texas, and North Carolina accounted for 256 of these bills.[27] During the first quarter of 2012, according to the National Conference of State Legislatures, 865 bills and resolutions relating to immigrants and refugees were introduced in 45 state legislatures and the District of Columbia. Overall, the most frequently recurring areas of targeted legislation during the first quarter of 2012 included law enforcement, employment, and public benefits. Many conservative pundits, like Samuel Huntington,[28] Tom Tancredo,[29] and Patrick Buchanan,[30] believe that a growing Latino population will usher in a "clash of civilizations" unless drastic political measures are undertaken. The growing fear that a divided United States of America is forthcoming, or already upon us, has led to many conversations and debates over legislation aimed at strengthening the enforcement of immigration laws and preserving our "American" way of life. Cultural and political perceptions linked to the apocalyptic "brown tide"[31] rising over our southern border are best revealed by contemporary attempts at political and legal immigration reform. This discursive policy arena belies matters pertaining to the completion of a border fence along the United States and Mexico, and extends into various aspects of our everyday lives.

The interplay between law enforcement, state and local lawmakers, and those targeted by immigration reform continues to illustrate the discursive tensions surrounding these policy efforts. *Arizona v. United States*, the 2012 Supreme Court case following the passage of Arizona's Senate Bill 1070, highlights just how intense these legal challenges can be. At the heart of the legal challenge imposed by the Obama administration were four key provisions. To illustrate the Obama administration's perceived overstep of Arizona's constitutional allowance, the Department of Justice lawsuit targeted Sections 3, 5(c), 6, and 2(b). Section 3 made failure to comply with federal alien registration requirements a state misdemeanor; §5(c) made it a misdemeanor for an unauthorized alien to seek or engage in work in the state; §6 authorized state and local officers to arrest without a warrant a person "the officer has probable cause to believe . . . has committed any public offense that makes the person removable from the United States"; and §2(b) required officers conducting a stop, detention, or arrest to make efforts, in some circumstances, to verify the person's immigration status with the federal government.

For the first three sections listed, Justice Anthony Kennedy, writing on behalf of the Court's majority, provided clear reasoning for the removal of these provisions. With respect to §6, Justice Kennedy wrote:

Section 6 attempts to provide state officers with even greater arrest authority, which they could exercise with no instruction from the Federal Government. This is not the system Congress created. Federal law specifies limited circumstances in which state officers may perform an immigration officer's functions. This includes instances where the Attorney General has granted that authority in a formal agreement with a state or local government. See, *e.g.,* §1357(g)(1). Although federal law permits state officers to "cooperate with the Attorney General in the identification, apprehension, detention, or removal of aliens not lawfully present in the United States," §1357(g)(10)(B), this does not encompass the unilateral decision to detain authorized by §6.[32]

In condemning the state's effort to expand arrest authority, Justice Kennedy minced no words in striking down this provision. The conflict that arose here stemmed from tension between local and federal authority. Kennedy argued:

> By authorizing state and local officers to make warrantless arrests of certain aliens suspected of being removable, §6 too creates an obstacle to federal law. . . . The federal scheme instructs when it is appropriate to arrest an alien during the removal process. The Attorney General in some circumstances will issue a warrant for trained federal immigration officers to execute. If no federal warrant has been issued, these officers have more limited authority.[33]

As Kennedy continued his series of arguments against Sections 3 and 5(c), his rationale focused on how Section 3 stands "as an obstacle to the federal regulatory system" and Section 5 "intrudes on the field of alien registration, a field in which Congress has left no room for States to regulate." As initially suspected by some, and later confirmed by the Supreme Court, much of the Arizona law overstepped its legal bounds by attempting to perform tasks only the federal government is authorized to perform.

When shifting the Court's attention to perhaps its most controversial provision, §2(b), Justice Kennedy's rationale took a rather peculiar turn. Dissenters criticizing §2(b) likened the expanded and unharnessed authority of local law enforcement to a license to racially profile.[34] To make clear, §2(b) allows:

> For any lawful contact made by a law enforcement official or a law enforcement agency of this state or a law enforcement official or a law enforcement agency of a county, city, town or other political subdivision of this state where reasonable suspicion exists that the person is an alien who is unlawfully present in the United States, a reasonable attempt shall be made, when practicable, to determine the immigration status of the person, except if the determination may hinder or obstruct an investigation. Any person who is arrested shall have the person's immigration status determined before the person is released. The person's immigration status shall be verified with the federal government pursuant to 8 United States Code Section 1373(c). A law enforcement official or agency . . . may not

solely consider race, color, or national origin in implementing the requirements of this subsection except to the extent permitted by the United States or Arizona Constitution.[35]

Of the many problems inherent in both the language and implementation of this law, the first begins with the authority that "reasonable suspicion" grants to local law enforcement who believe a "person is an alien who is unlawfully present in the United States." Early protests and demonstrations of this provision produced the popular t-shirt reading, "Do I look illegal?" Much of the same sentiment continues to linger. As mentioned above, many questions still exist over how officers would establish reasonable suspicion that a person is or is not in the country legally. While Senate Bill 1070 affirms that local law enforcement officers "may not solely consider race, color, or national origin," in its implementation, this caveat offers nothing more than a mirage. The bill's wording alone warrants much suspicion, inviting as it does questions regarding the specificities of its implementation and execution.

Again, when Kennedy began his initial affirmation of §2(b), his failure to realize or grapple with exactly *how* officers would validate reasonable suspicion that a person's presence in the United States is unlawful invited concern. Let's say a person is stopped for jaywalking in Tucson, or any other city or town within the state, and is unable to produce identification. At what point does an officer satisfy the "reasonable suspicion" burden of proof, allowing the officer to make a "reasonable attempt to verify [the jaywalker's] immigration status with ICE"? While it is true that the amended law states that officers and agencies cannot "solely consider race, color, or national origin," race and national origin *can* be two of many variables consulted when establishing "reasonable suspicion." With such elasticity and ambiguity, it is not without merit to infer that a person's accent, along with his or her race, could satisfy "reasonable suspicion" if that person were stopped for a nonimmigration issue and had no identification documents on hand. Oddly enough, this high degree of ambiguity within the interpretation of §2(b), especially as it pertains to matters of civil rights, received little attention from Kennedy.

Because the Latino population is the United States' fastest growing demographic group, possessing the ability to alter the political landscape by shifting many Republican-controlled congressional districts and states toward Democratic leadership, immigration reform has many far-reaching consequences. While many polls show that most office holders, office seekers, and constituents believe we have a "broken" system, there is a sharp divide when it comes to specific recommendations for fixing it. A Gallup poll released in February 2013 indicates that at least two-thirds of Americans favor five specific measures designed to address immigration issues, ranging from the 68 percent who would vote for increased government spending on security measures and enforcement at U.S. borders, to the 85 percent who would vote for a requirement that employers verify the immigration status of all new hires. More than seven in ten would vote for a pathway to citizenship for undocumented immigrants now living in this country.[36] Following the bombing of the Boston Marathon on April 15, 2013, a poll released by the *Washington Times* indicated that 75 percent of those polled believed—given what happened in Boston—that the immigration system "needs to be strengthened before we can move forward to immigration reform." Another 15 percent said there was no need to wait, and 10 percent were unsure or refused to answer.

The sentiment over immigration reform continues to waver slightly, but there is no wavering about whether or not our immigration system is in disarray. Congressional Republicans favor solutions that focus on strengthening the 1,969-mile U.S.-Mexico border, but they wish to do so without a pathway to citizenship for those who entered the United States undocumented or who have overstayed their visas. On the other hand, congressional Democrats would like to revamp the visa program to allow more high- and low-skilled workers into the country while providing a 13-year path to citizenship. Those who have entered the country undocumented would pay fines and back taxes.

Given our current state of political affairs, which came into existence during many years of congressional inaction, state and local governments have taken it upon themselves to craft their own reform policies, creating a rippling effect. Because of a lack of congressional leadership, growing political movements aimed at "taking our country back," and allegations of immigrants "taking our jobs" and draining our dwindling resources, the current political atmosphere lends itself to hasty action, often at the expense of deliberation or constituency involvement. As a result, we have become consumed by controversies that pit race against public policy, local against federal authority, and civil liberties against homeland security. Some assert that the United States has evolved into a postracial society, most notably demonstrated by the election of President Barack H. Obama. We reject this argument and seek to illustrate quite the opposite in reference to state-guided immigration policy and debate.

Our Arguments

As racial and ethnic demographics shift in the United States, so do so-called mounting concerns over how best to preserve American traditions, values, and laws. Political efforts to "take our country back," the passage of controversial state-level immigration laws, a lack of congressional coordination over immigration reform, and a weakening economy collectively amount to a perfect storm. Our chief goal in this book is to identify and analyze how political and legal debates over immigration reform in the United States produce policies that maliciously target Latinos, regardless of legal status. These debates continue to rely upon fear and paranoia, rather than facts.

At the core of this book is attention to law and policy, as opposed to mere headlines, as it is policy and the debates it produces that inform the headlines and subsequently introduce quarrels to the greater public. The perceived cultural and political lethality linked with Latin American immigrants, particularly those from Mexico, is the source of much attention and debate. Each chapter is devoted to analyzing the various domains housed under comprehensive immigration reform.

Chapter 1 analyzes the historical pairing of immigration reform with legislative movements pertaining to bilingual education. This chapter studies the historical development of bilingual education, highlighting its initial shortcomings in policy specificity, which allowed for the continuation of old antagonistic tactics into new discriminatory policies—especially for "national origin minorities." Chapter 2 focuses its attention on official language legislation, as 30 states currently have such laws. This chapter discusses recent state and federal movements pertaining to official language policy. One peculiar legal occurrence in particular occurred recently in San Luis, Arizona, when a city council candidate was removed from the ballot for not knowing "enough" English, resulting in the 2012 court case *Escamilla v. Cuello*. Chapter 3 analyzes the rise of local housing ordinances that seek to limit the inflow of immigrants into various townships. We analyze how proponents of these laws rhetorically reconfigure the legal concept of dwelling and housing rights for the purposes of immigration legislation. We also attend to how laws pertaining to renting have subtly begun to arise or alter in the name of immigration reform.

Chapter 4 explores the notion of borders as a rhetorical phenomenon, as "border security" debates appear solely in reference to the southern border (even though only 2 percent of the U.S.-Canada border is "secured," according to the Department of Homeland Security, and convicted terrorists—including those involved in the September 11 tragedy—have entered the United States from Canada). Chapter 5 attends to recent developments surrounding voting rights and immigration. Here, our attention turns to the recent rash of state-orchestrated voter identification laws, along with recent Supreme Court litigation. Chapter 6 provides policy recommendations for achieving comprehensive immigration reform, and the epilogue briefly discusses the state of voting rights following the 2013 Supreme Court case *Shelby County v. Holder.*

As the nation undergoes debates over how best to fix a "broken system," the number of policies introduced and referred to as "immigration reform" continues to expand. The success of this book is predicated on the understanding that immigration reform extends beyond issues pertaining to fencing the southern border, as more and more local governments are passing their own reform measures, and these measures constantly redefine and challenge what some consider to be immigration reform. The argument that bilingual education stunts an immigrant's assimilation process by encouraging "foreign allegiances"; the belief that declaring English as a state's official language (without providing resources for those seeking to improve their English) will magically make immigrants "better" citizens; and the fact that debates over "border security" rarely discuss our most porous border, the one between the United States and Canada, all illustrate how far-reaching these policies have become. Added to this evidence are widespread attempts at requiring proof of residency/citizenship in order to rent a house or apartment, the belief that voter identification laws will prohibit undocumented immigrants from voting, and other laws that substantiate the effects of local reform measures. All illustrate a changing direction in how we discuss and implement immigration reform in America, especially amidst a thriving Latino population. Our conversation starts with the peculiar political pairing of bilingual education and immigration law, as historically, this pairing has continuously resurfaced across the country.

Notes

1. Racial struggles in the United States have been the subject of many
    episodes, far too many to reiterate here. Often guided by the great bea-
    con of "freedom," both proponents and opponents of various racial
    grievances have claimed "freedom" as the basis for their "pursuit of
    happiness" and respective policy preferences. For example, in the
    1857 majority opinion in the *Dred Scott v. Sandford* case, Justice Taney
    argued that the Missouri Compromise was unconstitutional on the
    grounds that it violated the rights and freedom of slaveholding citizens
    as regarded their property: slaves. Freedom, writes Eric Foner, "helps
    bind our culture together and exposes the contradictions between what
    America claims to be and what it actually is." See, Eric Foner, *The
    Story of American Freedom* (New York: W.W. Norton, 1998).

2. See, Richard Drinnon, *Facing West: The Metaphysics of Indian-
    Hating and Empire-Building* (Minneapolis: University of Minnesota
    Press, 1980).

3. In the battle to prevent racial comingling, antimiscegenation statutes
    and court cases that upheld antimiscegenation were plentiful. See,
    Alfred Alvins, "Anti-Miscegenation Laws and the Fourteenth Amend-
    ment: The Original Intent," *Virginia Law Review* 52 no.7 (1966):
    1224–1255. James Kinney, *Amalgamation! Race, Sex and Rhetoric in
    the Nineteenth Century American Novel* (Westport: Greenwood Press,
    1985). Werner Sollors, *Interracialism: Black and White Intermar-
    riage in American History, Literature and Law* (New York: Oxford
    University Press, 2000). Elise Lemire, *Miscegenation: Making Race
    in America* (Philadelphia: University of Pennsylvania Press, 2002).

4. Arguments contending African American inferiority were numer-
    ous and widespread, especially in the nineteenth century. Arguments
    centering on human difference and inequality reached a new apex
    through the field of social science, and perhaps most notably through
    the "field" of "craniometry," or the measuring of human skulls and
    bones to prove innate white supremacy and African American infe-
    riority. For more on this, see, Stephen J. Gould, *The Mismeasure of
    Man* (New York: W.W. Norton & Company, 1981).

5. Jim Crow, or more specifically, the policies enacted and upheld as a
    result of racial and political posturing, can perhaps best be explained

by the following. See, Comer Vann Woodward, *The Strange Career of Jim Crow* (New York: Oxford University Press, 1960). Richard Wormser, *The Rise and Fall of Jim Crow* (New York: Macmillan, 2003). Michael J. Klarman, *From Jim Crow to Civil Rights: The Supreme Court and the Struggle for Racial Equality* (New York: Oxford University Press, 2004). Jane Dailey, *The Age of Jim Crow* (New York: W.W. Norton & Company, 2008).

6. Other examples include civil rights. While works in this area are far too numerous to list here, of particular interest are: Davis Houck and David Dixon, *Rhetoric, Religion and the Civil Rights Movement 1954–1965* (Waco, TX: Baylor University Press, 2006). James A. Aune & Enrique D. Rigsby, eds., *Civil Rights, Rhetoric and the American Presidency* (College Station: Texas A&M University Press, 2005). Garth Pauley, *The Modern Presidency and Civil Rights: Rhetoric on Race from Roosevelt to Nixon* (College Station: Texas A&M University Press, 2001).

7. See, Antoine Joseph, *The Dynamics Of Racial Progress: Economic Inequality and Race Relations Since Reconstruction* (New York: M.E. Sharpe, 2005).

8. See, Joe R. Feagin, Karyn D. McKinney, *The Many Costs of Racism* (Lanham, MD: Rowman & Littlefield, 2005).

9. See, Graham Richards, *Race, Racism and Psychology: Towards a Reflexive History* (New York: Routledge, 2004).

10. See, Desmond S. King, Rogers M. Smith, *Still a House Divided: Race and Politics in Obama's America* (Princeton, NJ: Princeton University Press, 2011).

11. See, Joe R. Feagin, *Racist America: Roots, Current Realities, and Future Reparations* (New York: Routledge, 2001).

12. The debate over reparations for descendants of slaves—including the controversy surrounding the Senate's "official" apology for slavery in 2009—has drawn much attention to and debate on the state of race relations in America. See the official apology: U.S. Congress, Senate, "A Concurrent Resolution Apologizing For the Enslavement and Racial Segregation of African Americans," S. Con. Res. 26. 111th Congress, 1st Session (June 18, 2009). On the reparations debate, see, Walter Block, "On Reparations to Blacks for Slavery," *Human Rights*

Review 3, no. 4 (2002): 53–73. Jacqueline Bacon, "Reading the Reparations Debate," *Quarterly Journal of Speech* 89:3 (2003): 171–195. Charles Ogletree Jr., "Repairing the Past: New Efforts in the Reparations Debate in America," *Harvard Civil Rights-Civil Liberties Law Review* 38 (2003): 279–320. Charles P. Henry, "The Politics of Racial Reparations," *Journal of Black Studies* 34, no. 2 (2003): 131–152.

13. See, Eugene Bardach, *A Practical Guide for Policy Analysis* (Washington, D.C.: CQ Press, 2009).

14. See, Joel Williamson, *The Crucible of Race: Black-White Relations in the American South Since Emancipation* (New York: Oxford University Press, 1984).

15. See, Donathan L. Brown, "In Defense of Unity & English-Only: On the Early Political Battles to 'Unite' the Nation," *Communication Law Review* 11, no. 1: 15–28.

16. Erika Lee, "The Chinese Exclusion Example: Race, Immigration, and American Gatekeeping, 1882–1924," *Journal of American Ethnic History*, p. 37.

17. Chinese Exclusion Act, 1882.

18. Lee, "The Chinese Exclusion Example: Race, Immigration, and American Gatekeeping, 1882–1924," 37.

19. Kitty Calavita, "The Paradoxes of Race, Class, Identity and 'Passing': Enforcing the Chinese Exclusion Acts, 1882–1910," *Law and Social Inquiry* 25, no. 1 (2000): 11.

20. Emergency Immigration Act of 1921.

21. Robert K. Murray, *The 103rd Ballot: Democrats and the Disaster in Madison Square Garden* (New York: Harper & Row, 1976), 7.

22. Mae Ngai, "The Architecture of Race in American Immigration Law: A Reexamination of the Immigration Act of 1924," *The Journal of American History* 86, no. 1 (1999): 69.

23. Ibid., p. 69–70.

24. See, Rodney Hero, "Multiple Theoretical Traditions in American Politics and Racial Policy Inequality," *Political Research Quarterly* 56, no.4 (2003): 401.

25. Just as a matter of reference, it should be noted that Carl Linnaeus can be referred to with two additional names, Carl von Linné and Carolus Linnaeus.

26. Of the many genres of pro-slavery argumentation, religious rhetoric in its defense was perhaps most dominant. For a more informed reading of this rhetorical transformation, see: Sylvester Johnson, *The Myth of Ham in Nineteenth-Century American Christianity* (New York: Palgrave Macmillan, 2004). David Goldenberg, *The Curse of Ham: Race and Slavery in Early Judaism, Christianity and Islam* (Princeton, NJ: Princeton University Press, 2003). Geo Armstrong, *The Christian Doctrine of Slavery* (Cambridge, MA: C. Scribner, 1857). Albert Barnes, *An Inquiry into the Scriptural Views of Slavery* (Philadelphia: Perkins & Purves, 1855).

27. "2012 Immigration-Related Laws, Bills and Resolutions in the States: Jan. 1–March 31, 2012," National Conference of State Legislatures. Accessed May 29, 2013. http://www.ncsl.org/issues-research /immig/2012-immigration-laws-bills-and-resolutions.aspx

28. Samuel Huntington, *Who Are We? The Challenges to America's National Identity* (New York: Simon & Schuster, 2004).

29. Tom Tancredo, *In Mortal Danger: The Battle for America's Border and Security* (Nashville: WND Books, 2006).

30. Patrick Buchannan, *The Death of the West: How Dying Populations and Immigrant Invasions Imperil Our Country and Civilization* (New York: St. Martin's Griffin, 2002).

31. See, Otto Santa Ana, *Brown Tide Rising: Metaphors of Latinos in Contemporary American Public Discourse* (Austin: University of Texas Press, 2002).

32. *Arizona v. United States, 567 U.S. ___ (2012).*

33. Ibid.

34. Donathan L. Brown, "An Invitation to Profile: Arizona v. United States," *International Journal of Discrimination and the Law* 12, no. 2 (2013): 117–127.

35. *Arizona v. United States, 567 U.S. ___ (2012).*

36. Frank Newport, "Americans Widely Support Immigration Reform Proposals," *Gallup Politics,* February 5, 2013. Accessed June 1, 2013. http://www.gallup.com/poll/160307/americans-widely-support -immigration-reform-proposals.aspx

1

Bilingual Education and Immigration Reform

To better understand the immigration reform movement in America is, partially, to better understand the landmark court cases and policy actions surrounding bilingual education. Bilingual education, says Guadalupe San Miguel Jr., is "one of the most contentious and misunderstood educational programs in the United States because it raises significant questions about national identity, federalism, power, ethnicity, and pedagogy."[1] Following World War II, the rise in America's Spanish-speaking population ushered in debate over the education of students whose primary language was not English. Because the teaching of foreign languages was largely excluded from many schools' curricula, Spanish-speaking students experienced widespread participatory exclusion, resulting in overarching disenfranchisement. (The same was true of Chinese-speaking students.) Students whose native language was not English were expected to achieve mastery of school curricula in a language system that was new and often confusing. Tensions began to mount for a change in pedagogical direction and an extension of civil rights by the sixties and seventies.

There was clear evidence that students whose dominant language was not English experienced second-class treatment. Proof ranging from educational exclusion to reprimand for not speaking English in school to physical altercations was widespread; this was particularly true of students from Spanish- and Chinese-speaking backgrounds. Many educators and activists believed that in order to achieve maximum inclusion and English proficiency, and to counteract a lack of educational opportunities, a bilingual education statute was long overdue. Efforts undertaken throughout the 1960s helped solidify a series of legislative and legal actions aimed at closing the linguistic divide. These policies and court decisions included: *Meyer v. Nebraska* (1923), the Bilingual Education Act of 1968, the 1970 proviso to Title VI of the Civil Rights Act of 1964, *Lau v. Nichols* (1974), Section 1703(f) of the Equal Educational Opportunity Act (1974), the 1988 Bilingual Education Act, and Title III of the 2002 No Child Left Behind Act. These policy outcomes and court decisions, writes David Marshall, "moved American law from a stance of prejudice toward bilingualism in education to one approaching affirmation of ethnicity and support for bilingualism."[2]

Meyer v. Nebraska

Both during and after World War I, a strong and united front of "American-ism" swept the nation. Immigrants, especially those of German descent, were met with great suspicion. Linguist Dennis Baron recounts this anti-German, English-only sentiment:

> Because of changing immigration patterns and a change in the pop-ular attitude toward Germany and its people, the status of German in the United States had shifted from immigrant mother tongue to that of a relatively unimportant supplemental or foreign language. . . . More and more private schools dropped German as the primary lan-guage of instruction and German congregations generally shifted to English for their worship.[3]

This anti-German backlash began to gain momentum, as did extreme fringes of the backlash. Anti-German sentiment was significant enough to cause many to burn books written in German on some fronts. Sauerkraut was renamed "liberty cabbage," much as French fries were renamed "free-dom fries" in some circles following September 11, 2001. The fear and blatant bigotry targeted toward people of German descent contributed to the development of the case before us now.

During the first half of the twentieth century, many states enacted pol-icies restricting when the instruction of "foreign languages"[4] could begin; some prohibited the teaching of foreign languages altogether.[5] Most nota-ble of these was a Nebraska law that made its way to the Supreme Court, marking the first time the Court addressed the topic of bilingual education.

The 1923 case *Meyer v. Nebraska* involved a Nebraska state law that prohibited the teaching in any school—whether private, public, denominational, or parochial—of any language other than English to any child who has not passed the eighth grade. The plaintiff, who taught in a Nebraska parochial school, was charged with unlawfully teaching German to a student who was but 10 years of age and had not passed the eighth grade.

The 1919 Nebraska law before the Court argued that to teach German or any language aside from English infringed upon a student's liberty as guaranteed under the Fourteenth Amendment. Those found guilty of violating this law, according to the state of Nebraska:

> Shall be deemed guilty of a misdemeanor and upon conviction, shall be subject to a fine of not less than twenty-five dollars ($25), nor more than one hundred dollars ($100) or be confined in the county jail for any period not exceeding thirty days for each offense.[6]

Here, in what some would refer to as America's first wave of linguistic hysteria, or nativism, English-only education was heavily regulated. Along with the Fourteenth Amendment, the foundation of the law rested on the state's argument over effect—that is, to allow children, especially children of "foreigners," to be taught a foreign language inculcated them with "foreign" ideas and beliefs, which could run counter to the best interests of America.

Writing on behalf of the court, Justice James McReynolds questioned the application of the Fourteenth Amendment and conversely argued that, as constructed and applied, Meyer's Fourteenth Amendment rights were in fact deprived as a result of the law. Justice McReynolds argued:

> While this Court has not attempted to define with exactness the liberty thus guaranteed, the term has received much consideration and some of the included things have been definitely stated. Without doubt, it denotes not merely freedom from bodily restraint, but also the right of the individual to contact, to engage in any of the common occupations of life, to acquire knowledge, to marry, establish a home and bring up children to worship God according to the dictates of his conscience, and generally to enjoy privileges, essential to the orderly pursuit of happiness by free men. The established doctrine is that this liberty may not be interfered with, under the

guise of protecting the public interest, by legislative action which is arbitrary or without reasonable relation to some purpose within the competency of the State to effect.[7]

While the Court found it unnecessary to "define with exactness" the liberty guaranteed by the Fourteenth Amendment, it did state that, "without doubt," the amendment extended to more than just freedom from bodily restraint. So long as the pursuit of happiness is within the boundaries of the law, all freedoms therein cannot be infringed upon. Furthermore, as McReynolds argued, whether regarding the teaching or learning of "foreign" languages or otherwise, "a desirable end cannot be prompted by prohibited means." Parents had a right to give their children an education, just as Meyer's right to teach was "within the liberty of the amendment."

Writing in the dissent were Justices Oliver Wendell Holmes Jr. and George Sutherland. Of all the justices, it was Holmes who was perhaps *the* weariest of his opinion. He noted:

It is with hesitation and unwillingness that I differ from my brethren with regard to a law like this. . . . I cannot bring my mind to believe that in some circumstances, and circumstances existing it is said in Nebraska, the statute might not be regarded as a responsible or even necessary method of reaching the desired result.[8]

However, despite his candor, Holmes argued, "I think I appreciate the objection to the law but it appears to me to present a question upon which men reasonably might differ and therefore I am unable to say that the Constitution . . . prevents the experiment being tried." The Meyer case appears to have sparked a role reversal amongst Justices Holmes and McReynolds, contrasting the "great civil libertarian" view some have of Holmes and the "arch conservative" notion some have of McReynolds.[9]

The Supreme Court held that Meyer's right to pursue the vocation of foreign-language instruction was protected under the Fourteenth Amendment, ultimately reversing the state's ruling. Not only did the Court declare that the prohibition or undue inhibition of either the use or teaching of a foreign language is unconstitutional, but the *Meyer* decision also marked the first time the Court extended the Fourteenth Amendment to personal liberties. The issue of bilingual education was by no means resolved, however, and Congress went to work in 1968 to craft the Bilingual Education Act.

Bilingual Education Act of 1968

As part of President Lyndon Johnson's "War on Poverty,"[10] Congress passed the Elementary and Secondary Education Act (ESEA) in 1965.[11] Through the dispersal of federal funds, ESEA was originally designed to implement compensatory and remedial programs for underprivileged children. This changed in 1968, however, when ESEA was amended to include bilingual education and renamed the Bilingual Education Act (BEA). It became law in 1968, marking the nation's first commitment to addressing the needs of students with limited English skills. Proponents argued that such legislation, along with bilingual education at large, "would promote academic achievement, thereby enabling Hispanics to participate more fully in the social, economic, and political life of the nation" and extending the rights of "language minority" students in America.[12]

The focus of the BEA, despite its championing, was left rather ambiguous. The BEA, writes Rachel Moran, "never clearly defined bilingual education, in part because of an unresolved ambiguity about the programs' proper objectives."[13] These proper objectives, explains James Crawford, pertained to "whether the act was [meant] to speed the transition to English or to promote bilingualism."[14] If nothing else, what we do have in the bill's actual language are 1) the findings of Congress regarding the state of language minority students; 2) a declaration of policy; and 3) a "uses of funds" clause, which closely resembles a quasi-line-itemed appropriations bill. In order to better illustrate these three areas of importance, we will focus on Sections I, 701, 702(b), 703, and 703(c).

At the core of one of America's most pervasive educational problems is the linguistic divide that disenfranchises many language minority students, so argued the findings of Congress. Section 701 laid out both the findings and purpose of House resolution 13103 as follows:

> This section expresses a congressional finding that an acute education problem in the United States concerns millions of children of limited English-speaking ability due to the fact that they come from environments where the dominant language is other than English, or where a language other than English is commonly used. It finds that little headway has been made on solving this problem and that there is an urgent need for comprehensive and cooperative action

now on the local, State, and Federal levels for new programs to assist these children.[15]

Before the BEA was signed into law on January 2, 1968, there existed no federally orchestrated outreach that concerned itself with closing the achievement gap associated with English-only instruction in schools. As a modest step forward, the BEA approached linguistic diversity with a vastly different tone from that of previous legislative sentiment. English-only proponents believed that learning and teaching "foreign languages," especially to children, would lead to a nation consumed in confusion.

Before President Johnson signed the act, bilingual education was in a state of disarray. Congress found that "little headway has been made on solving" the multiple problems produced when no attention is paid to how to achieve inclusion for all students. Given the dismal state of bilingual affairs that the BEA sought to counteract, Congress deemed it necessary to implement immediate "comprehensive and cooperative action" on the state, local, and federal levels in order to level the playing field for children. Section 701 acknowledged that problems existed; it stated those problems, which in turn brings us to the policies declaration—that is, exactly what this legislation sought to do and respond to.

The goal of Section 701 was not only to identify the bill's purpose, but also to define its cornerstone term, which receives frequent coverage within this discussion: "children of limited English-speaking ability." Because linguistic division was viewed as a significant hurdle against meeting the needs of these students, Section 701 simply followed the findings and purpose section with added specificity and clarity.

Drawing considerable distance from past anxieties and from the earlier *Meyer* case, in which teaching foreign languages to students who have not passed the eighth grade was in violation of state law, the BEA advanced a forward-facing orientation. As the bill made clear:

> Section 701 states the recognition of Congress to the special educational needs of youngsters who face the problem of having limited English-speaking ability and declares it a national policy to provide financial assistance to local educational agencies to develop and carry out new school programs designed to meet the special problems and to preserve and enhance the foreign language backgrounds and culture of these children. For the purpose of this title

'children of limited English-speaking ability' means children of
limited English-speaking ability because they come from environments where the dominant language is other than English or where
a language other than English is commonly used.[16]

Preserving and enhancing the foreign language background of students
through the allocation of federal funds now became a legislative necessity. In this landmark declaration, nonetheless, there existed a considerable degree of ambiguity over exactly how to "develop and carry out new
school programs" designed to meet the needs of these language minority
students.

What is imperative to note in the policies declaration is not only
its about-face from previous practice, but also the lingering vagueness
throughout the BEA's language regarding the preservation of language and
culture. On one hand, proponents could rejoice in the BEA's declaration,
while they simultaneously had reason to question its implementation—
that is, how state and local governing bodies would "develop and carry
out" such programs. However, as the policy was arranged, in keeping with
the traditional nature of House resolutions,[17] a "distribution of funds"
section comes next, explaining how and to whom such funds would be
available. This is followed by the specificities of the act in a discussion of
"operational programs."

Distribution of Funds & Operational Programs

The BEA briefly identifies three areas of consideration it uses as a guiding
light for allocating federal funds. It directs the "U.S. Commissioner of
Education" to consider:

> (1) the relative need of the States and areas within the States for
> programs pursuant to this title; (2) the number of children of limited
> English-speaking ability, aged 3 to 18, inclusive in each State, includ-
> ing migrant children, and (3) the desirability of the development of
> bilingual education programs for many different languages.[18]

Herein lie two points of tension, resulting in part from the statement's
brevity. The question of who gets what and why does get answered, though
in a shallow manner. This is the sole section discussing distribution, yet

there are no numeric qualifiers that establish what defines the "relative needs" of state and local districts. This is to say, statistically, what percentage of language minority students is needed to demonstrate what "relative needs" are? Furthermore, the same question applies to the "number of children of limited English-speaking ability": is there a threshold that must be met in order to receive these funds?

The BEA's distribution of funds clause places a considerable degree of trust and responsibility in the hands of the state. States have the onus of not only applying for funds, but also of developing and creating programs that "preserve and enhance the foreign language backgrounds and culture" of these children. How well the BEA was to succeed largely depended on how states would engage this access and achievement barrier.

Throughout Section 703, we are provided with brief, yet much-needed, explanations of the types of programs authorized as bilingual education. Again, what is of great significance in this language is how bilingual education programs are defined, as this continues to be a point of much contention today. Bilingual education programs, as the bill states, include:

> Instructions in the native language of the student and in English. Bilingual and bicultural education programs to acquaint students with the history and culture associated with each language. Efforts to attract and retain as teachers those persons who have an intimate knowledge and understanding of the children. Establish closer cooperation between the school and the home of the students. Preschool programs. Adult education programs. Comprehensive programs involving counselors, teachers' aides and other educational personnel who can contribute toward solving the problem of the children.[19]

As defined by the goals of the BEA, the success of its implementation is again heavily predicated on state and local efforts and outreach. Given the parameters of the BEA's operational language, its realization inevitably carries the possibility of varying state by state and district by district, all at the discretion of local officials.

Inevitably, the language of the BEA invites variances; these can be measured by gauging the levels of parent-student cooperation that schools foster, by curricula, or by some other means. The bill's language is extremely loose, which could lead to several results. On one hand, because the bill was not written with precision, local officials have the ability to implement very specific programs that best suit the needs of their students, which of course might differ from the needs of students in another district. On the other hand, school districts with strong dissenting views of the policy could take full advantage of that lack of specificity in the language. This is to say, those who oppose the policy can use its ambiguity to do as little as possible to meet the benchmarks of this federal act.

While Section 703 has the most specific discussion of what the grants provided under the BEA may be used for, it is Section 704 that provides the legal details pertaining to what and how federal funds may be used. Section 704(a) provides federal dollars for:

> Planning for and taking other steps leading to the development of programs offering high-quality educational opportunities designed to meet the special education needs of children of limited English-speaking ability in schools serving areas having concentrations of such children, including pilot projects designed to test the effectiveness of plans so developed and the development and dissemination of special instructional materials for use in bilingual education programs.[20]

Here, federal funds are not only available to achieve objectives relating to what Congress deemed to be one of the most acute educational problems in the United States, but locales are encouraged to take "other steps" toward meeting the needs of their language minority students through creative design. The demand to improve America's state of bilingual inclusion has led to much latitude in creation and implementation at the local level—whether with regards to measuring or testing for effectiveness through pilot programs or otherwise—was the focal point of Section 703 and 704.

Jointly, Sections 703 and 704 discuss student achievement and leave much room for improvisation at the state and local levels. However, while Section 704 is rather vague in discussing approach, Section 703 offers substantive suggestions as to what tools schools can or should consider. These aides include "teaching equipment and materials such as innovative computer-based learning systems, audiovisual devices and language laboratories."[21] In the bill's most direct passage on answering the question of "how"—that is, how are schools to achieve the desired outcomes of this bill?—state and local officials are provided with "forward-looking" examples of what federal dollars have been allocated for and what officials should consider when working toward closing the linguistic divide.

The Bilingual Education Act of 1964, later amended and expanded in 1968, was the first step the United States Congress took toward rectifying a lingering problem of inclusion for language minority children. While ambiguous in its language, the BEA was designed for specific crafting and execution by local school boards to better model the policy outcomes toward their particular populations of students. If any shortcomings ensued, in particular regarding discrimination and exclusion, the argument could be made that while the BEA provides a national framework for implementation, ultimately state and local entities are the stewards of their own demise or success, which brings us to our next point.

1970 proviso to Title VI of the Civil Rights Act of 1964

On May 25, 1970, Stanley Pottinger, then director of the Office for Civil Rights, authored a memorandum that was circulated to all school districts across the nation with more than 5 percent national origin minority group students (that is, those students born outside the United States who come from backgrounds where English is not their native tongue). The subject of this memo, "Identification of Discrimination and Denial of Services on the Basis of National Origin," sought to address one weakness prevalent in policy solutions to linguistic inclusion and education: pedagogical exclusion of national origin minority students. In many ways, Pottinger's landmark memo served as a progress report, discussing in clear terms the rather poor state of education for language minority children.

Pottinger's memo minced no words when stating the systemic problems uncovered during the Office for Civil Rights Title VI compliance review. Discrimination and denied opportunity were widespread, noted Pottinger, who saw very little change in access to equal-education opportunities for national origin minority children. He wrote, "Title VI compliance reviews conducted in school districts with large Spanish-surnamed student populations . . . have revealed a number of common practices which have the effect of denying equality of educational opportunity to Spanish-surnamed students."[22] Pottinger used his memo to address these deficiencies by identifying four major areas of concern pertaining to compliance with Title VI of the Civil Rights Act of 1964.[23]

The importance of this landmark memo resides not just in its adding of national origin to the federal discussion of discrimination and Latino politics. Additionally, in the 1974 *Lau v. Nichols* case, which will be discussed next, the Supreme Court ruling quoted two of Pottinger's key areas of concern. The first of Pottinger's four points noted that:

Where inability to speak and understand the English language excludes national origin-minority group children from effective participation in the educational program offered by a school district, the district must take affirmative steps to rectify the language deficiency in order to open its instructional program to these students.[24]

The Office for Civil Rights, in its review of Title VI compliancy, found that while race had been the subject of much federal discussion and some action, national origin had not. As Josué González and Ha Lam note, Pottinger's memo represented an attempt by the federal government "to go beyond race in its efforts to assure quality education for minority children and youth."[25] In context of the grander scheme of equal access, Pottinger called on local school boards to take "affirmative steps" to cease the proliferation of linguistic division that continued to disproportionately marginalize "Spanish surnamed students."

Pottinger's second area of concern involved academic tracking and the rationale employed by some school boards to place students with limited English proficiency in courses for children with mental disabilities. In Pottinger's words:

School districts must not assign national origin-minority group students to classes for the mentally retarded on the basis of criteria which essentially measure or evaluate English language skills; nor may school districts deny national origin-minority group children access to college preparatory courses on a basis directly related to the failure of the school system to inculcate English language skills.[26]

Again, while matters of implementation largely rested at the local level, school boards possessed the ability to effect bilingual inclusion as they saw fit, with regard to their specific locales and students. Apparently, as a result of this localized power, many districts simply placed students on academic tracks to which they did not belong. Instead of providing these students with the needed instruction and materials, many instructors placed these students in remedial courses, possibly seeking to mask their discriminatory practices. Not only were these practices in violation of the Civil Rights Act, but they duly worsened the education problem by seriously restricting the learning and inclusion of these students. The practice was akin to the hierarchical maxim of separate but equal.

This pattern of grouping gained further attention through Pottinger's third observation, also the second and final point cited by the Supreme Court in the *Lau* decision. In Pottinger's words,

> Any ability grouping or tracking system employed by the school system to deal with the special language skill needs of national origin-minority group children must be designed to meet such language skills as soon as possible and must not operate as an educational dead-end or permanent track.[27]

Instead of unloading their language minority students into dead-end situations or academic tracks, school boards must take action to meet the needs of their students and close the divide. As seen here, some school districts simply chose to place students in slower groups, putting them on track for continual failure. It can be argued that this practice continues to exist today.

In efforts to assure that all students are provided for and treated equally, parental involvement is critical. If the current pattern of strategic discrimination is to be broken, school districts must not only meet the needs of their students, but they must also involve their parents. When Anglo parents are notified about school activities and such, the same outreach must be made to the parents of national origin minority group students. School districts must take better steps to notify the parents of these students in a timely manner and in the language they understand. As Pottinger wrote, "Such notice in order to be adequate may have to be provided in a language other than English." Again, if full inclusion is to be achieved, school districts must take "affirmative steps" toward dismantling the discriminatory models they have created.

Pottinger's memo asked that each school district evaluate its current practices in light of the Office for Civil Rights' findings, in order to assess for compliance. Although this landmark document was very brief, it nevertheless attempted to establish corrective actions to be adopted and assessed regarding both parents and students of "national origin minority groups." Compared to the broad strokes the BEA used when discussing equality and inclusion, Pottinger's memo sought to clearly instruct school districts on this matter. Further, as noted above and as we shall now see, Pottinger's memo was instrumental in the 1974 *Lau v. Nichols* case.

Lau v. Nichols

Stemming from allegations that the San Francisco school system failed to provide English instruction to students of Chinese ancestry with limited English proficiency, *Lau v. Nichols* sought equal access for students from all language backgrounds. Of 2,800 students, the San Francisco school system only provided supplemental assistance to 1,000 students. As a result, a class action lawsuit was filed claiming that the San Francisco school system denied 1,800 students a "meaningful opportunity to participate in the public educational program and thus violates section 601 of the Civil Rights Act of 1964 . . . and the implementing regulations of the Department of Health, Education and Welfare," along with the rights guaranteed under the Fourteenth Amendment.[28]

The case had been denied relief by the initial district court and later reaffirmed by the court of appeals; the Supreme Court granted a petition for certiorari given the "public importance of the question presented." Following Stanley Pottinger's memo and the Office for Civil Rights' findings, equality for all students, regardless of background, must be met. According to the 1872 California Education Code (which began to undergo several changes beginning in 1967), specifically Section 71, English is the basic language for all school instruction, although the code does note that instruction may be given bilingually if or when the situation deems such necessary. The charge filed in *Lau v. Nichols* indicated that 1,800 non-English-speaking Chinese students were left without supplemental English instruction, presenting a clear need for bilingual instruction that was never addressed.

The previous courts upheld that there had been no violation of the Equal Protection Clause or Section 601 of the Civil Rights Act of 1964, as each student brings with him or her certain advantages and disadvantages completely separate from the school system. The courts claimed that, given the various cultural, social, and economic factors surrounding each student's experience, there was no way schools could be responsible for counteracting any deficiencies students possess. Responding to this argument and the question before the Supreme Court, Justice William Douglas delivered the opinion of the Court, while Justices Potter Stewart and Harry Blackmun authored concurring opinions.

Writing on behalf of the Court, Justice Douglas's first task was to declare grave dissent from the two lower courts' previous opinions, along with the aforementioned California Education Code. Wrote Justice Douglas, "There is no equality of treatment merely by providing students with the same facilities, textbooks, teachers, and curriculum, for students who do not understand English are effectively foreclosed from any meaningful education."[29] That is to say, students who do not understand English and are not provided with proper instruction cannot possibly participate in the same learning environment as those who fully comprehend English. To impose a standard before a student can grasp the basic skills needed inevitably limits that student's involvement and education.

Because the school district in question received federal dollars, it needed to abide by federal standards, including equality for all. Although Justice Douglas did not address the Equal Protection Clause argument advanced, violation of Section 601 of the Civil Rights Act was clear and present. Section 601 bans discrimination on the basis of race, national origin, or color in any program or activity receiving federal funds. It seemed obvious, Justice Douglas noted, "that the Chinese-speaking minority receive fewer benefits than the English-speaking majority from respondents' school system, which denies them a meaningful opportunity to participate in the educational program—all earmarks of the discrimination banned by regulation."[30] It is here that Justice Douglas cited Stanley Pottinger's 1970 memo in order to argue that districts must take "affirmative steps" to rectify a linguistic deficiency, when there is an inability to speak and understand English.

As the Court's ruling required no in-depth or fully sustained grappling with state or federal law, the decision was easily reached, largely based on the 1964 Civil Rights Act and Pottinger's memo. Quoting Senator Hubert Humphrey during a floor debate on the Civil Rights Act, Justice Douglas brought closure to his opinion, reciting, "Simple justice requires that public funds, to which all taxpayers of all races contribute, not be spent in any fashion which encourages, entrenches, subsidizes, or results in racial discrimination."

Justice Stewart's concurring opinion asked whether or not Section 601 alone would render illegal the expenditure of federal funds for these schools. While grappling with this question, Justice Stewart referred to the regulations in Pottinger's memo, particularly noting its adherence to Title VI of the Civil Rights Act. Stewart acknowledged that sufficient conditions had been met in regards to affirming Justice Douglas's decision. In his words:

> I think the guidelines here fairly meet the test. Moreover, in assessing the purposes of remedial legislation, we have found that departmental regulations and 'consistent administrative construction' are 'entitled to great weight.' . . . The Department has reasonably and consistently interpreted section 601 to require affirmative remedial efforts to give special attention to linguistically deprived children.[31]

Finding no inconsistency in the application of the law, Justice Stewart concurred with the Court on its ruling.

While Justice Stewart's remarks derived from questions of legal application and consistency, Justice Blackmun's concurring opinion sought to make clear one point. In his very brief four-sentence statement, two sentences in particular expressed Justice Blackmun's opinion. As he notes:

> I merely wish to make plain that, when, in another case, we are concerned with a very few youngsters, or with just a single child who speaks only German or Polish or Spanish or any language other than English, I would not regard today's decision, or the separate concurrence, as conclusive upon the issue whether the statute and the guidelines require the funded school district to provide special instruction. For me, numbers are at the heart of this case, and my concurrence is to be understood accordingly.[32]

In the eyes of Justice Blackmun, the large number of excluded students was the driving force that moved the Court to render its decision. Had this case involved far fewer students or perhaps another language, Justice Blackmun was not certain the decision would hold.

Overall, the *Lau* decision remains a landmark case for many reasons, but perhaps the most salient—lingual accommodation—is the one discussed here. The Supreme Court theoretically sought to end all debate over the lingering question as to whether or not the San Francisco school system violated Section 601 of the 1964 CRA. Not only was discrimination found, but the Court noted that it is simply not enough to provide the same education to children who are different if those students do not comprehend the language of instruction.

The *Lau* decision was historic in its approach to remedying the many problems faced by students with poor English-speaking skills. Accordingly, schools are now held accountable for providing students with adequate resources in order to close the linguistic divide. The case elevated the needs of limited English proficient students to the national stage, and in doing so, sought to make equal access to education a right, not a privilege. To codify the *Lau* decision into law, Congress quickly passed the Equal Education Opportunity Act of 1974.

Equal Education Opportunity Act of 1974

The Equal Educational Opportunities Act of 1974 (EEOA), like Title VI of the Civil Rights Act of 1964, had its origins in the civil rights struggles of the 1950s and 1960s. Following the landmark U.S. Supreme Court decision *Lau v. Nichols,* Congress codified *Lau* by passing the EEOA, 20 U.S. C. 1701-1720.

While the EEOA did not exclusively or exhaustively discuss bilingual education, there is one key passage on the subject that sought to follow the Supreme Court's lead from the *Lau* decision.[33] No state, it declared, shall deny equal educational opportunity to an individual on account of his or her race, color, sex, or national origin, through "the failure by an educational agency to take appropriate action to overcome language barriers that impede equal participation by its students in its instructional programs."[34] Based on the findings of the *Lau* decision and Pottinger's 1970 memo, Section 1703(f) of the EEOA sought to rid the lingering problem of the mistreatment of students whose native language is not English.

However, as in previous legislative attempts, there continued to exist a glaring omission of specificity. Neither Title VI of the Civil Rights Act, the *Lau* decision, nor the EEOA defined the meaning of "appropriate action to eliminate language barriers." Again, as prior legislative actions have illustrated, ambiguity generally allows either the continuation of discriminatory actions or no action at all—doing nothing is always a plausible policy "action."

At this point, the EEOA is a historical documentation of the continued efforts made on the federal level to extend equality to those whose native language is not English. Each of these legislative efforts sought to improve upon previously discovered weaknesses in either application or implementation. As each piece of historic legislation was signed into law and as each landmark court case was heard and ruled upon, another layer was added to the progression of bilingualism in America. From *Meyer* to *Lau* and from the BEA to our next point of focus, the Bilingual Education Act of 1988, each instance marks slow progress toward correcting past ambiguities and patterns of discrimination and exclusion.

The Bilingual Education Act of 1988

Following the 1970 findings on discrimination and bilingual education by the Office for Civil Rights, the *Lau* decision, and the 1974 EEOA, the 1988 BEA furthered the cause of bilingualism through the addition of new provisions. The BEA of 1988—part of Public Law 100-297, the Hawkins/Stafford Elementary and Secondary School Improvement Amendments—reauthorized bilingual education through September 1993. On April 19, 1988, the House of Representatives approved the bill (H.R. 1755) by an overwhelming margin of 397 to 1; the Senate followed suit and approved the bill the next day. On April 28, 1988, P.L. 100-297, as it soon became, was signed into law.

The 1988 BEA comprises of six sections: the introductory section and five sections labeled A-E. Our attention will focus on the new provisions for funding, the length of student participation in a program, and preservice activities. Because Part A contains the provisions on federal assistance for bilingual education and the specificities therein, it is the focus of our discussion.

The 1988 BEA authorized Congress to raise the previous ceiling on bilingual allocations to the tune of $200 million for the 1989 fiscal year. This allowed for greater accountability at the state and local levels regarding academic achievement for students enrolled in these programs. In keeping with Stanley Pottinger's memo (in particular, his observation on student placement in remedial courses), the 1988 BEA recognized that "regardless of the method of instruction, programs which serve limited English proficient students have the equally important goals of developing academic achievement and English proficiency."[35] School districts could no longer engage in the strategic placement of non-native English-speaking students in lower-track courses because of lingual deficiencies.

The gap, declared the BEA, must be closed through instruction and application.

Further action to address this dilemma means nothing if it is not accompanied by strategic changes that acknowledge the shortcomings leading to the 1988 BEA's legislative existence. Part A of this act discussed the intersection of federal funding and program establishment, operation, and improvement, the exact area of focus most in need of federal intervention. It gives us a great view into how Congress sought to strengthen bilingual education in America, by learning from past ambiguities and mistakes.

Transitional and Developmental Bilingual Education Programs

Transitional bilingual education programs were designed for limited English proficient (LEP) students in elementary and secondary schools. They were created to offer English instruction and, when necessary, instruction in the student's native language, in efforts to prevent non-English-speaking students from falling behind their peers while they master English. Applicants for federal grants to fund these programs must not only include parents and other representatives of the LEP children to be served, but these parents and representatives must comprise of a majority of such advisory councils. Because each situation is different, the 1988 BEA took steps to place authority in the hands of those who would know the needs of the student best. The 1988 BEA attempted to rectify discriminatory situations in which LEP students were not adequately provided for and parents were not included in the resolving of issues.

The language in the act recognizes past findings of subordination and strategically addresses them through less ambiguous language. In order for LEP students to be both included in mainstream classes and on track to meet standard grade promotion requirements, transitional programs must now provide grade-appropriate instruction along with the opportunity for LEP students to be included with non-LEP students. As subsection 4(b) of the act notes:

> In order to prevent segregation of children on the basis of national origin in programs of transitional bilingual education, and in order to broaden the understanding of children about languages and

cultural heritages other than their own, a program of transitional bilingual education may include the participation of children whose language is English, but in no event shall the percentage of such children exceed 40 percent.[36]

According to this new policy recommendation, largely drawn from the findings articulated in Pottinger's memo, inclusion is paramount. Not only is inclusion the prescribed legal route to counteracting past inequities, but it benefits all parties involved, allowing for a greater cultural understanding in what was once a highly segregated and fragmented environment.

Continuing along this path of correcting past wrongdoings, Subsection 4(d) adds greater specificity for LEP students in transitional bilingual education programs. These students shall, as the bill explains:

> if graded classes are used, be placed, to the extent practicable, in classes with children of approximately the same age and level of educational attainment. If children of significantly varying ages and levels of educational attainment are placed in the same class, the program . . . shall seek to ensure that each child is provided with instruction which is appropriate for such child's level of educational attainment.[37]

As opposed to the previous practice of placing and leaving LEP students in special education courses, this act called for age- and grade-appropriate class placement. What remains unique about the act's language is how it sought to enact inclusion. For example, if students are at different age and educational levels but in the same class, the LEP guidelines mandated that those children be provided with instruction and materials at each child's level. Given the discretion of local implementation via advisory councils, some aspects of this mandate will vary.

Developmental bilingual education programs differ in structure, although they are similar in scope. Developmental differs from transitional inasmuch as developmental provides both English and second-language instruction. A developmental program:

> Shall be designed to help children achieve competences in English and a second language, while mastering subject matter skills. Such instruction shall to the extent necessary, be in all courses or subjects

of study which will allow a child to meet grade-promotion and graduation standards.[38]

To better assist students in not only closing the linguistic divide, but—just as important—achieving subject mastery and graduating, such instruction is provided in all courses. Furthermore, the act mandates that whenever possible, classes in programs of developmental bilingual education must have an equal number of LEP and native English speakers.

While there are some differences between the scopes of transitional and developmental bilingual education programs, their aims are similar. They both intend to provide an inclusive yet carefully tailored education that meets the needs of LEP students, however those needs are defined by each local advisory council. Most notable of these programs are the reactionary language and strategic implementation procedures that have stemmed from previous legislative attempts and their outcomes. The next set of programs, "special alternative" and "family English literacy" programs, seeks to further the educational attainment of LEP students, in slightly different ways from those already discussed.

Special Alternative & Family English Literacy Programs

Unlike transitional and developmental programs, special alternative programs have specially designed curricula that reflect the particular lingual and instructional needs of enrolled students. These programs, according to the BEA:

> Shall provide, with respect to the years of study to which such program is applicable, structured English language instruction and special instructional services which will allow a child to achieve competence in the English language and to meet grade-promotion and graduation standards.[39]

Each classroom will address the needs of students on levels that are most fitting to them. Given the nature of this type of program, close observation and involvement at the local level are crucial if success is to be attained. The design and implementation of these programs are meant, of course, to build toward the ultimate goal of achieving subject mastery and meeting or exceeding graduation requirements.

The family literacy program, as implied by its name, entails a slight departure from the objectives and audience of the special alternative program. In this type of program, instruction is designed to aid both LEP adults and non-enrolled youth to achieve English competency. The program allows for instruction in either English only or in English and the student's native language. The act notes, "Where appropriate, such programs may include instruction on how parents and family members can facilitate the educational achievement" of LEP students.[40] Again, in a grave departure from and corrective to past acts of discrimination and sheer educational disregard, this provision encourages parental involvement.

The family English literacy program, in one sentence, provides services toward one other, unique goal, which none of the other programs offer. As the bill states:

> Such programs of instruction may include instruction designed to enable aliens who are otherwise eligible for temporary resident status under section 245A of the Immigration and Nationality Act to achieve a minimal understanding of ordinary English and a knowledge and understanding of history and government of the United States as required by section 312 of such Act.[41]

This program casts its net wide in efforts to promote English competency not only to students, but also to their immediate families and/or guardians. In order for parents and guardians to qualify for this program, preference is given to LEP students who are already enrolled in any program under the BEA. If the parents or guardians of LEP students are struggling with English competency, why not try to improve the skills of the entire household? The amendment seeks to achieve full inclusion in every sense possible by providing federal funds for the entire family.

Because the 1988 BEA sought to establish forward-looking programs and incorporation, major reforms were added to the aforementioned programs. The germane provisions included: (1) up to 25 percent of Part A funds could be used to fund special alternative instructional programs; (2) transitional bilingual education, special alternative instructional, and developmental programs could engage exclusively in preservice activities during the first 12 months of grants; and (3) there would be a three-year limit on a student's participation in transitional or special alternative programs. (Under special circumstances, the student could continue for up to two more years.) In part, these additions placed pressure on local school boards to produce results by articulating clear timetables for federal funding.

Despite being written with past discrimination and ambiguity in mind, the act has a rather terse nature, which can be interpreted as either positive or negative. As an amendment created to correct past findings, ideally one would hope its language was strategically employed to fill any gaps found to exist.

The 2002 No Child Left Behind Act

Passed by Congress on January 8, 2002, and signed into law by President George W. Bush, Public Law 107-110, commonly referred to as the No Child Left Behind Act (NCLB), represents the latest legislative reform addressing bilingual education. NCLB brought sweeping reform to schools nationwide, particularly through extensive annual testing to assess student and school achievement levels. With its specific demands for testing and its English language requirements, Title III of the act, entitled, "Language Instruction for Limited English Proficient and Immigrant Students," is of particular relevance to this conversation.

Title III: Language Instruction for Limited English Proficient Students

The No Child Left Behind Act stemmed from discussion and debate over the state of bilingual education in America writ large. It is often cited because of the new direction in which it took bilingual education. Unlike previous legislation, NCLB is multifaceted in its approach and specified goals. To begin, though, it is imperative to note the nine purposes the act identifies. The first three purposes simply reiterate language from the 1988 BEA—they outline that NCLB is dedicated to assisting LEP students develop "high quality" language instruction in order to meet the academic standards all children are expected to meet. Here, the goal is geared toward ensuring academic proficiency, with the overall aim to close the academic and lingual divide that once existed, and that arguably still permeates today.

Continuing on through the language of the bill, many of its stated purposes are quite familiar, incorporating past ideas and directions from previously discussed court cases and legislative acts. For example, purpose four seeks to "develop and enhance their [state educational agencies'] capacity to provide high-quality instructional programs designed to prepare limited English proficient children . . . to enter all-English instruction settings."[42] This language differs little from that of legislative precedence, and is just a continuation of previous attempts to transition LEP students into "mainstream" academic environments. Purposes five through seven pertain to transitioning students from special instruction courses into English-only courses, with the involvement and cooperation of local school boards and parents. NCLB indicates that this is not *the* solution, but part of the solution.

Without much close reading, one could be led to believe that the multiple purposes of the act just made it a reauthorization of the Elementary and Secondary Education Act; this could not be further from reality. While the already-mentioned purposes of NCLB advanced nothing new for the legislative state of bilingual education in America, purposes eight and nine did depart drastically from the act's previously assumed trajectory. That is to say, these final two purposes introduced the discussion that continues to draw much attention today: that of accountability.

As advocated by President George W. Bush and Secretary of Education Margaret Spellings, NCLB contained a fair amount of language regarding accountability and measurement of achievement. Purpose eight in Section A notes that part of the aim of the act was to "hold State educational agencies, local educational agencies, and schools accountable for increases in English proficiency and core academic content knowledge of limited English proficient children."[43] While no details are offered explaining how accountability would be measured or according to what standard(s), and while it only adds further lines of questioning to the act, purpose nine brings finality to the purposes clause. As it states, NCLB, in part, seeks "to provide State educational agencies with the flexibility to implement language instruction educational programs, based on scientifically based research . . . that the agencies believe to be the most effective for teaching English."[44] Exactly what qualifies as "scientifically based" educational programs, the act does not say. It ends the purposes clause on that note.

It is not until the end of Part A that we see the term "accountable" introduced, yet in subpart two, considerable space is dedicated to defining what and how "evaluations" will be used and measured. As the act states, at the end of every second fiscal year during which a grant is awarded, an evaluation must occur. It must include the following:

(1) A description of the programs and activities conducted by the entity with funds received under subpart 1 during the two immediately preceding fiscal years;

(2) A description of the progress made by children in learning the English language and meeting challenging State academic content and student academic achievement standards;

(3) The number and percentage of children in the programs and activities attaining English proficiency by the end of each school year, as determined by a valid and a reliable assessment of English proficiency; and

(4) A description of the programs made by children in meeting challenging State academic content and student academic achievement standards for each of the 2 years after such children are no longer receiving services under this part.[45]

In this part of the act, the language becomes much more focused and direct as the document moves toward perhaps its most controversial sections, those on evaluations and accountability. At their core, evaluations mirror academic progress reports for LEP programs and the students instructed in those programs.

After describing what these evaluations must include, NCLB goes into further detail regarding the use of evaluations, their components and measurements—all of which are treated with brief, separate clauses. First to be explained is the use of evaluations, which are intended:

(1) For improvement of programs and activities; (2) to determine the effectiveness of programs and activities in assisting children who are limited English proficient to attain English proficiency (as measured consistent with subsection (d)) and meet challenging State academic content and student academic achievement standards; and (3) in determining whether or not to continue funding for specific programs or activities.[46]

While by itself, this explanation of the "use of evaluations" is rather vague and leaves many questions unanswered, what is unequivocally clear is the final sentence of that clause, regarding the possibility of funding loss. Even with that possibility, questions still remain over (1) what exactly are the internal components of these evaluations; and (2) further insight into accountability measures and procedures. In what remains of this chapter, these areas of inquiry will be discussed inasmuch as the legislative language can provides us answers.

The evaluation components and arguably the surrounding goal of NCLB are guided by an underlying principle that all students, whether LEP or otherwise, must meet the same academic standards. In order to achieve that goal, so goes the language of the act, not only must schools provide information deemed necessary by the "state educational agency" (SEA), but evaluations must also declare how many students:

> (A) Are making progress in attaining English proficiency, including the percentages of children who have achieved English proficiency; (B) have transitioned into classrooms not tailored to limited English proficient children, and have a sufficient level of English proficiency to permit them to achieve in English and transition into classrooms not tailored to limited English proficient children . . . (D) [and] are not receiving waivers for the reading or language arts assessments under section 1111(b)(3)(C).[47]

In what reads like a direct response to the findings that spurred Stanley Pottinger's memo, along with language from the 1988 BEA, this description makes clear that evaluation components are largely concerned with gathering evidence of progress toward both increased English proficiency and the "mainstream" placement of LEP students. In seeking to achieve these benchmarks, and in the use of these evaluations for that purpose, accountability is key.

"Accountability" was one of the more familiar buzzwords associated with NCLB. Under this law, SEAs, through the reporting of evaluations and the establishment of English-language proficiency standards, monitor proficiency gains and content learning, creating statewide achievement objectives that are measurable annually. In the words of the act:

> Each state educational agency receiving a grant under subpart 1 shall hold eligible entities receiving a subgrant under such subpart accountable for meeting the annual measureable achievement objectives under subsection (a), including, making adequate yearly progress for limited English proficient children.[48]

Because measureable progress is demanded, in that all schools need to illustrate continual growth, there are significant consequences for schools that do not meet their state-specific benchmarks. This is discussed under the grand theme of "accountability" in the act.

NCLB provides very specific consequences in the event that a school, for two consecutive years, should fail to illustrate continual growth as measured by that school's state educational agency. First, the SEA will require the development of an improvement plan to ensure that the school meets its objections. Each improvement plan, as the act states, "shall specifically address the factors that prevented the entity from achieving such objectives."[49] Once the improvement plan is submitted, no further action by the state is required. However, should this improvement plan not lead to desirable results, the act outlines permissible actions; these are the source of most of the controversies surrounding NCLB.

The actions deemed proper and fitting by NCLB, following four consecutive years of failure to produce "annual measurable achievement objectives," can best be stated by the act itself. If an SEA determines that an entity has failed to meet its benchmarks, the SEA shall:

(a) Require such entity to modify the entity's curriculum, program, and method of instruction; or (b)(i) make a determination whether the entity shall continue to receive funds related to the entity's failure to meet such objectives; and (ii) require such entity to replace educational personnel relevant to the entity's failure to meet such objectives.[50]

The authority to fire employees, strip funding, and shift curricula if a certain measurable level of attainment is not met, forms the most controversial aspects of the act.[51] Who should be held "accountable" if the numbers do not meet a certain threshold? While NCLB believes and invests heavily in its chosen method for measuring achievement, critics contend that the empirical benchmarks need to be revisited, and that the stripping of funds accomplishes nothing positive for students.

The passage of NCLB represented the latest and most controversial legislative movement in the history of bilingualism in America. While in many ways NCLB served as a reauthorization of the Elementary and Secondary Education Act, this reauthorization came with sweeping reform along the lines of evaluations and accountability. As the act's language illustrates, NCLB articulates *what* must be accomplished, but is rather silent on *how* to accomplish those benchmarks. Critics of NCLB argue that such ambiguity creates an atmosphere of high-stakes testing without adequate preparation.[52]

Conclusion

Reviewing the history of bilingualism in America is of paramount importance if one is to discuss or debate English-only legislation. This chapter was written not only to investigate the diachronic development of landmark policies and court cases regarding bilingual education, but it was also written with the intent to include much of those policies' and cases' original language. Most historical scholarship in this area cites very little of the original language; this chapter was written to counteract that trend, eliminating the heavy use of paraphrasing.

Beginning with the *Meyer* decision and ending with NCLB makes it apparent that bilingualism in America has undergone and continues to undergo various shifts in policy and attitude. The history of bilingual education in America, in some forms and fashions, resembles our next area of focus: state-led efforts to limit the scope of bilingualism through the promotion and passage of English-only laws. A close reading of these efforts will illustrate the deeply rhetorical history surrounding the debate to legislate official language policy, especially in relation to immigration reform.

Notes

1. Guadalupe San Miguel Jr., *Contested Policy: The Rise and Fall of Federal Bilingual Education in the United States, 1960–2001* (Denton: University of North Texas, 2004), 1.

2. David Marshall and Gerda Bikales, *The Question of an Official Language: Language Rights and the English Language Amendment* (Ann Arbor: University of Michigan Press, 1986), 14.

3. Dennis Baron, *The English-Only Question: An Official Language for Americans?* (New Haven, CT: Yale University Press, 1990), 149.

4. When used in this regard, "foreign languages" refers to all languages other than English.

5. See, Carlos Ovanda, "Bilingual Education in the United States: His-
    torical Development and Current Issues," *Bilingual Research Jour-
    nal* 27, no. 1 (2003): 1–24.

6. 107 Neb. 657 (1919).

7. 262 U.S. 390 (1923).

8. 262 U.S. 390 (1923).

9. See, William Ross, "A Judicial Janus: *Meyer v. Nebraska* in Histor-
    ical Perspective," *University of Cincinnati Law Review* 57 (1988):
    1–25.

10. David Zarefsky, *President Johnson's War On Poverty: Rhetoric and
    History* (Tuscaloosa: University of Alabama Press, 2005).

11. United States Congress, *Elementary and Secondary Education
    Amendments of 1967*, Public Law 90-247; 81 Stat. 783 [H.R. 7819],
    90th Congress, 1st Session (January 2, 1968).

12. This statement in favor of the 1968 BEA was given as testimony by
    Rep. Edward Roybal during his 1967 Subcommittee on Education,
    under the larger guise of the House Committee on Education and
    Labor. See, *Bilingual Education Programs: Hearings on H.R. 9840
    and H.R. 10224 Before the General Subcommittee on Education
    of the House Committee on Education and Labor*, 90th Congress,
    1st Session, 144-47 (1967). To read more on the actual hearings
    themselves, see, *Bilingual Education Programs: Hearings Before
    the General Subcommittee on Education 90-1 on H.R. 9840, H.R.
    10224*, June 28, 29 (1967).

13. Rachel Moran, "Bilingual Education as a Status Conflict," *California
    Law Review* 75 (1987): 327.

14. James Crawford, *Bilingual Education: History, Politics, Theory, and
    Practice* (Los Angeles: Bilingual Education Services, Inc., 1995), 40.

15. United States Congress, *Elementary and Secondary Education
    Amendments of 1967*, Public Law 90-247; 81 Stat. 783 [H.R. 7819],
    90th Congress, 1st Session (January 2, 1968), p. 24.

16. Ibid, p. 24.

17. Within congressional protocol, generally those resolutions
    where financial allocation(s) are sought begin in the House of
    Representatives.

18. United States Congress, *Elementary and Secondary Education Amendments of 1967*. Public Law 90-247; 81 Stat. 783 [H.R. 7819], 90th Congress, 1st Session (January 2, 1968), p.25.

19. Ibid., p. 25.

20. Ibid., p. 29.

21. Ibid., p. 29.

22. United States Department of Health, Education, and Welfare, *DHEW Memo Regarding Language Minority Children* (Washington, D.C.: Federal Registry), 35.

23. See, Kenneth J. Meier and Joseph Stewart Jr., *The Politics of Hispanic Education: Un Paso Pa'lante y Dos Pa'Tras* (Albany: State University of New York Press, 1991).

24. United States Department of Health, Education, and Welfare, *DHEW Memo Regarding Language Minority Children* (Washington, D.C.: Federal Registry), 35.

25. Josué M. González and Ha Lam, "The *Lau v. Nichols* Supreme Court Decision," *Latino Education in the U.S.*, ed. Lourdes Diaz Soto (Lanham, MD: Rowman & Littlefield Education, 2007), 285.

26. United States Department of Health, Education, and Welfare, *DHEW Memo Regarding Language Minority Children* (Washington, D.C.: Federal Registry), 35.

27. Ibid.

28. *Lau v. Nichols*, 414 U.S. 563 (1974).

29. Ibid.

30. Ibid.

31. Ibid.

32. Ibid.

33. What should not be forgotten about this act is that many civil rights leaders and groups opposed the EEOA because it contained language that sought to stop busing in order to achieve segregated schools. The EEOA's companion piece of legislation was entitled the "Student Transportation Moratorium Act" and was intended by President Nixon to stop busing and preserve "neighborhood schools." For more on this, see Section 1703(c).

34. Equal Educational Opportunity Act, 20 USC Sec. 1703.

35. United States Congress, *The Hawkins/Stafford Elementary and Secondary School Improvement Amendments.* Public Law 100-297 [H.R. 1755], 96th Congress, 1st Session, April 28, 1988.

36. Ibid.

37. Ibid.

38. Ibid.

39. Ibid.

40. Ibid.

41. Ibid.

42. United States Congress, *English Language Acquisition, Language Enhancement, and Academic Achievement Act.* Public Law 107-110, 107th Congress, 1st Session, January 8, 2002.

43. Ibid.

44. Ibid.

45. Ibid.

46. Ibid.

47. Ibid.

48. Ibid.

49. Ibid.

50. Ibid.

51. See, Amy Reibach, "The Power Behind the Promise: Enforcing No Child Left Behind to Improve Education," *Boston College Law Review* (45) 667–704, 2004.

52. See, Paul Peterson, *No Child Left Behind? The Politics and Practice of Accountability* (Washington, D.C.: Brookings Institute Press, 2003).

2

Official Language Laws Amidst Immigration Reform

The framers of the Constitution took no action to "promote" or "protect" any official language.[1] No evidence exists to suggest the writers believed monolingualism or an official language could serve as society's social glue. The authoring and publication of both public and private documents in multiple languages is as old and "American" as the nation itself. From the Louisiana Constitution, which permitted laws to be published in French,[2] to California and Texas, which permitted laws to be published in Spanish,[3] bilingualism has always occupied a heavy presence in American political development. It was not until 1906 that there existed a requirement for naturalization that included speaking, reading, and writing English. Previously, it was sufficient to pledge allegiance to the Constitution.

As the pattern goes historically, "language laws, sentiments, and policies have been inextricably bound to immigration patterns and laws since colonial times," writes Bill Piatt; "foreigners" and their language have been the objects of great legal and political suspicion.[4] Generally linked to increasing numbers of "foreigners" entering the country, English-only debates oftentimes transform into crusades to keep America America. The political development of the English-only movement can be traced to the 1700s. In a 1753 letter to a friend, Benjamin Franklin famously expressed his fear in the rise of the German language—specifically in Pennsylvania, where he noted the number of street signs in German without English translation.[5] German immigrants, it was believed, would obscure "American" identity and erode national unity through their "refusal" to speak or learn English. In another instance, one of the recommendations of the

31

1868 congressional Indian Peace Commission, which had been chartered to seek peace with the Plains Indian tribes, was to establish English-only schooling for Native Americans.[6] The paranoia that accompanied the fear of a "foreign" takeover gained momentum throughout the 1900s, providing many of the talking points we continue to hear today from official language proponents.

Since the early 1900s, the fear of a "foreign" cultural and linguistic takeover has permeated American political rhetoric. In 1907, President Theodore Roosevelt expressed his thoughts on the matter, declaring, "We have room for but one language in this country, and that is the English language, for we intend to see that the crucible turns our people out as Americans, of American nationality and not as dwellers in a polyglot boarding house."[7] Although President Roosevelt's urging for a national language has yet to result in any sort of official ruling, it still resonates. A series of spirited 2006 congressional debates closely resembled Roosevelt's sentiments over immigration assimilation.

Based on historical precedence, the 2006 debates over immigration reform and the myriad amendments therein should come as no surprise. Like the debates before it, the 2006 congressional episode followed a well-established path. Generally linked to increasing numbers of "foreigners" entering the country, debates over immigration reform and official language policies have often transformed into crusades against the foreign foe. These fears are perhaps best captured and represented by the immigration reform policies lawmakers seek to enact and the debates they produce. In alignment with past policy attempts and debates, 2006 introduced measures aimed at both "securing the border" and mandating English as America's national language. House (House Resolution 4437) and Senate (S. 2611) immigration bills contained similar elements.

The House version of the bill alone produced much strife. The spring of 2006 bore witness to millions of Latinos protesting H.R. 4437 in the streets of cities across the nation. H.R. 4437, the Border Protection, Antiterrorism, and Illegal Immigration Control Act of 2005, was introduced on December 6, 2005, by Wisconsin Republican Congressman James Sensenbrenner. It was cosponsored by 35 House members, of whom 34 were Republicans.[8] The largest clusters of House supporters came from Texas and California, each of which provided six cosponsors. The bill, like previous attempts at immigration reform, contained numerous parts, or "titles," in this case totaling 13 in all. In the bill's initial title, "Securing

United States Borders," Section 101 directs the Secretary of Homeland Security to:

> take all appropriate actions to maintain operational control over the U.S. international land and maritime borders, including: (1) systematic surveillance using unmanned aerial vehicles (UAVs), ground-based sensors, satellites, radar coverage, and cameras; (2) physical infrastructure enhancements to prevent unlawful U.S. entry and facilitate United States Customs and Border Protection border access; (3) hiring and training additional Border Patrol agents; and (4) increasing deployment of United States Customs and Border Protection personnel to border areas with high levels of unlawful entry. Requires the Secretary to annually report to Congress respecting border control progress.[9]

As sponsors of the bill sought to "protect America's borders," much attention was given to the border between Mexico and the United States. Supporters (Republicans) of the bill, consciously or not, favored unprecedented militarized measures that would use largely untested technological advancements. If proponents succeeded in securing the bill's passage, the southern border would quite possibly resemble a combat zone. In efforts to "secure" America's border, war tactics would be employed against the enemy, that is, "illegal aliens."

Titles Two and Ten of the bill were among the most controversial. Sections 203 and 204 of Title Two discussed "combating alien smuggling and illegal entry and presence," unveiling new criminal penalties for illegal entrants. For instance, Section 203:

> makes illegal U.S. presence a crime. Increases prison penalties for first-time improper U.S. entry. Expands: (1) penalties for marriage and immigration-related entrepreneurship fraud; and (2) criminal penalties imposed upon aliens who illegally enter the United States or who are present illegally following convictions of certain crimes.[10]

While no details were offered regarding exactly how much such penalties would be increased, this section nonetheless raised many eyebrows, especially in light of Section 204, which "provides mandatory minimum sentences, with a specified affirmative defense exception, for aliens convicted of reentry after removal." Akin to state and local law enforcement campaigns like the "War on Drugs," H.R. 4437 sought to make a deep impact on how we talk about and enforce matters of undocumented immigration—namely, how we define and discuss Mexican immigration as a policy problem. Sections 1002 through 1004 of Title Ten contained language that would: 1) mandate the construction of at least two layers of reinforced fencing along with additional physical barriers, roads, lighting, cameras, and sensors in five specified zones along the U.S.-Mexico border, and 2) direct the secretary to conduct a study and report to Congress on the necessity and feasibility of constructing a barrier system along the northern U.S. land and maritime borders. Latino protesters' reactions to the bill, as Robert Suro and Gabriel Escobar note, "reverberated among supporters and gave rise to a sentiment among a majority of Latinos that immigrant marches were the beginning of a new Hispanic/Latino social movement that will go on for a long time."[11]

Following in similar fashion, minus the nationwide protests, the Senate's version, dubbed the Comprehensive Immigration Reform Act of 2006, was sponsored by Pennsylvania Republican Senator Arlen Specter, on April 7, 2006.[12] Senator Specter's bill enjoyed the support of six cosponsors: five Republicans and one Democrat, the late Massachusetts Senator Edward Kennedy. The bill contained nearly twice as many provisions as the House version and generally provided more specificity regarding how various programs would function. The Senate's version contained titles regarding "border enforcement," a "border tunnel prevention act," "interior enforcement," measures addressing "unlawful employment of aliens," and a program for "temporary guest workers," to name only a few.

Into the political atmosphere surrounding the Comprehensive Immigration Reform Act of 2006, on May 18 of that year, Oklahoma Republican U.S. Senator Jim Inhofe introduced Senate Amendment 4064, an amendment "to declare English as the national language of the United States and to promote the patriotic integration of prospective U.S. citizens." Inhofe—who represents a state where, in 2006, Latinos comprised 6.9 percent of the population—felt such a federal amendment was needed in order to guide immigrants toward assimilating to the "American" way of life.[13] According to the amendment, that way of life includes speaking English. On the issues, Inhofe represented the values of most fiscal and social conservatives. In 2002, for instance, he voted 'no' on a measure to add sexual orientation to the definition of hate crimes, and during the time of the 2006 debate, Inhofe voted 'yes' on a constitutional ban on same-sex marriage. He received a zero percent approval rating from the Human Rights Campaign and a 7 percent approval rating from the National Association for the Advancement of Colored People (NAACP).

Inhofe's English-only amendment received the support of 11 co-sponsors. Ten were Republicans from the states of West Virginia, Kentucky, Montana, Georgia, Wyoming, Alabama, South Carolina, and Arizona, along with both Republican senators from Tennessee and Oklahoma. Senate proponents took to the floor to urge their colleagues to pass the amendment. First to approach his colleagues was Inhofe himself. In an effort to shape what otherwise read as a purpose clause, Inhofe attempted to defend why such an amendment was needed, especially in light of the larger immigration reform debate. In his words:

> Basically, what it does is it recognizes the practical reality of the role of English as our national language. It states explicitly that English is our national language, providing English a status in law that it has not had before. It clarifies that there is no entitlement to receive Federal documents and services in languages other than English. It declares that any rights of a person and services or materials in languages other than English must be authorized or provided by law. It recognizes the decades of unbroken court opinions that civil rights laws protecting against national origin and discrimination do not create rights to Government services and materials in languages other than English, and establishes enhanced goals of the DHS as redesigned.[14]

For Senator Inhofe, federally declaring English as the national language was long overdue and desperately needed. Far too long had English either been ignored or not recognized as the uniting language that it is. The purpose of the amendment was not only to recognize English as America's language, but, in doing so, to place under scrutiny the rights of "language minorities" to receive governmental services in languages other than English. By citing no specific court cases when speaking of the "decades of unbroken court opinions" the amendment sought to rectify, Inhofe invited many questions from skeptics, which he did not address.

Despite being intended to clarify the role and purpose of his amendment, Inhofe's statements were clouded in ambiguity.

Although he did not acknowledge this, Senator Inhofe's opening comments raised many questions regarding the rights of national origin minorities, specifically as they related back to Title VI of the 1964 Civil Rights Act, Stanley Pottinger's landmark 1970 Title VI compliance memo, and the 1972 *Lau* decision. Alone, his statement that "there is no entitlement to receive Federal documents and services in languages other than English" would lead many to believe that the amendment would require significant changes to how and in what languages federal documents and services would be communicated, potentially harming the reach of the message. As a theoretical example, Inhofe represents a state located between the Rocky and Appalachian mountains, in an area colloquially referred to as "Tornado Alley." If a large-scale tornado, one that ranks as an F-4 on the Fujita scale of tornado intensity, were to strike and the Federal Emergency Management Agency (FEMA) were to be deployed, officials' ability to communicate information regarding disaster assistance in languages other than English would be curbed. That, at least, is what the amendment's language leads us to believe.[15] Without an account of the rights national origin minorities have, the language in Inhofe's amendment affirmed a racial and linguistic order regarding "the role" of English in America. Senator Inhofe's comments must be understood in the context of a larger debate over immigration from Mexico; racial, cultural, and linguistic hierarchical elements all exist within his rationale.

Senator Inhofe acknowledged the skepticism and dissent his amendment received from Senate Democrats and others, and offered a response. Regarding his "remaking" and articulation of the "American" people, Inhofe noted:

I would only say that this is something that is more significant probably to the American people than it is inside this Chamber. I know there is opposition to this. There are some people who don't believe that English should be our national language. If you look at some of the recent polling data, such as the Zogby poll in 2006, it found 84 percent of Americans, including 77 percent of Hispanics, believed that English should be the national language of Government operations. A poll of 91 percent of foreign-born Latino immigrants agreed that learning English is essential to succeeding in accordance with the United States, according to the 2002 Kaiser Family Foundation poll.[16]

Argued in this fashion, Inhofe presented his actions as no different from those of active or interest-based representation guided by the desires of his constituency.[17] Backed by overwhelming empirical data—in his mind—Inhofe depicted his actions as simply responding to the desires of the "American" people. However, his use of the 2002 Kaiser Family Foundation polling data to support his claims was a non sequitur, as his conclusion did not support his premise. To say that English should be recognized as our national language, and to conclude with a claim that 91 percent of foreign-born Latino immigrants agree that learning English is essential to success, did not support Inhofe's or any other English-only statute. If nothing else, the 2002 Kaiser poll he cited indicates that foreign-born Latino immigrants already know and overwhelmingly understand the importance of learning English, making such an amendment largely unnecessary.

Concerned over the nation's shifting demographics, Alabama Republican Senator Jeff Sessions rose in defense of the Inhofe amendment. Senator Sessions, representing a state that in 2006 reported less than a 3 percent Latino population, was focused on "uniting" all "Americans" under one nation, one flag, and, most important, one language. In this spirit, Senator Sessions remarked:

I thank the Senator from Oklahoma for his good work because we are now a Nation of people of different faiths, different skill sets, different backgrounds, different colors of skin, and different nationalities. Where we once were apart, now we have become Americans. The thing that makes this country effective is being able to communicate with one another in a common language. I think that is an ideal of America that is important. I think any Nation, historically, that has divisions based on language, begins to have a lot of complications and problems. So I am pleased that Senator Alexander and Senator Inhofe have worked hard on this, that they have come up with language that also includes more extensive training and learning on behalf of new citizens about what it means to be an American. No one has been more articulate over the years on this than Senator Alexander.[18]

As a "nation of people of different faiths, different skill sets, different backgrounds, different colors of skin, and different nationalities," the time had come to federally legislate "American" principles. If we, as a nation, were to mitigate the conflicts that linguistic heterogeneity brings, our first task would have to be one that establishes something resembling a racial and linguistic order. These hierarchical orders, like racial institutional orders, are "durable alliances of elite political actors, activist groups, and governing institutions united by agreement on racial policy."[19] Out of the fear that our nation was rapidly forgetting "what it means to be an American," proponents, representing the most powerful and prestigious chamber of Congress, justified their actions in efforts to protect "America" from the possible perils a changing national landscape might bring.

Creating one from many is an ambitious task, though from the standpoint of proponents, this could be accomplished through a declaration upholding the vital role English plays in America. Proponents of the measure followed in the tradition of a racial institutional order that oddly mirrored the Great Chain of Being, a conception in which the universe is "composed of an immense . . . number of links ranging in hierarchical order from the meagerest kind of existence . . . to the highest possible kind of creature."[20] Of the three basic components of the Great Chain of Being, one in particular was used frequently throughout the debate. Known as the Principle of Gradation, this linear hierarchical ranking of society, sometimes referred to by polygenists as the "natural order" ordained by God, is essentially an arrangement of beings placed from highest to lowest. To say, as Senator Sessions did, "I think everyone can support that [this] will help unify us as a nation and make sure we are one people, all Americans, adhering to the highest ideals of this great country,"[21] provides "structure and content to American racial identities," as Desmond King and Rogers Smith argue.[22] As a result, Spanish and Latinos, despite legal status, have become politically delegated to the lower rungs of the American racial order.

All too often, legislative solutions written with the intent to "solve" or "protect" the policy preferences of elite political actors have resulted in the formation of sociopolitical and economic barricades constructed to defend against "the other"—that is, societies supposedly threatening menace at that time. Whether these groups are Native Americans, women, African Americans, or otherwise, their perceived threats to "American" stability are articulated and executed through numerous policy barricades. I believe Jennifer Hochschild is correct when identifying the relationship between governmental structures, policy processes, and racial statuses in America. These structures and processes control, define, and redefine how racial orders are upheld or changed through public policy.[23]

The strategic and restrictive framing of the "American" people, in an attempt to uphold a racial institutional order thought to benefit those labeled as "white," reveals a unique yet longstanding relationship between race, national identity, and policy outcomes. To this end, Tennessee Republican Senator Lamar Alexander, a cosponsor of the amendment, took to the Senate floor to state:

> This amendment is as important as any amendment which is being offered because it helps take our magnificent diversity and make it something even more magnificent. It recognizes that only a few things unite us: our principles, found in our founding documents, and our common language. We are proud of where we have come from, where our ancestors have come from, but to make this land of immigrants truly one country, we must have and honor our national language, our common language, and that language is English.[24]

It was this statement by Senator Alexander that was perhaps most revealing of the belief that homogeneity is a, if not *the*, precursor to societal order. Saying that our nation's diversity could be made into "something even more magnificent," or perhaps something better unified, by means of the amendment, while simultaneously linking unity with "our founding documents," presented yet another non sequitur. If Senator Alexander was referring to the Constitution, or possibly the Bill of Rights, when describing the "founding documents" from which we derive "our" principles, then the question now becomes, "Whose unity is he speaking about?" These founding principles and documents vigorously fought for the preservation of an Anglo racial order, as evidenced by Indian removal[25] and antimiscegenation statutes,[26] to name only a few examples. Like the Great Chain of Being, Senator Alexander's advocacy privileged the recognition and application of supposed "ideal American principles" as those beliefs and values that occupy the highest rung, where again, the Spanish language and inevitably Latinos represent all that is lower.

Although both immigration reform measures failed, the 2006 debate represents both a timely and timeless congressional illustration of what happens when immigration reform meets racial politics. Despite Congress's difficulty in passing comprehensive immigration reform and Republicans' lackluster ability to persuade Democrats to endorse a national language bill, official language legislation is alive and well. The quest for so-called "unity" continues to gain momentum on the state level; English is the official language in 30 states. A glimpse inside the recent rhetorical developments of this movement sheds a light on how race and immigration policies are crafted, and on the sorts of the debates they produce.

State Legislatures and Official Language Laws

Attempts at passing official language legislation offer great insight into how many state legislatures choose to frame issues surrounding immigrants and immigration. A failed 2011 attempt to make English the official language of Pennsylvania provides one of many good examples. Two measures, the Pennsylvania Official Language Act, introduced by Representative Rose Marie Swanger (R-Lebanon County), and House Bill 888, or the Official Language Act, introduced by Representative Scott Perry (R-York), both sought to streamline and expedite the immigrant assimilation process.

The legislative language in both measures was identical, as the bills' chief architects sought maximum impact and exposure. Each bill, in its "legislative findings" section, asserted eight axioms:

(1) The people of the United States have brought to this nation the cultural heritage of many nations.

(2) The people of the United States, despite their many differences, have lived together harmoniously and productively as citizens of one nation.

(3) The traditional and common language of the United States and of this Commonwealth is English.

(4) A knowledge of the common language is essential to full exercise of constitutional freedoms, informed and knowledgeable empowerment as voters, citizen checks against government abuses and individual prosperity and independence.

(5) The English language has been our strongest bond to one another as fellow citizens and has contributed substantially to national unity and societal cohesiveness.

(6) English has been this nation's language by custom only and warrants special legal protection.

(7) Government has a fiduciary responsibility to the citizenry to ensure that it operates as efficiently as possible, and the growth of multiple language bureaucracies and printing represents an abrogation of this fiduciary responsibility.

(8) The Commonwealth and its municipalities and the Federal Government also have a responsibility to ensure that citizens have opportunities to learn English.[27]

Each so-called axiom, or "legislative finding," revealed the discursive assumptions steering the wheel of this legislative vehicle. At finding two, we witness perhaps the most misguided and deceptive claim of them all. At no point in our existence could we claim that the English language has safeguarded the nation against movements threatening to disrupt societal peace and productivity. Issues over cultural diversity continue to divide, rather than unite. Some believe the nation is heading on a cultural collision course with Latino immigrants, whereas now is the time to reclaim and rearticulate all that it means to be "American."

Continuing down this path, axiom four represented another misinformed claim regarding the constitutional rights of people with limited English proficiency. As mentioned earlier, survey data supports the claim that immigrants, particularly those from Latin America, understand the vital role that English plays in U.S. society. Axiom four is therefore very misleading and applies a large dosage of historical and legal amnesia. This supposed axiom critically overlooks one constitutional safeguard, resulting from the landmark 1970 case *Negrón v. New York*.

On March 10, 1967, Rogelio Nieves Negrón was sentenced in the county court of Suffolk County to a term of 20 years to life after a jury found him guilty of murder in the second degree, which judgment was affirmed. *Negrón v. New York*, the ensuing case, pertained to whether or not the state court was obligated to advise Negrón of his legal rights. Was the court required to inform Negrón that he was entitled to a court-appointed interpreter to translate the testimony of the English-speaking witnesses, and did its failure to so advise Negrón and to appoint such an interpreter deprive him of his constitutional rights under the Sixth and Fourteenth Amendments? In writing on behalf of the court, Judge Irving Kaufman argued:

It is axiomatic that the Sixth Amendment's guarantee of a right to be confronted with adverse witnesses, now also applicable to the states through the Fourteenth Amendment . . . includes the right to cross-examine those witnesses as 'an essential and fundamental requirement for the kind of fair trial which is this country's constitutional goal.' But the right that was denied Negrón seems to us even more consequential than the right of confrontation. And it is equally imperative that every criminal defendant—if the right to be present is to have meaning—possess sufficient present ability to consult with his lawyer with a reasonable degree of rational understanding . . . Negrón's language disability was obvious, not just a possibility, and it was as debilitating to his ability to participate in the trial as a mental disease or defect. But it was more readily "curable" than any mental disorder. The least we can require is that a court, put on notice of a defendant's severe language difficulty, make unmistakably clear to him that he has a right to have a competent translator assist him, at state expense if need be, throughout his trial.[28]

Contrary to what the language bills before the Pennsylvania state legislature claimed, it is quite evident that, in more ways than one, constitutional representation extends to those with limited linguistic proficiency. Congress made this permanent in 1978 with the passage of the Federal Court Interpreter's Act. The onus to fully engage in due process—along with other constitutional safeguards—is not solely on the individual. Even speaking a "common language," as history has repeatedly proven, does not ensure the full protection of all the rights and promises guaranteed under law. The false impression that English is the automatic gateway to political participation, social inclusion, and upward mobility denies the existence of countervailing forces such as discrimination and the discursive and oftentimes veiled crevasses that harbor racism.

As calls for immigrant assimilation continue, so does the nativism that frequently accompanies these efforts. When, in 2012, Oklahoma became the latest state to make English its official language,[29] the decision was mired in great controversy. What began as a cost-cutting crusade to save Oklahoma tax dollars quickly transformed into a prescriptive measure geared toward achieving linguistic homogeneity. This movement toward supposed fiscal responsibility established the political momentum needed for Oklahoma lawmakers to introduce the Oklahoma Taxpayer and Citizen

Protection Act of 2007. Consistent with historical patterns, the act was touted as a combined savings mechanism and immigration reform measure. In 2007, this was the most punitive immigration law in the United States, and Governor Brad Henry promised aggressive enforcement.

The Oklahoma Taxpayer and Citizen Protection Act of 2007 states:

> The State of Oklahoma finds that illegal immigration is causing economic hardship and lawlessness in this state and that illegal immigration is encouraged when public agencies within this state provide public benefits without verifying immigration status. The State of Oklahoma further finds that when illegal immigrants have been harbored and sheltered in this state and encouraged to reside in this state through the issuance of identification cards that are issued without verifying immigration status, these practices impede and obstruct the enforcement of federal immigration law, undermine the security of our borders, and impermissibly restrict the privileges and immunities of the citizens of Oklahoma. Therefore, the people of the State of Oklahoma declare that it is a compelling public interest of this state to discourage illegal immigration by requiring all agencies within this state to fully cooperate with federal immigration authorities in the enforcement of federal immigration laws. The State of Oklahoma also finds that other measures are necessary to ensure the integrity of various governmental programs and services.[30]

Needless to say, the passage and vowed enforcement of this law came with much tension and divisiveness. This degree of polarization, writes Cass Sunstein, "often occurs because of people's failure to adjust their reactions to the skewed compositions of the groups in which they find themselves. . . . This tendency can get us into a lot of trouble in many areas, wrapping our judgments not only about politics but also about health, money, and religion."[31] The unsupported claim of lawlessness resulting from a growing "illegal" immigrant population throughout the state enforced a political atmosphere steeped in suspicion, leading to what Leo Chavez refers to as the "Latino threat." As a discourse, the "Latino threat" is a danger to society caused by Latinos' supposed unwillingness to conform to societal norms and expectations.[32] Key to this rhetorical practice of classification, writes Edward Schiappa, is "the ability to identify certain sensations as the same and others as different, thereby allowing for firm differences to be created and defined."[33] As a result of our supposedly threatening differences, limits must be imposed.

In accordance with the Oklahoma law, limits were imposed through four mandates:

A. It shall be unlawful for any person to transport, move, or attempt to transport in the State of Oklahoma any alien knowing or in reckless disregard of the fact that the alien has come to, entered, or remained in the United States in violation of law, in further-ance of the illegal presence of the alien in the United States.

B. It shall be unlawful for any person to conceal, harbor, or shel-ter from detection any alien in any place within the State of Oklahoma, including any building or means of transportation, knowing or in reckless disregard of the fact that the alien has come to, entered, or remained in the United States in violation of law.

C. Nothing in this section shall be construed so as to prohibit or restrict the provision of any state or local public bene-fit described in 8 U.S.C., Section 1621(b), or regulated pub-lic health services provided by a private charity using private funds.

D. Any person violating the provisions of subsections A or B of this section shall, upon conviction, be guilty of a felony pun-ishable by imprisonment in the custody of the Department of Corrections for not less than one (1) year, or by a fine of not less than One Thousand Dollars ($1,000.00), or by both such fine and imprisonment.[34]

The national sentiment leading up to 2007 paved the way for the smooth passage of this legislative vehicle, which secured an 88–9 mar-gin in the Oklahoma House and a 41–6 margin in the Oklahoma Senate. According to Republican State Representative Randy Terrill, the bill's chief architect, "The states have always been the great laboratories of democracy. Whether it was welfare reform in the mid- to late-1990s or whether it's immigration in 2007, people shouldn't be surprised that when the federal government can't or won't act, people of the state of

Oklahoma will step up to the plate and hit the home run."[35] Terrill believed the sanctions of this law were a great legislative victory, coming as they did in a time of supposed unprecedented levels of "illegal" immigrant activity and unrest.

This new immigration law laid the groundwork for the unveiling of an official language initiative that had nothing to do with economics. Indeed, Oklahoma's three-part series to mandate an official language—House Bill 2252, House Joint Resolution 1042, and State Ballot Question 751—represented the latest "remedy" offered to counteract the perceived decline in immigrant assimilation. Fueling this perception was the elusive definition of what it means to be an "American." American identity, according to Leonie Huddy, "does not mean the same thing to all Americans. And it is the meaning of American identity, not its existence, that determines its political consequences."[36] Leading up to the controversy surrounding State Ballot Question 751, Oklahoma's ballot proposal for an official language, were two House resolutions, House Bill 2252 and House Joint Resolution 1042, both sponsored by Representative Terrill.

Introduced in February 2009, House Bill 2252 was prompted, in part, by a federal investigation of the Oklahoma Department of Public Safety over allegations that the agency violated the civil rights of two Iranian immigrants who had not been offered written driver's license exams in Farsi. Troubled by the investigation, Oklahoma lawmakers quickly drew up House Bill 2252, a measure that would require driver's license tests to be provided only in English; the requirement that the Department of Public Safety offer driver's license tests in Spanish would be repealed. In defense of his proposed bill, Terrill noted, "The state has spent about $22,000 to print Spanish-language manuals and has paid nearly $7,000 for translation services. That could increase as more than 20 people last year requested tests in other languages, such as Arabic and Russian, while Representative Mike Christian, R-Oklahoma City, believed it's common sense, arguing that, if they can't speak English, they can't read the signs."[37] At face value, this could appear to be simply a cost-cutting measure aimed at reducing state spending during an economic downturn, but that is far from accurate.

Supporters of the measure ultimately secured its passage, and the focus soon moved away from fiscal concerns to immigration and assimilation. Van Tran notes, "In 2000, 13 percent of the U.S. population or 35.2 million people self-identified as of Latino descent. To put this into historical perspective, the current level reflects a four-fold increase from 1960 and a two-fold increase from 1980 when it was 3.6 percent and 6.9 percent of the total population, respectively."[38] In a press release issued after the passage of House Bill 2252, Representative Terrill shared his concerns about those figures: "In a year of budget cuts, it makes no sense to spend extra money on Spanish-language drivers' tests that serve no legitimate public policy purpose. Providing this special accommodation to non-English speakers indirectly encourages illegal immigration and prevents assimilation of legal immigrants."[39] Of course Terrill offered no support for his claim. Instead, we are simply to assume that language diversity threatens social and political cohesion. In this case, the Spanish language falls victim to the rhetorical efforts of enemy construction. As Gina Petonito explains, "All conflicts have situations where one group casts the other as enemy . . . draw[ing] from available cultural resources to construct the other as a villainous foe."[40] For Terrill, the foe that culturally and economically plagued Oklahoma must be eliminated at all political costs.

House Bill 2252 was taken one step further by HJR 1042, introduced less than one month later. This proposed measure sought to make English the state's official language. With the exception of the Native American languages the state provides accommodations for, HJR 1042 understood English to be the "common and unifying language" of the State of Oklahoma, and as such all official actions would be conducted in English, except when otherwise required by federal law. When taken to vote, Terrill's measure passed by a 66–32 margin, sending a proposed constitutional amendment to voters in November of 2010. Following the bill's historical passage, Terrill argued, "As our common American language, English and the 'melting pot' process it supports has made the United States the most successful multi-ethnic nation in history." However, he continued, "Unfortunately, the drive to linguistically Balkanize our nation makes it harder for legal immigrants to assimilate while wasting limited taxpayer dollars."[41] Republican Representative George Faught explained that his support was in direct response to Oklahomans' frustrations with the growing influence of Spanish throughout the state, declaring, "It's time to give them what they want, and to stop wasting limited taxpayer dollars."[42] As the portrayed enemies of linguistic unity, Latinos, Murray Edelman explains, become "identifiable persons or stereotypes of persons to whom evil traits, intentions, or actions can be attributed," despite lack of any evidence to support such sweeping claims.[43] Obtrusively constructed around cultural and behavioral outliers, enemies are usually defined in opposition to how we view ourselves, denying the possibility of resemblance.

The rise in the state's Latino population has ushered in fears over a new Latino majority-minority in some areas, which would offset some congressional safe seats. Use of the Spanish language "in parts of the country with a heavy Latino concentration," posits Van Tran:

> has raised concerns over its potential divisive effect on American national identity and social cohesion. However, this debate often assumes that English acquisition occurs at the cost of Spanish abandonment, despite a long tradition of research that points to the potential beneficial and synergistic effects of bilingualism on cognitive development and academic outcomes among Latino students.[44]

Once the political maneuvering had taken place in the halls of the state legislature, the stage was set for the main event. What had been a measure aimed at reducing the state's spending evolved into a campaign against the purported cultural and linguistic shortcomings that Oklahoma's Latino community was supposedly imposing on "our" society.

With a steady stream of unsubstantiated apocalyptic appeals aimed at the state's Latino community, lawmakers authored Ballot Question 751, which stated the following:

> This measure amends the state constitution. It adds a new article to the constitution. That article deals with the state's official actions. It dictates the language to be used in taking official state action. It requires that official state actions be in English. Native American languages could also be used. When federal law requires, other languages could also be used. These language requirements apply to the state's 'official actions.' The term 'official actions' is not defined. The Legislature could pass laws determining the application of the language requirements. The Legislature would also pass laws implementing and enforcing the language requirements. No lawsuit based on state law could be brought on the basis of a state agency's failure to use a language other than English. Nor could such a lawsuit be brought against political subdivisions of the state.[45]

While the bill's language was written in efforts to suppress the influence of the Spanish language, from the perspective of the voter, all that was actually known was that a vote in support of the ballot question would make English the state's official language. Republican State Representative Harry Coates said, "The bill just makes a statement that we want to conduct business in English."[46] Despite its ambiguity, Ballot Question 751 enjoyed a nearly 76 percent approval in the November 2010 general election.

Most troubling throughout the legislative life of this debate was that Representative Terrill, his cosponsors, and those who supported the bill offered no support to their sweeping claims. Instead, onlookers were left with the residual message that language diversity threatens social and political cohesion. Furthermore, many of Terrill's arguments ignored most existing data illustrating that "all in all, the evidence of powerful currents of acculturation is simply undeniable in the realm of language."[47] As seen here, the arguments offered by the bill's proponents suffered from glaring omissions of evidence. With no evidence to support even the cornerstone correlation between Latino immigrants and English negligence, many questions remained unanswered. For instance, Terrill did not address a 2007 Pew Hispanic Center survey titled "English Use Among Hispanics in the United States."[48] If he had, he would have had to contend with data illustrating a counter-reality to his claim. As reported, "Latinos believe that English is necessary for success in the United States"; when asked whether adult Latinos "need to learn English to succeed in the United States, or can they succeed even if they only speak Spanish," 89 percent responded that they understood the importance of learning English. Slightly more Spanish-dominant Latinos (92 percent) also echoed this belief. In a 2012 survey, also by the Pew Research Hispanic Center, 87 percent of Latinos indicated a belief that Latino immigrants need to learn English to succeed in the U.S.[49]

Throughout these and similar campaigns, questions of belonging and societal absorption are guided by shortsighted beliefs that Spanish and English cannot coexist harmoniously, and a rigid, one-way system of cultural subtraction is our only salvation. No other state has passed a similar measure since the Oklahoma law, but this does not mean we are witnessing a slow decline in such legislation. Even when English is read, written, and spoken "sufficiently well," we are not necessarily safeguarded against political and legal tensions, as our next discussion confirms.

When English is not Enough

As the debate over immigration reform intensifies, so do efforts to regulate/restrict all languages deemed "foreign." In Arizona, officeholders and seekers who do not read, write, speak, and understand English "sufficiently well" risk having their candidacies revoked. This was the case with Alejandrina Cabrera, a former city council candidate in the southern Arizona border city of San Luis. Upon being labeled "not sufficiently fluent" in English by the Arizona Superior Court in Yuma County, she was removed from the ballot. While Arizona's 1910 Enabling Act requires officeholders and seekers to "read, write, speak, and understand English sufficiently well," it does not specify or quantify proficiency; nor does it articulate ways to measure fluency. This ambiguity informed the 2012 case *Escamilla v. Cuello*,[50] which further directed suspicion toward a state legislature already engulfed in a political crisis over both its enactment of immigration laws (Senate Bill 1070)[51] and its banning of ethnic studies classes in public schools.[52]

While most documents point to 1988 as Arizona's first instance of attempting to secure an official language, there is evidence suggesting that Arizona sought to make English its official language even prior to becoming a state in the union. In anticipation of statehood, the 1910 adoption of the Arizona Constitution included numerous sections and subsections regarding the construction and maintenance of the state apparatus, on matters such as public education and achieving the "perfect toleration of religious sentiment." At face value, many of the stated purposes and goals of the 1910 Arizona Constitution are to be expected. Some, however, raise serious concerns not only about the state's founding nativist principles but also about how such principles—especially those pertaining to race and therefore to the Latino community—are selectively cited and enforced today. At the center of the current controversy over what defines English fluency is Section 20 of Arizona's Enabling Act, which declares:

> That said State shall never enact any law restricting or abridging the right of suffrage on account of race, color, or previous condition of servitude, and that [the] ability to read, write, speak, and understand the English language sufficiently well to conduct the duties of the office without the aid of an interpreter shall be

a necessary qualification for all state officers and members of the state legislature.[53]

Given the argument that two Arizona courts pursued to remove Alejandrina Cabrera's name from the ballot in consultation with Section 20, a closer examination of issues pertaining to "official" and "national language" policies and their peculiar correlation to race and immigration is warranted.[54] The ambiguity surrounding what it means to "understand the English language sufficiently well" links the past to the present, providing the legal elasticity needed to execute questionable maneuvers against a particular group of people. Here, the paranoid style "represents an old and recurrent mode of expression in our public life, which has frequently been linked with movements of suspicious discontent" against those viewed and defined by lawmakers as so-called threats to our overall well-being.[55] The 1910 law established the legal basis for paranoia and distrust because there is no way to gauge, quantify, or otherwise assess the meaning of "sufficiently well." Such vagueness allows for the legal maneuverability needed to deny the absorption and incorporation of those groups of people that lawmakers deem undesirable.

Much like Arizona Senate Bill 1070, which possesses an addendum that prohibits racial profiling, Arizona's Enabling Act executes a sleight-of-hand maneuver in its wording. On face value, some may find comfort in the declaration that discrimination by race, color, or previous condition of servitude is discouraged. However, when considered alongside the widespread withholding of literary (i.e., literary tests for voting), let alone educational, inclusion for various immigrant groups and peoples of color, the clause requiring officeholders and -seekers to "read, write, speak, and understand the English language sufficiently well" falls very short of anything remotely liberating. Even with the legal safeguard against racial profiling written into Arizona's immigration law, allegations of profiling and harassment at the hands of local law enforcement continue to run rampant, particularly in reference to the state's Latino population.[56] While the Enabling Act appears to be color blind, American political development articulates a counter-reality, one that highlights the subtle formations of disenfranchisement.

From the outset, the Enabling Act possessed a peculiar political history that continues to evade any serious dialogue, especially pertaining to race and ethnicity. In 1850, the Territory of New Mexico (which included the present state of Arizona) was added to the union. Thirteen years later, New Mexico and Arizona were separated as territories, then in 1906, Congress passed a joint statehood bill for them, stipulating that rejection of joint statehood by the voters of either territory would prevent its enactment. To express their disdain for such a measure, dissenters went to Congress in the hopes of preventing joint statehood. In stating the rationale behind their objection, they argued along racial and ethnic lines, positing:

> The decided racial difference between the people of New Mexico, who are not only different in race and largely in language, but have entirely different customs, laws and ideals and would have but little prospect of successful amalgamation . . . [and] the objection of the people of Arizona, 95 percent of whom are Americans, to the probability of the control of public affairs by people of a different race, many of whom do not speak the English language, and who outnumber the people of Arizona two to one.[57]

Following the Treaty of Guadalupe Hidalgo in 1848, when Mexican nationals were offered the option of receiving American citizenship or relocating to Mexico, close to 90 percent chose American citizenship. Additionally, the treaty defended various political, religious, and civil rights of Spanish-speaking colonists by protecting their culture and language. The nativist sentiment underlying protests of joint statehood, which cited racial and linguistic differences as reasons for separation, carried well into the crafting of Arizona's Enabling Act. It struck a defining chord in how Arizona sought to distinguish itself from New Mexico.

With joint statehood for New Mexico and Arizona no longer a viable option, Congress passed, and President William Taft signed, the Enabling Act, allowing Arizona to draft its own constitution. The various provisions of the act included the prohibition of the sale of "intoxicating liquors" to Native Americans, a disclaimer regarding the state's "right" to public lands belonging to either the federal government or Native Americans, and the notorious requirement that all state officials be able to read, write, speak, and understand the English language. Said best by David Berman, "Congress appeared anxious to improve the state's image, encourage the assimilation of Indians, Hispanics and blacks into the Anglo culture, and, at the same time, protect their interests and well-being."[58] Racial paranoia was the bonding element that amalgamated Arizona's efforts toward statehood, largely contributing to the controversy at hand.

It was this historical legacy surrounding the state's Enabling Act that halted city council candidate Alejendrena Cabrera's run for the position; her rejection from the ballot was duly assisted by the questionable actions of the Arizona Superior Court in Yuma County. What began as a typical campaign for city council in the border town of San Luis ended on a far less typical note. (In San Luis, political controversy is the norm, as evidenced by the 24 recall attempts of local officeholders since 2001.[59]) The state law requiring candidates to "read, write, speak, and understand English sufficiently well" leaves many questions unanswered, including:

- Who is to decide what "sufficiently well" means?
- How, if possible, can "sufficiently well" be quantified or measured?
- Just how fluent must Arizona officeholders and -seekers be?

Although the law did not establish any standards for fluency, Cabrera's incumbent challenger, San Luis Mayor Juan Carlos Escamilla, filed a lawsuit challenging Cabrera's eligibility on the grounds that she allegedly lacked English fluency.

In efforts to gauge whether or not Cabrera's English proficiency complied with the 1910 law, Arizona Superior Court Judge John Nelson first framed the context of the legal challenge by articulating what *he* believed to be the relevant concerns before the court. Judge Nelson explained:

The only issue before the Court is whether Respondent Cabrera satisfies the requirement of A.R.S. § 38-201(C) [the 1910 law] that she is able to speak, write and read the English language with sufficient proficiency. . . . However, the issue of proper interpretation of A.R.S. § 38-201 is an issue of first impression, as the statute is not the subject of any reported Arizona appellate decision. In interpreting a statute, a court must look to the legislative intent, but little evidence of legislative intent has been provided to the Court. A.R.S. § 38-201(C) would be rendered meaningless if, as suggested by Respondent Cabrera, it were interpreted as having no standard or only requiring minimal or bare proficiency at speaking, reading, and writing in the English language. The standard to be applied under

A.R.S. § 38-201(C) . . . must be in the context of the political office at issue, here City Councilman for the City of San Luis, Arizona.[60]

According to the U.S. Census Bureau, 98.7 percent of the population in San Luis, Arizona, is Latino, and 87.9 percent of the population speaks a language other than English at home. An interpretation of the statute within the context of "the political office at issue, here City Councilman for the City of San Luis, Arizona" must acknowledge and account for this reality. For instance, former San Luis City Councilman Carlos Bernal described, "My [English] pronunciation was weak; it's rare to have council members who have a 100 percent grasp of the English language. There have been very few."[61] Understanding A.R.S. § 38-201(C) within the context Judge Nelson outlined creates an arbitrary standard of English fluency that provides a legal pathway to other such cases, especially in places where Spanish is prevalent. Given the lack of benchmarks, measures, or matrices to assess English proficiency, it is impossible to definitively interpret the law. Equally troubling is Judge Nelson's articulation of the challenge introduced by Cabrera, as the dispute was not whether A.R.S. § 38-201(C) required "minimal or bare proficiency."

To assist with the court's efforts to determine compliancy with A.R.S. § 38-201(C), linguistic expert William Gregory Eggington of Brigham Young University was hired to test Cabrera's English proficiency, adding another wrinkle to the case. What many thought would be a fairly objective and scientific method of assessment turned out to possess neither of those qualities; the hiring of Professor Eggington only added further doubt to the execution of justice for Cabrera. According to court documents, prior to conducting a series of three English proficiency tests at the law offices of Garcia, Hengl, Kinsey and Villarreal, P.L.C. (the firm representing Cabrera), Eggington was informed of Cabrera's poor hearing. Yet he failed to make accommodations, in the first of many oversights throughout the case.

Despite having no established benchmark to articulate proficiency, Eggington proceeded and presented findings indicating that Cabrera failed to meet the minimum level of English skill needed to be in compliance with A.R.S. § 38-201(C). Oddly enough, though Judge Nelson argued that "the standard to be applied under A.R.S. § 38-201(C) must be in the context of the political office at issue . . . for the City of San Luis, Arizona," Eggington testified that he never conducted the research necessary to establish a baseline for someone seeking the office of city councilperson for San Luis. Furthermore, Eggington testified to never having visited San Luis, and to not taking into consideration the "Hispanic English" dialect of southern Arizona. While Eggington testified that Cabrera read English between a ninth and tenth grade level (at or above the reading level of most U.S. newspapers and magazines), he never tested her writing abilities, according to court documents. Despite the numerous shortcomings in the expert's evidence, and despite Cabrera's demonstrated willingness to both testify and read a San Luis council meeting agenda and minutes in English, Judge Nelson concluded, "The Court finds [Eggington's] testimony to be compelling and adopts it." He continued, "The Court finds that Respondent Cabrera does not satisfy the requirement of A.R.S. § 38-201(C) that she possesses the ability to speak, read, and write the English language with sufficient proficiency to perform as a City Councilman for the City of San Luis." [62]

In light of Judge Nelson's decision to remove Cabrera from the ballot, Cabrera's legal team presented the Arizona Supreme Court with five issues that clarified their request for an appeal. Unsurprisingly, three of the challenges pertained to the peculiar establishment and articulation of an English-language proficiency standard that injected trivial specificity into an otherwise ambiguous "sufficient proficiency" clause. These objections included:

> Whether the trial court erred in interpreting A.R.S. § 38-201(C) to impose a proficiency standard specific to a member of City Council for the City of San Luis, Arizona, then misapplied it to the evidence produced at trial?

> Whether the trial court erred in admitting and relying upon Dr. Eggington's opinions and in the testimony of Appellant in granting the injunction?

> Whether the test adopted by the trial court is in violation of Appellant's constitutional right to participate in government?[63]

When examined closer, these points of objection raise serious concerns over how the court ruled Cabrera unfit to run for public office. One concern pertains to how the court established and ultimately accepted an English proficiency standard that was mostly created by Eggington, an Australian sociolinguist. Among other troubling declarations, this sociolinguist testified that he had never visited any part of the southwest U.S. border or studied its people or their English dialect, let alone had he not studied or visited San Luis, Arizona.

Additionally, Cabrera's legal team argued in its appeal, "Appellant knows of no statute, case or other law that provides for or otherwise permits a trial court to adopt an English proficiency standard that will only be applied to that case, based upon unverified opinions and unaccepted testing methodologies."[64] If the Arizona Superior Court in Yuma County can apply an arbitrary standard, there is nothing stopping other state courts from creating and enforcing their own proficiency standards; this is akin to the superficial litmus tests, such as literacy tests, used throughout history to disenfranchise and discourage the political participation of people of color. Such tests have been outlawed, mostly following the passage of the Voting Rights Act of 1965, on account of their overt prejudicial intentions. Therefore, the question of whether or not the tests adopted by the court to gauge Cabrera's proficiency violated the Equal Protection Clause of the Fourteenth Amendment, at least in the court's eyes, is irrelevant.

The heightened level of paranoia in this case invites much skepticism over its handling and the objectivity surrounding it. Despite Eggington's inability to prove that Cabrera was "unable to speak, write, and read the English language," the court attempted to superficially assess Cabrera's level of English-language proficiency. Furthermore, during the trial, Eggington admitted that one of the three tests administered was "experimental," never having been used before as evidence in a civil or criminal trial. This statement calls into question whether or not the court observed the "*Frye* rule," which states that the proponent of scientific evidence must show the evidence's underlying reliability.[65] Nonetheless, regardless of concerns raised over the validity of Eggington's "expert" testimony and tests, his evidence was not disqualified. Rather, it was cited by Judge Nelson when affirming his ruling to strike Cabrera's name from the ballot. Ignoring the aforementioned shortcomings, the Arizona Supreme Court signed a short order affirming the lower court's decision.

Conclusion

Since 2012, legislative attempts to declare English the official language of various states continue to gain sustainable momentum. Purportedly supported by unsubstantiated claims over low levels of cultural and linguistic assimilation by Latin American immigrants, these attempts are generating great interest. In Carroll County, Maryland, for instance, the Latino population has grown by more than 300 percent since 2000 (about 3 percent of the county's population) according to the *Baltimore Sun*. As a direct result, the all-Republican Board of County Commissioners has begun debating the need for an official language law. Lawmakers in Carroll County advanced axioms similar to those found in the successful 2011 Pennsylvania official language law, House Bill 361.

> **WHEREAS,** the Board of County Commissioners of Carroll County, Maryland, has determined that amendments to certain sections of the Code are necessary to advance the public health, safety, and welfare;
>
> **WHEREAS,** the English language is the common language of Carroll County, Maryland and of the United States of America;
>
> **WHEREAS,** the use of a common language removes barriers of misunderstanding and helps to unify the citizens of Carroll County, the State of Maryland, and the United States of America, and helps to enable the full economic and civic participation of all its citizens, regardless of national origin, creed, race, or other characteristics, and thus a compelling governmental interest exists in promoting, preserving, and strengthening the use of the English language;
>
> **WHEREAS,** proficiency in the English language, as well as other languages, benefits Carroll County both economically and culturally and should be encouraged;
>
> **WHEREAS,** in addition to any other ways to promote proficiency in the English language, the Board of County Commissioners of Carroll County can promote proficiency in English by using the English language in its official actions and activities;
>
> **WHEREAS,** the Board of County Commissioners of Carroll County recognizes the need to protect and preserve the rights of those who speak only the English language to use or obtain governmental programs, services, and benefits;
>
> **WHEREAS,** the Board of County Commissioners of Carroll County can reduce costs and promote efficiency in its roles as

employer and as a government accountable to its citizens by using the English language in its official actions and activities; and

WHEREAS, the Board of County Commissioners of Carroll County, Maryland, desires to designate the English language as the official language of Carroll County, and for that purpose, it is necessary to adopt an ordinance.[66]

In a series of legislative findings that has little coherence or evidence, the axioms released by the Carroll County Board of County Commissioners contradicts reality. Lawmakers argued that, "The use of a common language removes barriers of misunderstanding and helps to unify the citizens of Carroll County, the State of Maryland, and the United States of America," and, "Proficiency in the English language, as well as other languages, benefits Carroll County both economically and culturally and should be encouraged," but failed to substantiate or discuss specific issues related to Carroll County. Are we to believe, based on their proclamation, that the English language is under attack and losing its footing in the county, state, and country? Or are we to praise the economic and cultural benefits associated with bilingualism? This type of dichotomy riddles the ordinance, prompting dissenters to question the lawmakers' justification. Are there documented cases that illustrate the tensions or "barriers of misunderstanding" between English and other languages, or is the movement in Maryland yet another poorly justified example of a deep-seated political and cultural paranoia that fraudulently associates immigrants, immigration, and cultural obscurity?

Around the country, rising Latino populations are motivating expanding political attempts toward assimilation. Most recently in Arizona, barely a year following *Escamilla v. Cuello*, lawmakers in the Arizona House entertained House Bill 2283, an addendum to the state's existing official language law that would ban state agencies from mailing out information in any language other than English. (Non-English translations would be posted online rather than mailed.) If an agency of the state is required to issue or disseminate any material other than voting information, the proposed bill states that it may:

1. Only issue or disseminate the publication, document, or material by posting it on a government internet website and maintaining a printed copy in the state agency's office.

2. Include on the English language version of the publication, document or material, a conspicuous notice of the address of the internet website and the location of the agency office where the version of the publication, document or material in a language other than English is posted and maintained.[67]

Banning such non-English mailings effectively precludes Arizona's substantial Spanish-speaking population from receiving government services and information. Instead of promoting English-language education, Arizona excluded its large limited-English-speaking population by making English the official state language in 2006. Access to computers and Internet service places this proposal on shaky grounds, but it nonetheless shows the peculiar state of affairs revolving around many state-led attempts at "preserving and enhancing" the role of English in our society.

In New York State, Senate Bill 1902, introduced in January 2013 by Republican state senator Mike Nozzolio, follows a rhetorical tradition that leads official language proponents to believe that diversity uncontained—that is, without governmental intervention—will cause sociopolitical chaos. As written, Senate Bill 1902 affirms:

That, the state is comprised of individuals from many ethnic, cultural and linguistic backgrounds, and continues to benefit from this rich diversity. Throughout the history of New York and the United States the common thread binding individuals of differing backgrounds has been the English language. Command of the English language is necessary to participate in and take full advantage of the opportunities afforded by American life. Absent a rudimentary command of the English language, citizens of this state are not able to make their voices heard in the legislative process, effectively exercise their right to vote, or fully understand the rights afforded [to] them by the United States and New York Constitutions. Such citizens also have a more difficult time finding gainful employment, affordable housing, health insurance, and otherwise availing themselves of the full benefits of American life for themselves and their families.[68]

Seemingly ignoring societal variables that have been proven to divide, such as access to education and the ever-widening socioeconomic gap, proponents insist that language is the bridge to all opportunities. Unfortunately, even when a linguistic divide is eliminated, other variables like race, socioeconomics, gender, and sexual orientation avail themselves as targets for discrimination. Moreover, to even argue that "throughout the history of New York and the United States the common thread binding individuals of differing backgrounds has been the English language" indicates severe historical amnesia. In relation to this peculiar line of argumentation, Donaldo Macedo contends:

> First, if English is the most effective educational language, how can we explain why over 60 million Americans are illiterate or functionally illiterate? Second, if English Only education can guarantee linguistic minorities a better future, as educators like William Bennett promise, why do the majority of Black Americans, whose ancestors have been speaking English for over two hundred years, find themselves still relegated to the ghettos?[69]

To say that knowing English will fully liberate a group from the margins of society is both ahistorical and absent of reality, yet this belief fuels an expanding movement, as shifting demographics continue to weigh heavily on the minds of many lawmakers.

As seen throughout the history of immigration reform movements, calls for official language legislation have followed in lockstep with shifts in how America handles its newcomers. What remains peculiar about this debate is that nowhere has a single language declaration been proven to ameliorate or credited with ameliorating national disunity or instability. Proponents of official language legislation present their advocacy as not only responding to the will of constituents, but also as acting upon a greater calling to unify America. This repetition of proof insisting that an official language is the *best* safeguard toward achieving prosperity for immigrants represents what Ernest Bormann refers to as a fantasy type, or "a stock scenario repeated again and again by the same characters or by similar characters."[70] English is *the* prerequisite for achieving economic prosperity, social and cultural acceptance, and societal democratic participation. Within this type of fantasy is the preservation of an ideology that understands linguistic heterogeneity to be divisive for national unity and destructive for immigrant prosperity.

As argued by proponents of English as the official language, in defense against societal chaos, homogeneity emerges as the precursor to order. Assimilation serves as society's safeguard, identifying and eradicating those behaviors that fall outside the margins of "normalcy." Such an ideology has an unfortunate by-product: notes Amardo Rodriguez, it "blocks any possibility of a genuinely new and different discussion of human potentiality."[71] At the foundation of the belief in assimilation is a shallow worldview or, more accurately, a fear of diversity left uncontained. The eradication of supposedly obtrusive cultural markers, stated or not, is the goal of assimilation. What arises from this paralyzing paradigm is the perception of diversity as a threatening menace.[72] The perceived lethality of linguistic pluralism only reinforces a justificatory ontology steeped in division, in which, according to Robert Lieberman, "some groups are systemically favored while others are systematically deprived."[73] Once this supposed duality between order (English) and chaos (non-English) forms, calls for and coercions toward assimilation are sure to follow.

In keeping with the theme of perceptions of social lethality, we now visit the ongoing developments surrounding local housing ordinances, in particular attempts to establish the legal definition of a dwelling, and the peculiar alterations to occupancy limits that followed.

Notes

1   See, Donathan L. Brown, "In Defense of Unity & English-Only: On the Early Political Battles to 'Unite' the Nation," *Communication Law Review* 11, no. 1 (2001), 15–28.

2.   See, Vernon Valentine Palmer (ed.), *Mixed Jurisdictions Worldwide: The Third Legal Family* (Cambridge: Cambridge University Press, 2012).

3.   See, Nicolas Kanellos and Helvetia Martell, *Hispanic Periodicals in the United States, Origins to 1960: A Brief History and Comprehensive Bibliography* (Houston: Arte Publico Press, 2000).

4.   See, Bill Piatt, *Only English? Law & Language Policy in the United States* (Albuquerque: University of New Mexico Press, 1990), 13.

5.   See, Robert MacNeil and William Cran. *Do You Speak American?* (New York: Random House, 2007).

6. David Wilkins and Heidi Stark, *American Indian Politics and the American Political System* (Lanham, MD: Rowman & Littlefield, 2010).

7. Theodore Roosevelt, *Works*, vol. XXIV (New York: Charles Scribner's Sons, 1926).

8. United States Congress, *Border Protection, Antiterrorism, and Illegal Immigration Control Act of 2005.* 109th Congress, 1st Session, December 6, 2005.

9. Ibid.

10. Ibid.

11. Matt Barreto, Sylvia Manzano, Ricardo Ramirez, and Kathy Rim, "Mobilization, Participation, and Solidaridad: Latino Participation in the 2006 Immigration Protest Rallies," *Urban Affairs Review* 44, no. 5 (2009): 737.

12. United States Congress, *Comprehensive Immigration Reform Act of 2006*, 109th Congress, 1st Session, April 7, 2006. .

13. United States Census Bureau, *Oklahoma Quick Facts.* Accessed April 9, 2013. http://quickfacts.census.gov/qfd/states/40000.html.

14. United States Congress, *Comprehensive Immigration Reform Act of 2006*, 109th Congress, 1st Session, April 7, 2006.

15. For more information on precisely how the Federal Emergency Management Agency provides a unified national response to disasters and emergencies, the *National Incident Management System* (NIMS) has a template for disaster management and response details.

16. United States Congress, *Comprehensive Immigration Reform Act of 2006*, 109th Congress, 1st Session, April 7, 2006.

17. See, Representative Bureaucracy in the following essays: Frederick Mosher, *Democracy and the Public Service* (New York: Oxford University Press, 1968). Kenneth Meier, "Representative Bureaucracy: A Theoretical and Empirical Exposition," in *Research in Public Administration* vol. II, ed. James Perry (San Francisco: Jossey-Bass, 1993), 1–36. Kenneth J. Meier, "Latinos and Representative Bureaucracy: Testing the Thompson and Henderson Hypotheses," *Journal of Public Administration Research and Theory* 3, 4 (1993): 393–414. Julie Dolan and David Rosenbloom, *Representative Bureaucracy:*

Classical Readings and Continuing Controversies (Amonk, NY: ME Sharpe, 2003). Kenneth Meier and Daniel P. Hawes, "Ethnic Conflict in France: A Case of Representative Bureaucracy?" *American Review of Public Administration* 4 (2008): 1–26.

18. United States Congress, *Comprehensive Immigration Reform Act of 2006*, 109th Congress, 1st Session, April 7, 2006.

19. Desmond King and Rogers Smith, "Strange Bedfellows? Polarized Politics? The Quest for Racial Equity in Contemporary America," *Political Research Quarterly* 61, no. 4 (2008): 686.

20. Arthur Lovejoy, *The Great Chain of Being: A Study of the History of an Idea* (New York: Harper & Brothers, 1936), 59.

21. United States Congress, *Comprehensive Immigration Reform Act of 2006*, 109th Congress, 1st Session, April 7, 2006.

22. King and Smith, "Strange Bedfellows? Polarized Politics? The Quest for Racial Equity in Contemporary America," 686.

23. See, Jennifer Hochschild, "You Win Some, You Lose Some: Explaining the Pattern of Success and Failure in the Second Reconstruction," *Taking Stock: American Government in the Twentieth Century*, ed. Morton Keller and R. Shep Melnick (New York: Cambridge University Press, 1999), 220.

24. United States Congress, *Comprehensive Immigration Reform Act of 2006*, 109th Congress, 1st Session, April 7, 2006.

25. Richard Drinnon, *Facing West: The Metaphysics of Indian-Hating and Empire-Building* (Minneapolis: University of Minnesota Press, 1980).

26. In the battle to prevent racial comingling, anti-miscegenation statutes and court cases that upheld anti-miscegenation were plentiful. See, Alfred Alvins, "Anti-Miscegenation Laws and the Fourteenth Amendment: The Original Intent," *Virginia Law Review* 52, no.7 (1966): 1224–1255. James Kinney, *Amalgamation! Race, Sex and Rhetoric in the Nineteenth-Century American Novel* (Westport, CT: Greenwood Press, 1985). Werner Sollors, *Interracialism: Black and White Intermarriage in American History, Literature and Law* (Oxford, UK: Oxford University Press, 2000). Elise Lemire, *Miscegenation: Making Race in America* (Philadelphia: University of Pennsylvania Press, 2002).

27. Pennsylvania House Bill 361 (2011).

28. *United States Ex. Rel. Negron v. State of New York, 434 F.2d 386,1970.*

29. See, Donathan L. Brown, "Legislating Language in the Name of National Unity: An Oklahoma Story," *International Journal of Discrimination and the Law* 12, no. 3 (2013): 4–17.

30. *Oklahoma House Bill 1804,* (2007).

31. Cass Sunstein, *Going to Extremes: How Like Minds Unite and Divide* (New York: Oxford University Press, 2009).

32. Leo Chavez, *The Latino Threat: Constructing Immigrants, Citizens, and the Nation* (Stanford: Stanford University Press, 2008).

33. Edward Schiappa, *Defining Reality: Definitions and the Politics of Meaning* (Carbondale: Southern Illinois University Press, 2003).

34. *Oklahoma House Bill 1804* (2007).

35. Stephen Dinan and Jerry Seper, [No Title,] *Washington Times,* November 3, 2007: A01.

36. Leonie Huddy, "From Social to Political Identity: A Critical Examination of Social Identity Theory," *Political Psychology*, 22, no. 1 (2001): 130.

37. Michael McNutt, "Two Language Measures Move Forward in the House," *The Oklahoman*, February 19, 2009: 12A.

38. Van Tran, "English Gain vs. Social Loss? Language Assimilation among Second-Generation Latinos in Young Adulthood," *Social Forces* 89, no. 1 (2010): 257.

39. McNutt, "Two Language Measures Move Forward in the House," *The Oklahoman*, February 19, 2009: 12A.

40. Gina Petonito, "Racial Discourse and Enemy Construction: Justifying the Internment 'Solution' to the 'Japanese Problem' During World War II," Patrick Coy and Lynn Woehrle, eds., *Social Conflicts and Collective Identities* (Lanham, MD: Rowman & Littlefield, 2000).

41. McNutt, "Two Language Measures Move Forward in the House," *The Oklahoman*, February 19, 2009: 12A.

42. Ibid.

43. Murray Edelman, *Constructing the Political Spectacle* (Chicago: University of Chicago Press, 1988).

44. Tran, "English Gain vs. Social Loss? Language Assimilation among Second-Generation Latinos in Young Adulthood," *Social Forces* 89, no. 1 (2010): 258–259.

45. *Oklahoma State Question 751, the English is the Official Language of Oklahoma Act* (2010).

46. Bruce Hoebrock, "English on the Ballot as the State's Official Language," *Tulsa World*, September 19, 2010: A19.

47. Richard Alba and Victor Nee, *Remaking the American Mainstream: Assimilation and Contemporary Immigration* (Cambridge, MA: Harvard University Press, 2003).

48. "English Use Among Hispanics in the United States." Pew Hispanic Center, 2007.

49. Paul Taylor, Mark Hugo Lopez, Jessica Hamar Martinez, and Gabriel Velasco, "When Labels Don't Fit: Hispanics and Their Views of Identity." Pew Hispanic Center, 2012.

50. See, Donathan L. Brown, "When English is Not Enough: *Cabrera v. Cuello.*" *Harvard Journal of Hispanic Policy* 25, no. 1 (2013): 49–68.

51. See, Donathan L. Brown, "An Invitation to Profile: *Arizona v. United States,*" *International Journal of Discrimination and the Law* 12, no. 2 (2012): 117–127.

52. See, Jeff Biggers, *State Out of the Union: Arizona and the Final Showdown Over the American Dream* (New York: Nation Books, 2012).

53. Article 28, Section I, Arizona Constitution.

54. See, Robert Lieberman, *Shaping Race Policy: The United States in Comparative Perspective* (Princeton, NJ: Princeton University Press, 2005).

55. Richard Hofstadter, *The Paranoid Style in American Politics and Other Essays* (Cambridge: Harvard University Press, 1965).

56. See, Otto Santa Ana and Celeste González de Bustamante, eds., *Arizona Firestorm: Global Immigration Realities, National Media, and Provincial Politics* (Lanham, MD: Rowman and Littlefield Publishers, 2012).

57. U.S. Congress, Senate, *Congressional Record*, 61st Cong., 2d Sess. (1910): 109.

58. David Berman, *Arizona Politics and Government: The Quest for Autonomy, Democracy and Development* (Lincoln: University of Nebraska Press, 1998), 31.

59. See, Ricardo Lopez, "Arizona Supreme Court Bars Candidate with Limited English." *Los Angeles Times*, February 8, 2012. Accessed April 14, 2012. http://articles.latimes.com/2012/feb/08/nation/la-na -san-luis-english-20120208.

60. Escamilla v. Cuello, CV-12-0039 (2012).

61. Lopez, "Arizona Supreme Court Bars Candidate with Limited English." *Los Angeles Times,* February 8, 2012. Accessed April 14, 2012. http://articles.latimes.com/2012/feb/08/nation/la-na-san-luis -english-20120208.

62. Escamilla v. Cuello, CV-12-0039 (2012).

63. Ibid.

64. Ibid.

65. Frye v. United States, 293 F. 1013, 1014 (App. D.C. Dec. 03, 1923).

66. Carroll County, Maryland Ordinance 2013-01, 2013.

67. Arizona House Bill 2283, 2013.

68. New York Senate Bill 1902, 2013.

69. Donaldo Macedo, *Literacies of Power: What Americans Are Not Allowed to Know* (Boulder, CO: Westview Press, 1994), 126.

70. Ernest Borman, *Force of Fantasy: Restoring the American Dream* (Carbondale: Southern Illinois University Press, 2001), 7.

71. Amardo Rodriguez, *Diversity: Mestizos, Latinos and the Promise of Possibilities* (Mountain View, CA: Floricanto Press, 2007), 73.

72. Amardo Rodriguez, *Revisioning Diversity in Communication Studies* (Leicester, UK: Troubador Publishers, 2010).

73. Robert Lieberman, *Shaping Race Policy: The United States in Comparative Perspective* (Princeton: Princeton University Press, 2005).

3

Housing Ordinances and Immigration Policy

Metaphors matter in understanding the direction of immigration debates and policy. Indeed, metaphors of pollution and contamination figure prominently in immigration discourses and representations.[1] Immigrants, in particular undocumented immigrants, often appear in such discourses like viruses seeking to exploit a healthy host species. The metaphors of pollution and contamination assume that the interests of the different species are inherently incompatible. Survival of the viruses presumably involves draining the host species of vital resources. On the other hand, survival of the host species requires repelling these viruses.

Metaphors of pollution and contamination ultimately place immigrants (both documented and undocumented) and citizens on opposite sides in a violent conflict that encourages the latter to enact policy to stop immigrants from flourishing; such flourishing would come at the expense of the community harboring these supposed viruses and parasites. This conviction can be vividly seen in the latest policy strategy that immigration opponents are employing to stop the prosperity of undocumented immigrants. Cities and local municipalities are increasingly enacting housing ordinances that specifically ban the renting of apartments and homes to undocumented immigrants.[2] The goal is to stop these cities and municipalities from becoming hosts to undocumented immigrants, and also to stop tenants from harboring such immigrants.

Many of the housing ordinances now sweeping the country mirror the 2006 Illegal Immigration Relief Act of San Bernardino, California. Specifically, the language of Section Seven of the San Bernardino ordinance has become commonplace in many housing ordinances. It establishes that:

> Illegal aliens are prohibited from leasing or renting property. Any property owner or renter/tenant/lessee in control of property, who allows an illegal alien to use, rent or lease their property shall be in violation of this section, irrespective of such person's intent, knowledge or negligence, said violation hereby being expressly declared a strict liability offense. Property owner is hereby required to submit a copy of the lease or rental agreement to the City Clerk's Office within 45 days of execution. Any person or entity that violates this section shall be subject to a fine of not less than $1,000.[3]

All of the versions of these new housing ordinances require prospective tenants to provide the local municipality with some kind of documentation to verify their immigration status. What constitutes proper legal documentation differs, at least in part, across ordinances. Nearly all ordinances impose harsh sanctions on landlords who continue to rent dwellings to individuals who never submitted the necessary documentation. The goal of these new immigration ordinances is to make the supposed harboring of undocumented immigrants impossible, presumably to stop immigrants from "draining" town resources.

This goal is captured unambiguously in Section Six under the heading "Business Permits, Contracts or Grants." Here, the San Bernardino ordinance states that:

> Any for profit entity, including acts committed by its parent company or subsidiaries, that aids and abets illegal aliens or illegal immigration shall be denied approval of a business permit, the renewal of a business permit, city contracts or grants for a period not less than five years from its last offense. Aiding and abetting shall include, but not be limited to, the hiring or attempted hiring of illegal aliens, renting or leasing to illegal aliens, or funding or aiding in the establishment of a day laborer center that does not verify legal work status. Any act that aids and abets illegal aliens within the United States, not just within the City limits, will constitute a violation.[4]

These city and town housing and immigration ordinances had origins in a 2006 report from the Center for Immigration Studies, which claimed to provide "immigration policymakers, the academic community, news media, and concerned citizens with reliable information about the social, economic, environmental, security, and fiscal consequences of legal and illegal immigration into the United States." The report, "Attrition Through Enforcement: A Cost-Effective Strategy to Shrink the Illegal Population," aimed to counter the claim that forcibly removing the 11 million plus undocumented immigrants in the United States was unworkable and, therefore, the only reasonable solution was to legalize those persons through an amnesty program. According to the report, such a program would be most "likely to result in large numbers of ineligible individuals receiving status, including terrorists, and will spawn new illegal immigration."[5]

Besides enacting new housing ordinances that explicitly target undocumented immigrants, cities and local municipalities are also establishing occupancy regulations and provisions; although these make no mention of undocumented immigrants, they do directly target that population. The new regulations claim to focus only on stopping "overcrowding" and regulating "maximum occupancy." Many aim to limit occupancy size by legally and narrowly defining what constitutes a family unit. For example, in the city of Manassas, Virginia, an overcrowding ordinance limits municipal definitions of "family" to include only immediate relatives. Isabelle M. Thabault, Director of the Fair Housing Project at the Washington Lawyers' Committee, notes, "When Manassas changed the definition of 'family' to prevent extended families from living together, it essentially made a common Hispanic family structure illegal."[6] As Daniel Eduardo Guzman explains, these new ordinances pose a serious threat to undocumented immigrants, as immigration opponents know that courts generally defer to towns and cities on matters of dwelling as long as enforcement appears to be nondiscriminatory. As a result, these new ordinances have "been reasonably effective"—immigrant families, and Latino immigrant families in particular, "tend to maintain numerically larger households than the average American family." This tendency, along with the fact that many immigrant households (and especially Latino households) are composed exclusively of male laborers, contributes to many "immigrant households violating occupancy ordinances."[7]

The notion of harboring features prominently in all the new housing ordinances that target undocumented immigrants. Harboring is generally defined in these ordinances as "to let, lease, or rent a dwelling unit to an illegal alien." The city of Escondido, California, passed Ordinance No. 2006-38 R, an "ordinance of the city of Escondido, California establishing penalties for the harboring of illegal aliens." The ordinance penalizes any owner of a dwelling unit who "harbors an illegal alien in the dwelling unit, knowing or in reckless disregard of the fact that an alien has come to, entered, or remains in the United States in violation of law."[8] Moreover, "the City finds that it is in the best interest of and will serve and benefit the health, safety and welfare of the public and law-abiding business entities and property owners to adopt policies and procedures to deter and prevent the harboring of illegal aliens, and criminal activity by illegal aliens."[9]

Probably the most prominent mention of harboring in these new housing ordinances appears in one from Hazleton, Pennsylvania, which declares that:

> unlawful employment, the harboring of illegal aliens in dwelling units in the City of Hazleton, and crime committed by illegal aliens harm the health, safety and welfare of authorized U.S. workers and legal residents in the City of Hazleton. Illegal immigration leads to higher crime rates, subjects our hospitals to fiscal hardship and legal residents to substandard quality of care, contributes to other burdens on public services, increasing their cost and diminishing their availability to legal residents, and diminishes our overall quality of life.[10]

In response to these supposed "findings" that appear without any kind of supporting evidence, Hazelton's immigration act:

> seeks to secure to those lawfully present in the United States and this City, whether or not they are citizens of the United States, the right to live in peace free from the threat [of] crime, to enjoy the public services provided by this city without being burdened by the cost of providing goods, support and services to aliens unlawfully present in the United States, and to be free of the debilitating effects on their economic and social wellbeing imposed by the influx of illegal aliens to the city.[11]

The ordinance allows any city resident to file a complaint with Hazleton's Code Enforcement Office alleging that a property owner is "harboring" a tenant who is an "illegal alien."

In September 2010, the Third Circuit of the United States Court of Appeals ruled against the City of Hazleton in a challenge against its new immigration act. They argued that "deciding which aliens may live in the United States has always been the prerogative of the federal government," later noting that the Supreme Court has long ruled that no state or locality has any power to "regulate immigration" and thereby determine "who should or should not be admitted into the country, and the conditions under which a legal entrant may remain."[12] As for the harboring provision, the court ruled that "the federal prohibition against harboring has never been interpreted to apply so broadly as to encompass the typical landlord/tenant relationship." Instead, the court defined harboring as conduct "tending to substantially facilitate an alien's remaining in the United States illegally and to prevent government authorities from detecting the alien's unlawful presence."[13] Harboring therefore requires:

> some act of obstruction that reduces the likelihood the government will discover the alien's presence. It is highly unlikely that a landlord's renting of an apartment to an alien lacking lawful immigration status could ever, without more, satisfy this definition of harboring. Renting an apartment in the normal course of business is not in and of itself conduct that prevents the government from detecting an alien's presence.

Although the court acknowledged that other courts of appeals have held that a showing of concealment is unnecessary, the Court could find no case "in which someone has been convicted of 'harboring' merely because s/he rented an apartment to someone s/he knew (or had reason to know) was not legally in the United States."[14] The Court concluded that:

> It appears plain that the purpose of these housing provisions is to ensure that aliens lacking legal immigration status reside somewhere other than Hazleton. It is this power to effectively prohibit residency based on immigration status that is so clearly within the exclusive domain of the federal government.[15]

But Hazleton and all the other cities and local municipalities with similar housing and immigration ordinances may yet prevail, as in 2011 the Supreme Court advised the Court of Appeals to reconsider its ruling.[16] Even if these harboring provisions are eventually determined to be legally sound, what about their moral foundation? As Jill Esbenshade writes in a report that examines the impact of these ordinances on immigrant populations across the country, these

> ordinances also bring into question whether it is . . . humane to deprive dependent children of shelter. Roughly 4.9 million children in the United States live in households headed by undocumented immigrants. About 3.1 million of these children are U.S.-born citizens. Over 40 percent of the households targeted by such ordinances include children and almost one-third include U.S.-citizen children.[17]

Since Hazelton

Now states are also increasingly enacting immigration laws with housing provisions that presumably bar the harboring of undocumented immigrants. In the case of Arizona's immigration law of 2010, interestingly called the Support Our Law Enforcement and Safe Neighborhoods Act, the goal was to make any kind of harboring impossible. Janice Brewer, Arizona's Republican Governor, argued that the law was necessary to save the state from devolving into lawlessness because of increasing numbers of undocumented immigrants "pouring" into the state. As she declared:

> This bill strengthens the laws of our state, protects all of us, every Arizona citizen and everyone here in our state lawfully. . . . I've decided to sign Senate Bill 1070 into law because, though many people disagree, I firmly believe it represents what's best for Arizona. Border-related violence and crime due to illegal immigration are critically important issues to the people of our state, to my Administration and to me, as your Governor and as a citizen. There is no higher priority than protecting the citizens of Arizona. We cannot sacrifice our safety to the murderous greed of drug cartels. We cannot stand idly by as drop houses, kidnappings and violence compromise our quality of life. We cannot delay while the destruction happening south of our international border creeps its way north. . . . As committed as I am to protecting our state from crime associated with illegal immigration I am EQUALLY committed to holding law enforcement accountable should this statute

ever be misused to violate an individual's rights. Respect for the rule of law means respect for every law. I have led that way every day in every office I have ever held. That will not change. I have also spent my career in service to Arizona working to bring people together, no matter the color of their skin and no matter the depth of our disagreements. This bill—and this issue—will be no exception.[18]

Following the passage of the bill, its critics found little solace in Governor Brewer's declaration of equal treatment under the law, as many questions were raised but few answered. Chief among those questions was one pertaining to racial profiling—race was one variable that would factor into the enforcement of the law.[19] Critics questioned whether state officials, who had a recently tarnished race relations record, could be trusted to faithfully execute their duties without violating civil rights.

For Arizona Republican State Representative Russell Pearce, the chief sponsor of the bill, immigrants are nothing but "invaders of American sovereignty and it can't be tolerated. I believe in the rule of law. I've always believed in the rule of law. We're a nation of laws."[20] As always, for opponents of immigration, the fear was anarchy. By supposedly encouraging anarchy, immigrants threaten the social and moral integrity of the United States. Although they acknowledged that the new law was harsh and punitive, many supporters contended that it was "a necessary evil." The lack of policy and action at the federal level left Governor Brewer and the legislature with, presumably, no other choice. For the Governor and many legislators, "something had to be done" to deal with "the crisis caused by illegal immigration and Arizona's porous border."

Proponents of Arizona's new immigration law believed that only such a restrictive law would be capable of stemming the flow of immigrants into Arizona and solving a "crisis" that "the federal government has refused to fix." The law contained nearly all the same punitive provisions against harboring undocumented immigrants that would soon appear in other immigration laws sweeping the country at the state level. It was also laden with many other provisions that aimed to discourage undocumented immigrants from settling in Arizona, such as the language prohibiting "anyone from transporting, moving, concealing, or harboring persons who the alleged violator knows to be illegally in the United States, as well as encouraging or inducing aliens to come to Arizona illegally."[21]

In direct contradiction of all the lawlessness that is supposedly threatening to engulf Arizona, the rate of violent crime at the border, and across
the state, has actually been declining. According to "On Border Violence,
Truth Pales Compared to Ideas,"

> statistics show that even as Arizona's population swelled, buoyed in
> part by illegal immigrants funneling across the border, violent crime
> rates declined, to 447 incidents per 100,000 residents in 2008, the
> most recent year for which comprehensive data are available from
> the F.B.I. In 2000, the rate was 532 incidents per 100,000. Nation-
> ally, the crime rate declined to 455 incidents per 100,000 people,
> from 507 in 2000.[22]

There is clearly no positive relationship between the supposed harboring
of undocumented immigrants and moral depravity.

Still, local and federal advocates of immigration laws with harboring provisions claim that this and other corrosive relationships exist. San
Bernardino's immigration bill begins with the supposed finding "that illegal immigration leads to higher crime rates, contributes to overcrowded
classrooms and failing schools, subjects our hospitals to fiscal hardship
and legal residents to substandard quality of care, and destroys our neighborhoods and diminishes our overall quality of life." However, in contrast
to these supposed findings, Thomas Vicino writes, "Crime rates are at an
all-time low, and school officials haven't a clue what prompted claims
of overcrowding."[23] In Escondido, California, the immigration law also
begins with the supposed finding that "the harboring of illegal aliens in
dwelling units in the City, and crime committed by illegal aliens harm the
health, safety and welfare of legal residents in the City," yet according to
a report from the Immigration Policy Center, "Despite council claims that
crime rates were growing in the city, the crime rate in Escondido dropped
by 10 percent between 1998 and 2002 and dropped again between 2004
and 2005, according to the FBI Crime Index."[24] In Hazleton, during court
proceedings, city officials "claimed that undocumented immigrants were
responsible for bankrupting the city, driving up healthcare costs and
increasing local crime." However, an article from the American Civil
Liberties Union contradicts this: "The evidence at trial showed that from
2000–2005, Latino immigrants actually helped to transform a huge city
budget deficit into a surplus . . . the private hospital system made a $4
million profit and . . . the crime rate actually fell."[25]

Moreover, there is no correlation between the supposed harboring of undocumented immigrants and unemployment. As a report by Jill Esbenshade explains:

> Around two-thirds of ordinance locales (68 percent) had unemployment rates at or below the national average in 2000, as did 64 percent of the 25 largest localities in 2005 for which unemployment data was available. Between1990 and 2000, the unemployment rate actually decreased by an average of 0.2 percent in these localities, compared to a decrease of 0.4 percent nationwide.[26]

In fact, Esbenshade writes, "Many of the city governments that have fought hardest for ordinances—like Escondido, California—have actually seen declines in local unemployment rates in recent years."[27]

Nonetheless, many states continue to introduce new immigration laws to stop the supposed harboring of undocumented immigrants. Alabama's 2011 immigration law, the Alabama Taxpayer and Citizen Protection Act, is noteworthy in many regards. It begins with the declaration that "the State of Alabama finds that illegal immigration is causing economic hardship and lawlessness in this state and that illegal immigration is encouraged when public agencies within this state provide public benefits without verifying immigration status."[28] The state also "finds that certain practices currently allowed in this state impede and obstruct the enforcement of federal immigration law, undermine the security of our borders, and impermissibly restrict the privileges and immunities of the citizens of Alabama."[29]

The new Alabama immigration law required, among other things, the Attorney General of Alabama to attempt to negotiate a Memorandum of Agreement with certain aims, including:

> to criminalize certain behavior relating to concealing, harboring, shielding, or attempting to conceal, harbor, or shield unauthorized aliens and to provide penalties;
>
> to prohibit certain deductible business expenses; to make it a discriminatory practice for a business entity or employer to fail to hire a legally present job applicant or discharge an employee while retaining an employee who is an unauthorized alien under certain conditions;
>
> to require public schools to determine the citizenship and immigration status of students enrolling;

to prohibit a landlord from knowingly entering into a rental agreement to harbor an illegal alien and provide penalties.[30]

The Alabama immigration law, which legal scholars view as the most
comprehensive and punitive in the history of the United States, passed
overwhelmingly in both chambers of the Alabama legislature, with a significant majority of local and national support. Republican State Senator
Scott Beason, chairman of the State Senate's Rules Committee and a sponsor of the law, noted that the Alabama legislature needed to "empty the
clip" on the immigration issue, arguing, "We have plenty of needs from
our own people. They come first." For many of its sponsors, the aim of the
law was to ensure an exodus of immigrants out of Alabama by making life
unbearable for them. As always, aliens are cast negatively—in this case,
they are depicted as being greedy and unfair.

Alabama Republican Representative Mo Brooks confirmed this goal:
"Those are the intended consequences [the exodus of immigrants] of Alabama's legislation with respect to illegal aliens. The bottom line is illegal
aliens consume far more of our tax resources than they generate."[31] Continuing, Brooks argued, "We don't have the money in America to keep
paying for the education of everybody else's children from around the
world. We simply don't have the financial resources to do that."[32] Brooks
also claims that undocumented immigrants "commit heinous crimes
against American citizens." According to him, the main purpose of the
law was to remove undocumented immigrants from Alabama, and the legislation would achieve its goal. "These aren't unintended consequences,"
he stated; "We want illegal aliens out of the state of Alabama and I want
illegal aliens out of the United States of America."[33] Republican Representative Micky Hammon, another prominent sponsor of the new bill, posited
that immigrants "were coming in here like thieves in the night and taking
our jobs and tax revenue."[34] For Republican State Senator Rusty Glover,
who voted for the law and is also a history teacher, "It's heartbreaking to
read about [children being pulled out of school], but it's going to be an
immigration bill or it's not going to be one."[35] It was also going to be an
immigration bill without any sponsor being obligated to show evidence to
support any of the supposed findings.

Alabama's immigration law was also comprehensive about requiring residents to uphold the law or face harsh sanctions. These sanctions
appeared as follows:

A person who is a United States citizen or an alien who is lawfully present in the United States and is a resident of this state may bring an action in circuit court to challenge any official or head of an agency of this state or political subdivision thereof . . . that adopts or implements a policy or practice that is in violation of 8 U.S.C. § 1373 or 8 U.S.C. § 1644. If there is a judicial finding that an official or head of an agency, including, but not limited to, an officer of a court in this state, has violated this section, the court shall order that the officer, official, or head of an agency pay a civil penalty of not less than one thousand dollars ($1,000) and not more than five thousand dollars ($5,000) for each day that the policy or practice has remained in effect after the filing of an action pursuant to this section. Every person working for the State of Alabama or a political subdivision thereof . . . shall have a duty to report violations of this act. Any person who willfully fails to report any violation of this act when the person knows that this act is being violated shall be guilty of obstructing governmental operations as defined in Section 13A-10-2 of the Code of Alabama 1975. No official or agency of this state or any political subdivision thereof . . . may adopt a policy or practice that limits or restricts the enforcement of federal immigration laws by limiting communication between its officers and federal immigration officials in violation of 8 U.S.C. § 1373 or 8 U.S.C. § 1644, or that restricts its officers in the enforcement of this act. All state officials, agencies, and personnel . . . fully comply with and, to the full extent permitted by law, support the enforcement of federal law prohibiting the entry into, presence, or residence in the United States of aliens in violation of federal immigration law.[36]

As illustrated thus far in this chapter and throughout those preceding it, immigration reform continues to undergo peculiar twists and turns. In Alabama, the immigration reform crusade places a legal onus on every citizen, every lawfully admitted "alien," and even state officials to report anything they witness that might be in conflict with the law. Those who fail to do so become subject to legal action, specifically regarding the potential obstruction of governmental operations.

Interestingly enough, this political/legal notion of stopping an entity from harboring perceived threats to a community has deep roots in U.S.

policy—namely, it harks back to the Fugitive Slave Act (FSA) of 1850. Sections of the Alabama immigration law are nearly fully exchangeable with sections of the FSA. For instance, the latter criminalizes any person who:

> shall knowingly and willingly obstruct, hinder, or prevent such claimant, his agent or attorney, or any person or persons lawfully assisting him, her, or them, from arresting such a fugitive from service or labor . . . or shall harbor or conceal such fugitive . . . shall, for either of said offences, be subject to a fine not exceeding one thousand dollars, and imprisonment not exceeding six months.[37]

Similarly, Section 13 of the Alabama immigration law criminalizes persons who:

> (1) Conceal, harbor, or shield or attempt to conceal, harbor, or shield an alien from detection in any place in this state; (2) Encourage or induce an alien to come to or reside in this state if the person knows or recklessly disregards the fact that such coming to, entering, or residing in the United States is or will be in violation of federal law; (3) Transport, or attempt to transport, or conspire to transport in this state an alien in furtherance of the unlawful presence of the alien in the United States; (4) Harbor an alien unlawfully present in the United States by entering into a rental agreement . . . with an alien to provide accommodations, if the person knows or recklessly disregards the fact that the alien is unlawfully present in the United States.[38]

Unfortunately, this is merely one of many such comparisons.

The Fugitive Slave Act of 1850 and the Alabama law share very similar approaches to local law enforcement strategies and abilities. The FSA made clear that:

> It shall be the duty of all marshals and deputy marshals to obey and execute all warrants and precepts issued under the provisions of this act, when to them directed; and should any marshal or deputy marshal refuse to receive such warrant, or other process . . . he shall, on conviction thereof, be fined in the sum of one thousand dollars. . . . and after arrest of such fugitive . . . should such fugitive escape, whether with or without the assent of such marshal or his deputy,

such marshal shall be liable, on his official bond, to be prosecuted for the benefit of such claimant, for the full value of the service or labor of said fugitive in the State, Territory, or District whence he escaped.[39]

Meanwhile, the Alabama law mandates that "no official or agency of this state or any political subdivision thereof . . . may adopt a policy or practice that limits or restricts the enforcement of federal immigration laws by limiting communication between its officers and federal immigration officials . . . or that restricts its officers in the enforcement of this act." Furthermore, "All state officials, agencies, and personnel . . . shall fully comply with and, to the full extent permitted by law, support the enforcement of federal law prohibiting the entry into, presence, or residence in the United States of aliens in violation of federal immigration law."[40]

Probably most revealing is the fact that both laws strip either slaves or undocumented immigrants of equal legal protection. In the Fugitive Slave Act, no slave can bear witness against a citizen in any court proceeding. According to Alabama law, citizens have no obligation to uphold any employment contract with an undocumented immigrant, and thus "shall not be liable for any claims made against the business entity or employer by the terminated employee [undocumented immigrant]."[41] Under these laws, slaves and undocumented immigrants have no comparable moral worth to that of citizens and are therefore entitled to no equal legal protection. But what is the moral worth of any law that purposely seeks to deny equal rights to and protection of all peoples? How could such laws be assumed to be morally just and, in the case of the new immigration laws, believed by many judges to be in harmony with the U.S. Constitution? And what is the moral worth of any person who would uphold a law that purposefully denies equal rights and protection to all? This is the challenge the FSA poses to the new set of immigration laws. Who would now claim that people were being morally just by upholding a law that was morally unjust, denying as it did equal protection to all human beings? On the other hand, if slaves and abolitionists were morally just in deliberately violating the Fugitive Slave Act, then are undocumented immigrants no less morally just for disobeying any immigration law that deprives them of equal rights—such as the right to housing—and protection?

The U.S. Constitution is founded on the premise that all human beings are born with certain inalienable rights, which have nothing to do with race, ethnicity, gender, or resident status. These are rights that simply come with being human—thus the phrase "inalienable rights." The Constitution mandates that no law should deprive any person of these rights. According to the Fourteenth Amendment, "No state shall make or enforce any law which shall abridge the privileges or immunities of citizens of the United States; nor shall any State deprive any person of life, liberty, or property, without due process of law; nor deny to any person within its jurisdiction the equal protection of the laws."[42] The amendment makes an important distinction between citizens and persons by deliberately moving from language about citizens to language about persons when invoking our inalienable right to life, liberty, and property. In the Constitution, person trumps citizen. No state can make or enforce any law that abridges "the privileges or immunities of citizens of the United States"; no state can "deprive any person [again, 'any person'] of life, liberty, or property, without due process of law; nor deny to any person [again, 'any person'] within its jurisdiction the equal protection of the laws."

Thus the right of equal protection to "any person" rather than merely "citizens of the United States" is paramount. It is the cornerstone of our democracy and is responsible for the moral evolution of our social, legal, political, and educational systems. The Equal Protection Clause means that laws must be moral, and laws, by offering equal protection to all regardless of legal status, are inherently so. This forms the foundation of our notions of decency and fairness. Indeed, the Equal Protection Clause best reflects our morality, enforcing as it does both our belief that all human beings, by being born with certain inalienable rights, are deserving of various protections, and our commitment to guarantee those protections. This is supposedly what our legal system is fundamentally about—that is, guaranteeing equal protection to all, regardless of race, ethnicity, or immigration status—and it is why the abolitionist, civil rights, and women's rights movements all challenged the courts to do what was morally just by upholding the principle that all persons possess certain inalienable rights. What are we to make of the fact that every new immigration law violates the Equal Protection Clause by denying persons the right to have others honor contracts and the rights to shelter, water, and any means to sustain themselves? What are we to make of the fact that upholding these morally unjust laws makes us morally unjust? That is, these laws aim to stop us from doing what is morally just. They do not uphold the laws that require equal protection to all. What is the possibility of life when a law—such as the Alabama immigration law—criminalizes a person for "knowingly" applying for work so as to afford food and shelter? The Constitution morally—rather than merely legally—obligates us to treat all human beings—rather than merely our fellow citizens—with the dignity and respect all of us would demand of each other. It is, again, this obligation that led to the abolitionist movement, the civil rights movement, the women's movement, the gay rights movement, and the disability rights movement. All these movements faced enormous struggles and involved tremendous sacrifices. What would the United States be now without them and without the willingness of so many persons to disobey laws that were morally unjust?

The notion that all persons, rather than merely all citizens, are deserving of equal rights and protections is behind the sanctuary city ordinances being passed by many cities and local municipalities. These prohibit local authorities, especially law enforcement departments, from: using local funds and resources to enforce immigration laws; inquiring about the legal status of immigrants and reporting such information to federal authorities; and blocking cooperation with federal agencies in regards to the identification and deportation of undocumented immigrants. This latter is in violation of a 1996 federal law, the Illegal Immigration Reform and Immigrant Responsibility Act, which requires local governments to cooperate with the Department of Homeland Security's Immigration and Customs Enforcement (ICE).

Sanctuary city ordinances normally come with language originally found in a policy initiated in Los Angeles by the Chief of Police in 1979, which states, "Officers shall not initiate police action with the objective of discovering the alien status of a person. Officers shall not arrest nor book persons for violation of title 8, section 1325 of the United States Immigration code (Illegal Entry)."[43] This policy is based on the recognition that undocumented immigrants are not willing to report crimes, out of fear of being apprehended and deported. It also recognizes that undocumented immigrants are especially criminally vulnerable because, again, of their unwillingness to report crimes to police. As Ron Miller, Police Chief of Topeka, Kansas, notes, "We cannot police a community that will not talk to us."[44] In a 2009 Police Foundation report, "70 percent of police chiefs surveyed believe that immigrant crime victims are less likely to contact local police than other members of the community."[45] According to Lynn Tramonte, "These findings led the Police Foundation to conclude

that police should focus on criminal laws, not civil immigration enforcement, and engage in a dialogue with representatives of the immigrant community to ensure that immigrants work with state and local police when
they are victims of or witnesses to crime."[46] For sanctuary city advocates,
access to police services (as well as health services) is vital to guaranteeing fundamental rights and protections as found in the Constitution.
Among the many other cities that now have sanctuary city ordinances are:
Chandler and Phoenix, Arizona; Fresno, Los Angeles, Davis, National
City, San Diego, San Francisco, Sonoma County, and Long Beach, Cali-
fornia; Hartford and New Haven, Connecticut; Miami, Florida; Evanston,
Chicago, and Cicero, Illinois; Denver, Colorado; New Orleans, Louisiana;
Cambridge and Orleans, Massachusetts; Portland, Maine; Baltimore and
Takoma Park, Maryland; Ann Arbor and Detroit, Michigan; Minneapolis,
Minnesota; Newark, Trenton, Jersey City, and Union City, New Jersey;
Durham, North Carolina; Albuquerque, Aztec, and Santa Fe, New Mex-
ico; Albany and New York City, New York; Ashland, Gaston, and Marion
County, Oregon; Austin, Houston, and Katy, Texas; Virginia Beach, Vir-
ginia; Seattle, Washington; and Madison, Wisconsin.

In 1996, Congress moved to end these ordinances by passing the Illegal
Immigration Reform and Immigrant Responsibility Act and the Personal
Responsibility and Work Opportunity Reconciliation Act; these withhold
federal funds to cities and local municipalities with such ordinances. A
legal challenge to these laws by New York City found no success. Various
members of Congress have made legislative attempts over the years to end
sanctuary city ordinances by denying access to other kinds of funds and
resources.[47] States have also begun to enact laws prohibiting cities and
local municipalities from passing sanctuary city ordinances.[48]

Texas legislators recently passed legislation denying state funds to
cities and local municipalities with these ordinances. Representative Jose
Aliseda (R-Beeville), a Latino immigrant and prominent supporter of the
legislation, said that, "As a legal Mexican immigrant who understands that
the American Dream must be protected, I was proud to support and vote
for this legislation. The reality is that this bill simply puts Texas teeth on
federal law which was signed by President Clinton in 1996. . . . HB 12 is
good policy and good for Texas."[49] Recent polls also show that a majority
of Americans support federal legislation ending sanctuary ordinances and
support withholding federal funds from cities and local municipalities that
refuse to comply with such laws. To avoid the withholding of federal and

state funds, many cities and local municipalities with sanctuary ordinances now publicly claim only to embody the ordinances in spirit.

Sanctuary city debates have become, fundamentally, issues of law and order. Opponents contend that these ordinances undermine law and order by preventing police from enforcing federal law; they point to crimes committed by undocumented immigrants as evidence. On the other hand, proponents argue that these ordinances promote law and order by encouraging all persons, without threat of penalty, to come forward and report crimes, and to be actively involved in maintaining order. Although the term "sanctuary city" has no set legal definition, the notion of sanctuary means provision and protection—as in, being provided with a space that is safe and nurturing. What have been lost in sanctuary city debates are the obligations of a city or local municipality, based on the Fourteenth Amendment, to be a safe and nurturing place for all persons, rather than merely all citizens. These sanctuary ordinances put cities in violation of the amendment that assumes that all persons are entitled to life, liberty, and property. How could these rights be guaranteed when people are denied access to housing as well as the police?

They Must Go: On Immigration & Deportation

Globally, the political/legal directive to deport individuals back to their countries of origin has been used with increasing frequency. The French government expelled nearly 30,000 "illegal migrants" in 2009, and it has promised to deport more, including some 30,000 Roma. In the United States, under the presidency of Barack Obama, the colloquial title "Deportation Nation" has been used to describe our state of affairs. Explained best by Michael Shear of the *New York Times*:

> In four years, Mr. Obama's administration has deported as many illegal immigrants as the administration of George W. Bush did in his two terms, largely by embracing, expanding and refining Bush-era programs to find people and send them home. By the end of this year [2013], deportations under Mr. Obama are on track to reach two million, or nearly the same number of deportations in the United States from 1892 to 1997. Since 2010, the government has deported more than 200,000 parents of children who are United States citizens.[50]

One option always at the disposal of governments is the removal of individuals. Once we begin to deny housing and employment, and once we fail to orchestrate a federal immigration overhaul, piecemeal "solutions" become commonplace. As a consequence of failed congressional leadership, states begin to implement policies that critics argue amount to racial profiling. With no federal organization on the matter, some states see deportation as one of the best short-term solutions.

Although President Obama, having seen his approval ratings among a growing Latino constituency plummet, ordered an easing of deportations, a June 2013 vote in the House of Representatives changed that directive. In House Resolution 5855, Iowa Republican Congressman Steven King introduced a measure that, among other things, reversed President Obama's orders on deportation. This appropriations bill for the Department of Homeland Security included several controversial measures. Title II of the bill, "Security, Enforcement and Investigations," as it pertained to U.S. Customs and Border Patrol, was the main source of tension. Buried within the 100-page bill, the law stated:

> That the Border Patrol shall maintain an active duty presence of not less than 21,370 full-time equivalent agents protecting the borders of the United States in the fiscal year. . . . That of the total amount available, not less than $1,600,000,000 shall be available to identify aliens convicted of a crime who may be deportable, and to remove them from the United States once they are judged deportable. . . . Provided further, that of the total amount provided, not less than $2,749,840,000 is for detention and removal operations, including transportation of unaccompanied minor aliens, of which not less than $91,460,000 shall be for alternatives to detention.[51]

Passed along party lines, this bill would have begun to provide a clear path for U.S. Immigration and Customs Enforcement (ICE) to target more undocumented immigrants than what President Obama initially directed. As the bill was written, undocumented immigrants who were brought to the country as children would be eligible for deportation. In a statement condemning the bill, President Obama argued that, "It asks law enforcement to treat these Dreamers the same way as they would violent criminals. It's wrong. It's not who we are. And it will not become law," affirming he would reject the provision.[52] Nonetheless, as evidenced by sagging poll numbers, many immigrant groups believe that much of the damage has already been done.

As a supposed precaution against violent criminals and other "illegal" undesirables, deportation still remains on the table as a policy choice. Increasingly calling for local and federal sharing of information pertaining to immigration status, some lawmakers believe that deportation exists as a great deterrent against society's unwanted. However, what escapes much conversation are the detailed accounts of deportations and near-deportations gone wrong. In the 2010 case *Galarza v. Szalczyk*, Ernesto Galarza, a New Jersey-born U.S. citizen of Puerto Rican descent, was held illegally for three days in the Lehigh County Prison. Galarza had been mistakenly swept up in a series of drug arrests by Allentown police aimed at, among others, the construction contractor for whom he worked for, an immigrant from the Dominican Republic. Galarza had nothing to do with the crimes, but he was jailed along with other arrestees. Galarza was not released because the ICE had issued an immigration detainer against him, directing prison officials to hold him while it investigated whether he could be deported to the Dominican Republic—even though his social security card and Pennsylvania driver's license were in his wallet at the time of his arrest (and in the prison's possession during his detention), Galarza was not told why he was being held.[53] He was later acquitted of any wrongdoing.

From the outset, the case was riddled with errors and gross negligence. During the booking process, Mr. Galarza told Lehigh County prison officials that he was born in New Jersey. Prison officials took his fingerprints and confiscated and stored his wallet, which contained his Pennsylvania driver's license, social security card, debit card, and health insurance card. At some point on Friday, November 21, 2008, ICE agent Mark Szalczyk, acting on information relayed by Detective Christie Correa, filled out an immigration "detainer" form and faxed it to Lehigh County. The immigration detainer falsely described Galarza as a suspected "alien" and citizen of the Dominican Republic. Oddly enough, the detainer was not accompanied by a warrant, an affidavit of probable cause, a removal order, or any other evidentiary support.

Galarza was later notified that he would not be released because he was the subject of "a detainer." Unfortunately, the prison official did not specify what kind of detainer was preventing his release, nor did he provide Galarza with a copy or any additional information. When Galarza protested, the prison official told him that he would have to wait through the entire weekend and speak with a prison counselor the following Monday. Upon speaking with a prison counselor, and upon the arrival of two ICE officers, Galarza was immediately released and the detainer was canceled.

Sadly, this is just one of many emerging examples of unlawful detention and close-call deportations in attempts at misguided "solutions." In *Quezada v. Mink* (2010), a partial settlement of a federal court lawsuit filed in 2010, the United States was made to pay $50,000 to ACLU client Luis Quezada, who spent 47 days illegally imprisoned in a Jefferson County, Colorado, jail in 2009 simply because federal authorities wanted to investigate whether he was violating immigration laws.[54] Plaintiffs in the case *Cacho v. Gusman* (2011), like those in the *Quezada* case, argued that they were held for indefinite periods of time without legal authority because they were believed to be undocumented immigrants. The amount of litigation falling into this category exposes an imperfect system that violates the constitutional rights of those who are suspected to be undocumented.[55]

Metaphorically, immigrants have become deviants, regardless of legal status. As seen in just the few cases above, even with verifiable evidence, suspicion outweighs reality. Criminality continues to pervade our conversations over housing rights, deportation, and border security; our debates have become obscured, with no end in sight.

Conclusion

We are metaphorical beings. We conceive the world through metaphors. We perceive the world through metaphors. We organize the world through metaphors. We experience the world through metaphors. It is because of metaphors that language matters. The notion that language shapes our social worlds should really mean that metaphors shape our social worlds. In other words, the fact that language is inherently metaphorical means language influences how we perceive, conceptualize, and relate to the world. Because metaphors matter, the kinds of metaphors found in immigration policy discourses are important. We presumably have an immigration system that is "broken." Immigrants are a "drain" on our resources, there is a "flood" of immigrants upon us, and the country is facing nothing less than an "invasion." There are also metaphors of "pollution," "contamination," "balkanization," "infection," and "infestation." In a review of media representations, David Cisneros found that "metaphors of immigrants often portray them as objects or threats to society, whether biological, physical, or social. On the other hand, metaphors of immigration concretize the problem through cognitive comparisons to other physical or social ills."[56] By shaping our social worlds, metaphors shape and influence how we perceive, communicate with, and experience each other.

Metaphors embody and reflect ideological positions. Cisneros explains, "As repositories of cultural understandings, metaphors are some of the principal tools with which dominant ideologies and prejudices are represented and reinforced."[57] Moreover, in shaping what we perceive to be true and possible, metaphors affect what we believe and imagine. For example, framing immigration discourse in terms of "illegal aliens," "border security," and "amnesty," according to George Lakoff and Sam Ferguson, "focuses entirely on the immigrants and the administrative agencies charged with overseeing immigration law." This framing "dehumanizes" immigrants and "pre-empts" a consideration of "broader social and economic concerns" (such as foreign economic policy and international human rights).[58] Put differently, to claim that immigrants are a "drain" on our resources is by no means a neutral description of immigrants—that is, it is not a description devoid of biases and prejudices. Metaphors end all illusions of objectivity.

There is an inseparable relationship between language, being, and our thoughts. That each influences and shapes the other means that changing one also involves changing the other. According to David Bohm, "Our thought system chops up the world into pieces. It splinters the world. It separates and divides everything into conflicting pieces," such as meaning vs. ambiguity, order vs. chaos, ignorance vs. knowledge, citizen vs. immigrant, and so forth.[59] What emerges is a thought system that assumes a world laden with conflict, a thought system that puts us in constant battle with the world, a thought system that torments our being with all manner of unnecessary and unhealthy tension, and a thought system that infuses all of this division, separation, and fragmentation into our language. Ultimately, what emerge are a thought system, a language system, and a manner of being that together only make for death and destruction. This thought system has given rise to the metaphors of pollution and contamination that set up a violent conflict between immigrants (supposed parasites) and citizens (supposed healthy hosts). It also makes any proper resolution to this conflict all but impossible. The best that can be achieved is a compromise that mutually serves the material and practical needs of both sides. However, as soon as the conditions that sustain such a compromise break down, violent struggle—as history has shown again and again—becomes all but inevitable. Immigration policy discourse lacks metaphors that reflect and can bring forth new thought systems that would release us from the conflict between citizen and immigrant. We would do well to look at metaphors that recognize our ecological foundation.

Ecologically, there is no such thing as a native or foreign species. All species are invasive, as all species have origins elsewhere. As anthropologist Hugh Raffles explains:

> Like humans, plants and animals travel, often in ways beyond our knowledge and control. They arrive unannounced, encounter unfamiliar conditions and proceed to remake each other and their surroundings. Designating some as native and others as alien denies this ecological and genetic dynamism. It draws an arbitrary historical line based as much on aesthetics, morality and politics as on science, a line that creates a mythic time of purity before places were polluted by interlopers.[60]

Species survive and flourish by moving from place to place, always in search of new resources and more fecund environs. Ecologically, movement is status quo. Without moving from place to place, species would perish; if this were to occur across species, all the diversity that abounds in the world would disappear. Thus, diversity means movement. Movement brings new challenges, new resources, new capacities, new capabilities. Movement vitalizes ecologies by pushing them to do new and different things. It impedes mediocrity.

Invasive species survive and flourish by adapting and adjusting to the constraints of new ecologies. This requires such species to develop capacities and capabilities that strengthen the integrity and resiliency of the new ecology. That all ecologies have constraints means that every species must work within such constraints. No ecology can sustain any species that acts otherwise. Because constraints are always pushing and pressing up against invasive species, species are always challenging and contesting these constraints. This tension is vital for the survival of all ecologies. It makes diversity possible. By adapting and adjusting, invasive species become new species, and new species ultimately make for new ecologies. According to Raffles:

Non-native plants and animals have transformed the American landscape in unmistakably positive ways. Honeybees were introduced from Europe in the 1600s, and new stocks from elsewhere in the world have landed at least eight times since. They succeeded in making themselves indispensable, economically and symbolically. In the process, they made us grateful that they arrived, stayed and found their place.[61]

This is just one of many examples illustrating how diversity emerges in the natural world. Arguably, this ecological perspective gives us a more constructive way of framing the relationship between citizens and immigrants, and of making immigration policy.

The debates over spatial aspects like housing ordinances continue to intensify. In the chapter that follows, we shift our attention to another growing aspect of this policy arena: border crossing.

Notes

1. David Cisneros, "Contaminated Communities: The Metaphor of Immigrant as Pollutant in Media Representations of Immigration," *Rhetoric & Public Affairs* 11, no. 4 (2008): 569–602.

2. Daniel Guzman, "There Is No Shelter Here: Anti-Immigration Ordinances and Comprehensive Reform," *Cornell Journal of Law and Public Policy* 20 (2010): 399–439.

3. Illegal Immigration Relief Act of San Bernardino, CA, 2006.

4. Ibid.

5. Jessica Vaughan, "A Cost-Effective Strategy to Shrink the Illegal Population," Center for Immigration Studies, April 2006. Accessed June 2, 2013. http://www.cis.org/Enforcement-IllegalPopulation.

6. Guzman, "There Is No Shelter Here: Anti-Immigration Ordinances and Comprehensive Reform," *Cornell Journal of Law and Public Policy* 20 (2010): 415.

7. Ibid., 415.

8. Ordinance No. 2006-38 R.

9. Ibid.

10. *Lozano v City of Hazleton* No. 07-3531 (2010).

11.　Ibid.

12.　Ibid.

13.　Ibid.

14.　Ibid.

15.　Ibid.

16.　Kent Jackson, "Court Tosses Ruling Against Hazleton Immigration Law," *Citizens Voice,* June 7, 2011. Accessed June 2, 2013. http://citizensvoice.com/news/court-tosses-ruling-against-hazleton -immigration-law-1.1158009.

17.　Jill Esbenshade, "Division and Dislocation: Regulating Immigration Through Local Housing Ordinances," Immigration Policy Center, 2007. Accessed March 2, 2012. http://www.immigrationpolicy.org/ special-reports/division-and-dislocation-regulating-immigration -through-local-housing-ordinances.

18.　Janice K. Brewer, "Statement by Governor Jan Brewer," April 23, 2010. Accessed, June 2, 2013. http://azgovernor.gov/dms/upload/ PR_042310_StatementByGovernorOnSB1070.pdf.

19.　See, Donathan L. Brown, "An Invitation to Profile: *Arizona v. United States,*" *International Journal of Discrimination and the Law* 12, no. 2 (2012): 117–127.

20.　Ted Robbins, "The Man Behind Arizona's Toughest Immigrant Laws," National Public Radio, March 12, 2008. Accessed June 2, 2013. http:// www.npr.org/templates/story/story.php?storyId=88125098.

21.　Arizona Senate Bill 1070 (2010).

22.　Randal Archibold, "On Border Violence, Truth Pales Compared to Ideas," *New York Times*, June 19, 2010. Accessed June 2, 2013. http://www.nytimes.com/2010/06/20/us/20crime.html?pagewanted =all&_r=0.

23.　Thomas Vicino, *Suburban Crossroads: The Fight for Local Control of Immigration Policy* (Lanham, MD: Rowman and Littlefield, 2012).

24.　Jill Esbenshade, "Division and Dislocation: Regulating Immigration Through Local Housing Ordinances," Immigration Policy Center, 2007. Accessed March 2, 2012. http://www.immigrationpolicy .org/special-reports/division-and-dislocation-regulating-immigration -through-local-housing-ordinances.

25. "Hazleton, PA Anti-Immigrant Law Is Unconstitutional, Federal Appeals Court Rules," American Civil Liberties Union, September 9, 2010. Accessed June 4, 2013. http://www.aclu.org/immigrants-rights/ hazleton-pa-anti-immigrant-law-unconstitutional-federal-appeals -court-rules.

26. Esbenshade, "Division and Dislocation: Regulating Immigration Through Local Housing Ordinances." Immigration Policy Center, 2007. Accessed March 2, 2012. http://www.immigrationpolicy.org/ special-reports/division-and-dislocation-regulating-immigration -through-local-housing-ordinances.

27. Ibid.

28. Beason-Hammon Alabama Taxpayer & Citizen Protection Act (Act 2011-535).

29. Ibid.

30. Ibid.

31. Alexander Trowbridge & Mackenzie Weinger. "Alabama immigration law is working, Rep. Mo Brooks says." *Politico*, October 6, 2011. Accessed June 9, 2013. http://www.politico.com/news/stories/ 1011/65351.html.

32. Ibid.

33. Ibid.

34. Ibid.

35. Ibid.

36. Beason-Hammon Alabama Taxpayer & Citizen Protection Act (Act 2011-535).

37. Fugitive Slave Act, accessed, June 5, 2013. http://avalon.law.yale .edu/19th_century/fugitive.asp.

38. Beason-Hammon Alabama Taxpayer & Citizen Protection Act (Act 2011-535).

39. Fugitive Slave Act. Accessed June 5, 2013. http://avalon.law.yale .edu/19th_century/fugitive.asp.

40. Beason-Hammon Alabama Taxpayer & Citizen Protection Act (Act 2011-535).

41. Ibid.

42.   14th Amendment, *United States Constitution*, 1787.

43.   Office of Chief of Police Special Order NO. 40, Accessed June 9, 2013. http://keepstuff.homestead.com/Spec40orig.html.

44.   Lynn Tramonte, "Debunking the Myth of 'Sanctuary Cities': Community Policing Policies Protect Americans." *Immigration Policy Center*, April 2011. Accessed June 10, 2013. http://www.immigration policy.org/sites/default/files/docs/Community_Policing_Policies _Protect_American_042611_update.pdf.

45.   Ibid.

46.   Ibid.

47.   Edwin Mora, "House Bill Seeks to Deny 'Sanctuary Cities' Immigration Enforcement Funds," *CNS News*, May 14, 2012. Accessed June 10, 2013. http://cnsnews.com/news/article/house-bill-seeks-deny -sanctuary-cities-immigration-enforcement-funds#sthash.TTW spKZY.dpuf.

48.   Jesse McKinley, "Immigration Protection Rules Draw Fire," *New York Times,* November 12, 2006. Accessed June 11, 2013. http:// www.nytimes.com/2006/11/12/us/12sanctuary.html?_r=0.

49.   "Legislative Update: Texas House Passes Sanctuary Cities Bill." Accessed, June 11, 2013. http://www.texasgop.org/posts/153 -legislative-update-texas-house-passes-sanctuary-cities-bill .

50.   Michael Shear, "Seeing Citizenship Path Near, Activists Push Obama to Slow Deportations," *New York Times*, February 23, 2013: 12.

51.   H.R. 5855 (2013).

52.   Stephen Dinan, "GOP Votes to Life Deportation Limits; Signals Trouble for Broader Reform Bill." *Washington Times*, June 7, 2013: 3.

53.   *Galarza v. Szalczyk et al*, 5:10-cv-06815 (2012).

54.   *Quezada v. Mink*, No. 10-0879 (2010).

55.   *Cacho et al v. Gusman*, 2:11-cv-00225 (2011).

56.   David Cisneros, "Contaminated Communities: The Metaphor of Immigrant as Pollutant in Media Representations of Immigration," *Rhetoric & Public Affairs* 11, no.v4 (2008): 569–602.

57.   Ibid., 571.

58. George Lakoff & Sam Ferguson, "The Framing of Immigration." *Rockridge Institute*, 2006. Accessed June 11, 2013. http://economic refugee.wordpress.com/what-does-economic-refugee-mean.

59. David Bohm, *Thought As A System* (New York: Routledge, 1994).

60. Hugh Raffles, "What to Do About Invasive Species," *New York Times*, April 9, 2011. Accessed June 12, 2013.http://www.nytimes .com/2011/04/10/opinion/l10species.html.

61. Ibid.

4

Borders and Immigration Policy

Both sides of the political spectrum in the United States generally assume that building a wall on the U.S.-Mexico border is vital to a comprehensive immigration policy. Polls also consistently show that an overwhelming majority of Americans believe that enhanced border security measures are an important component of any immigration policy.

The Secure Fence Act of 2006 reflects this kind of popular support. This act mandated that the Secretary of Homeland Security "take all actions the Secretary determines necessary and appropriate to achieve and maintain operational control over the entire international land and maritime borders of the United States."[1] This included:

(1) systematic surveillance of the international land and maritime borders of the United States through more effective use of personnel and technology, such as unmanned aerial vehicles, ground-based sensors, satellites, radar coverage, and cameras; and

(2) physical infrastructure enhancements to prevent unlawful entry by aliens into the United States and facilitate access to the international land and maritime borders by United States Customs and Border Protection, such as additional checkpoints, all weather access roads, and vehicle barriers.[2]

To fulfill these obligations, the Secretary of Homeland Security "shall provide for at least 2 layers of reinforced fencing, the installation of additional physical barriers, roads, lighting, cameras, and sensors" that covers nearly

700 miles, leaving about 1,300 miles of the border with Mexico uncovered. Congress approved $1.2 billion to begin construction; the full fence is estimated to cost $6 billion. Upon passage of the act, Senate majority leader Bill Frist (R-Tenn.) said, "Fortifying our borders is an integral component of national security. We can't afford to wait."[3] But a *Washington Post* report stated:

> The measure was pushed hard by House Republican leaders, who badly wanted to pass a piece of legislation that would make good on their promises to get tough on illegal immigrants, despite warnings from critics that a multibillion-dollar fence would do little to address the underlying economic, social and law enforcement problems, or to prevent others from slipping across the border.[4]

Upon signing the Secure Fence Act into law, President Bush noted:

> Ours is a nation of immigrants. We're also a nation of law. Unfortunately, the United States has not been in complete control of its borders for decades and, therefore, illegal immigration has been on the rise. We have a responsibility to address these challenges. We have a responsibility to enforce our laws. We have a responsibility to secure our borders. We take this responsibility seriously.[5]

President Bush also noted that, "Since I took office we have more than doubled funding for border security—from $4.6 billion in 2001 to $10.4 billion this year. We've increased the number of Border Patrol agents from about 9,000 to more than 12,000, and by the end of 2008, we will have doubled the number of Border Patrol agents during my presidency."[6] But even supporters of the Secure Fence Act recognized the difficulty of implementation. Colin Hanna, president of the conservative public policy nonprofit organization Let Freedom Ring, said that without a proper fence, "attempting to secure the entire 1,951 mile U.S.-Mexican border would require over 100,000 Border Patrol agents, a financial and administrative impossibility."[7] In fact, "Even if good technology is employed—cameras, drones and the like—securing the border with manpower and technology alone is still a practical impossibility."[8] Similarly, W. Ralph Basham, past commissioner of U.S. Customs and Border Protection, contended that building a fence along the border is the "dumbest" of all ideas.

Nevertheless, a new Bipartisan Framework for Comprehensive Immigration Reform coming out of the U.S. Senate is planning to introduce immigration legislation that "will provide a tough, fair, and practical roadmap to address the status of unauthorized immigrants in the United States that is contingent upon our success in securing our borders."[9] In order to "fulfill the basic governmental function of securing our borders, we will continue the increased efforts of the Border Patrol by providing them with the latest technology, infrastructure, and personnel needed to prevent, detect, and apprehend every unauthorized entrant." The Bipartisan Framework makes no mention of completing the fence along the U.S.-Mexico border, nor does it make any kind of promise to provide the necessary funds to hire the thousands of new border patrol agents who would "prevent, detect, and apprehend every unauthorized entrant."[10]

The primary assumption found in immigration debates is that, besides being necessary, borders are good. In making a case that any new immigration policy must put the interests of citizens over those of undocumented immigrants, Stephen Macedo, professor of politics and director of the Center for Human Values at Princeton University, contends that "borders are morally significant because they bound systems of collective self-governance."[11] Macedo claims that out of this bounding, citizens come to have "powerful obligations of mutual concern and respect, and mutual justification, to one another because they are joined together—as constituents members of a sovereign people—in creating binding political institutions that determine patterns of opportunities and rewards for all."[12] This obligation, Macedo argues, requires the government to put the interests and well-being of citizens first and foremost when making immigration policy. In other words, besides defining and reflecting our obligations to different persons, borders also protect the interests of citizens by stopping aliens from exploiting the "opportunities and rewards" that citizens have mutually created. This is why, for Macedo, borders are "morally significant" and must be recognized as so by policymakers.

Borders also presumably ensure nationhood by giving us an identity through the demarcation of territory. Those who are of our territory theoretically share our values, our beliefs, our customs, and our traditions. So being American is ultimately about being of a certain territory and sharing things with other persons from that territory. As Joseph Nevins explains, "It is impossible to understand the production and importance of national boundaries, and their almost sacred nature in many parts of the world, without understanding nationalism and the changing conceptions of territory."[13] In immigration debates, identity is bound up with territory, meaning that identity is presumably impossible without a connection to a physical and geographical space. This, again, is supposedly how borders give us an identity and allow community and nationhood. Conversely, the lack of highly secured borders presumably constitutes a threat to our identity, our nation, and the traditions and institutions that make both possible. It also, according to this argument, represents weakness, indicating a lack of resolve to do all that is necessary to protect our borders, and in turn to protect our values and beliefs, traditions and institutions. The unwillingness to defend and protect one's borders is commonly perceived as the beginning of a nation's decline and disintegration.

A lack of secured borders presumably allows peoples from supposedly backward nations and civilizations to "pour" into our territory, exploit our resources, and disrupt the values, beliefs, traditions, and institutions that make our nation "great," "exceptional," and "extraordinary." According to this line of thinking, without assimilation, balkanization and disintegration are inevitable. An absence of secured borders gives us no ability to control who or how many persons from different places enter our territory. This is why a secured border is commonly assumed to be a vital component of any immigration policy. To protect our borders is supposedly to protect the values, beliefs, traditions, and institutions that create our identity, nation, and ultimately our civilization. Nevins writes, "Borders are metaphors for and [a] manifestation of how we perceive the world and act within it."[14] In this way, borders "describe ongoing processes of construction of different types of geographically and historically specific divisions and zones of contact between territories, ones that reflect power relations between groups and that have very real impact on people's lives."[15]

This border narrative shapes and drives U.S. immigration policy. It is why many members of Congress insist that securing our borders must come first in any new immigration policy. This narrative appears vividly and alarmingly in the writings of immigration opponents. For instance, writing in the aftermath of September 11, Samuel Huntington, once chairman of the Harvard Academy for International and Area Studies and Albert J. Weatherhead III University Professor at Harvard University, warned of the United States disintegrating and collapsing as a result of the rise of immigrants from non-European nations. He called for a new push to protect the "American Creed." According to Huntington, the "American

Creed," as initially formulated by Thomas Jefferson and later elaborated upon by many others, "is widely viewed" as the defining element of American identity. This creed, argued Huntington, "was the product of the distinct Anglo-Protestant culture of the founding settlers of America in the seventeenth and eighteenth centuries." Key elements of that culture included "the English language; Christianity; religious commitment; English concepts of the rule of law, responsibility of rulers, and the rights of individuals; and the dissenting Protestant values of individualism, the work ethic, and the belief that humans have the ability and duty to try to create a heaven on earth."[16] Huntington believes that following September 11, "Americans should recommit themselves to the Anglo-Protestant culture, traditions, and values that for three and half centuries have been embraced by Americans of all races, ethnicities, and religions and that have been the source of their liberty, unity, power, prosperity, and moral leadership as a force for good in the world."[17]

Huntington also claimed that Latino immigration poses the greatest threat to the territorial, cultural, and political integrity of the United States. He writes:

> The American people who achieved independence in the late eighteenth century were few and homogenous: overwhelmingly white (thanks to the exclusion of blacks and Indians from citizenship), British and Protestant, broadly sharing a common culture, and overwhelmingly committed to the political principles embodied in the Declaration of Independence, the Constitution, and other founding documents.[18]

Huntington calls for immediate and severe actions to neutralize all of these threats, which constitute the greatest challenge to our "existing cultural, political, legal, commercial, and educational systems," and "to the historical, cultural, and linguistic identity" of the United States.

Patrick Buchanan echoed Huntington's many fears and warnings about what the new immigration trends would mean for the future of the country. According to Buchanan, the United States is morally and politically "decomposing" and is on a path to "national suicide" as a result of a coming "Third World invasion." Citing figures from the U.S. Census Bureau, Buchanan writes, "Hispanics, 1 percent of the U.S. population in 1950, are now 14.4 percent. Since 2000, their numbers have soared 25 percent to 45 million. The U.S. Asian population grew by 24 percent since 2000, as the number of white kids of school age fell 4 percent. Half the children five and younger today are minority children."[19] Also,

> By 2050 the number of African-Americans and Hispanics will have almost doubled from today's 85 million, to 160 million. The future seems more ominous than it did in the hopeful days of civil rights. For these burgeoning scores of millions will not long accept second-class accommodations in the affluent society, where they are the emerging majority.[20]

Buchanan is also concerned about the apparent unwillingness of immigrants to learn English and about various U.S. institutions encouraging this unwillingness. He writes, "In Chicago's schools, children are taught in two hundred languages. Five million of the 9 million people in Los Angeles County speak a language other than English in their homes."[21] Like Huntington, Buchanan believes that this kind of language diversity will ultimately bring chaos and disunity to the United States; he therefore insists on English being declared the national language. He believes that language commonality, rather than language diversity, is necessary for the creation of any great society. In fact, according to Buchanan, "No great republic or empire . . . ever arose because it embraced democracy, diversity, and equality."[22] He wants the United States to immediately and drastically curb the number of immigrants legally admitted every year, build a great wall on the border with Mexico, and deny amnesty to the 12-20 million undocumented immigrants already in the country.

Mike Huckabee, Governor of Arkansas from 1996 to 2007, claims that securing the border with Mexico must be the "first step" in any immigration policy. Securing the border is "about enforcing the law. And the law has a purpose: to make our country stronger and safer for everyone."[23] By subverting the laws that presumably make "our country stronger and safer for everyone," undocumented immigrants, claims Huckabee, erode the integrity of "our country" and put us all at risk. He writes, "The job of the federal government is to define and defend our borders. We can't be free if we aren't safe, and we aren't safe if our boundaries are ignored routinely by those without respect for our laws."[24] He also claims that the federal government's unwillingness to secure the U.S.-Mexico border is why, in the first quarter of 2010, "almost 1,200 bills and resolutions dealing with immigration were proposed in forty-five states."[25] For Huckabee, "Securing our border is a broader concept than simply preventing people from crossing. It includes discouraging people from approaching the border in the first place. Illegals must view our border not as an obstacle to overcome but as a dead end with no opportunity for them on the other side."[26] Ultimately, "This is our country; we have to decide who comes here and who stays here."[27] Huckabee points to California as "a perfect example of what happens when we are overrun by uneducated, unskilled people who are a burden rather than as asset."[28]

James Edwards, in a paper titled "A Biblical Perspective On Immigration Policy," part of a volume that grew out of a Princeton University symposium on immigration policy, contends that the Bible legitimizes an immigration policy with aggressive border security. He claims that "civil government is divinely instituted for the protection of the innocent and the punishment of the guilty."[29] This obligates the government to do all that is necessary to maintain law and order, such as using "the sword" (or "coercive force") "to defend the nation against foreign invaders."[30] According to Edwards, "Magistrates and statesmen have an obligation to protect their own communities and if necessary to use the coercive power of the state to achieve this aim. This obligation includes the obligation to patrol national borders and to enforce immigration laws that are directed at the public good."[31] Edwards argues that the failure of government to fulfill this supposedly vital function threatens the law and order that are crucial for protecting the public good. Thus, writes Edwards,

> The rightful power of the sword includes policing the nation's borders, as well as the arrest and deportation of immigrant lawbreakers, even when their only violation is of immigration status. The state is duty-bound to act in this manner because of the illegal aliens' disregard for legitimately constituted authority and the adverse effect of his immigration upon the citizens whom the government is duty-bound to protect.[32]

In addition to his belief that undocumented immigrants undermine law and order, Edwards claims that the enormity and diversity of current immigration hinder the "common culture" and "cohesiveness" necessary for community and nationhood. This presumably establishes further proof that border security is an important function of government.

When these various rhetorical arenas converge, the collision course becomes most pronounced and finely articulated during nation political events. This was the case during the 2012 GOP presidential primary, in which the issue of immigration reform by means of border security played a prominent role.

All The President's Men & Women

Much debate on border security has resulted from the April 2010 passage of Arizona's "tough" immigration law, the Support Our Law Enforcement and Safe Neighborhoods Act, and from news coverage surrounding the self-proclaimed "toughest" sheriff in America, Joe Arpaio.[33] Securing our borders—a concept that generally refers to one border, not necessarily both—has been a guaranteed catalyst for many single-issue voters, whose expressed concerns revolve around "taking our jobs," not speaking "our" language, or otherwise. Border security and immigration reform over-all continue to feature prominently, leading to various forms of political posturing. For instance, in the close 2010 Senate race in Nevada between Republican challenger Sharron Angle and Democratic incumbent Harry Reid, Angle took advantage of the immigration issue by releasing a highly controversial campaign ad. Entitled "Best Friend," Angle's 30-second September 2010 spot claimed, amongst other charges, that, "Illegals are sneaking across our border, putting America's safety and jobs at risk." The ad sought to inject civil unrest and criminality into the immigration debate. While the commercial was notorious for its depiction of "illegal aliens" (all Latinos), it captured the urgency of the moment and afforded Angle the national spotlight. She nearly defeated Senator Reid.[34]

In Louisiana, in what appeared to be a carbon copy of the Sharon Angle ad, Republican incumbent Senator David Vitter released his October 2010 "Welcome Prize" ad. Vitter accused his opponent, Democrat Charlie Melancon, of both making it easier for "illegals" to get welfare checks and other taxpayer-funded benefits, and voting against a bill that would allow police to arrest "illegals." Also with Latino actors playing the role of "illegals," Vitter's ad, like Angle's, seized the moment of the immigration movement in an ultimately successful effort to sail past his opponent. The growing concern over a "broken" immigration system by means of open borders continues to occupy much thought and debate.

In the 2012 Republican campaign to unseat President Obama, both Texas Governor Rick Perry and Minnesota Congresswoman Michelle Bachmann immediately began to spar over immigration reform and border security. Polling data, perceived debate performance, and fundraising dollars all illustrate that Governor Perry's campaign sunk fast. Once believed to be a strong contender, he suffered a series of early setbacks from which he never fully recovered. Brushing aside Perry's comments linking social security to a federally operated Ponzi scheme, his failure to recall which three federal departments he would eliminate if elected president, and other outtakes, no single issue crippled his candidacy more than immigration.

During the September FOX News GOP Debate in Florida, Perry came under his greatest attack by rivals, who accused him of being "soft" on "illegal immigration." Perry's immigration reform credibility came under great scrutiny—he was blamed for providing a "magnet" for "illegal immigrants" in 2001 when he signed the Texas Dream Act, which allowed students who had attended at least three years of school at a Texas high school to receive in-state tuition for Texas colleges and universities. Perry's 2001 actions opened the floodgates for criticism, providing rivals with the opportunity to portray him as "soft" on immigration. While attempting to stand firm and defend his platform, Governor Perry took stiff criticism from former Massachusetts Governor Mitt Romney, former Pennsylvania Senator Rick Santorum, and Minnesota congresswoman Michele Bachmann. Defending his 2001 support of the Texas Dream Act, he argued, "If you say that we should not educate children that have come into our state for no other reason than they were brought here through no fault of their own, I don't think you have a heart." His goal, he said, was to prevent these children from becoming a "drag" on society,[35] later adding, "I'm proud that we are having those individuals be contributing members of our society rather than telling them 'you go be on the government dole.'"[36]

Encouraged by loud boos from the audience, Rick Santorum did not address whether or not children of undocumented immigrants should be allowed to attend such colleges and universities. Instead he positioned his criticism of Perry by asking, "Why should they be given preferential treatment as an illegal in this country?" But the sound bite of the debate came from former Massachusetts Governor Mitt Romney. Not convinced that Governor Perry was in tune with conservative voters and their rhetorical vision of immigration reform, Romney argued that being against "illegal immigration" does not mean you do not have a heart; "it means that you have a heart, and a brain." This became the sound bite now and perhaps forever associated with Perry's "soft" stance on immigration.

For Governor Perry, the bleeding did not stop, as both Bachmann and Romney took aim at him. Despite the near-unanimous vow by candidates to further construct a border fence to deter "illegal" immigration, Perry was again the "outsider." In his words, "The idea you're going to build a wall from Brownsville to El Paso and extend it another 800 miles to Tijuana is just not reality. . . . What we've got to have is more boots on the ground."[37] Bachmann, in her swipe at Governor Perry, declared that not only would she build a fence, but "we will not have taxpayer-subsidized benefits for illegal immigrants or their children." The statement drew much applause. As seen through the eyes of Rick Santorum, Perry's "soft" approach to immigration greatly harmed the Texas governor's candidacy and has contributed to a shrinking community of Perry supporters. In Santorum's words, "People want someone they can trust to take care of a big issue in this country, and Rick Perry is . . . committed to continuing the status quo when it comes to illegal immigration."[38] Santorum's statement also alluded to Perry's refusal to comment on Arizona's immigration law, other than to say that it would not be the right law for Texas.

This campaign season saw the emergence of key issues that candidates had to be prepared to address, in order to lead the nation and guide the world. Because constituents looked for candidates they could visualize as making the "tough" decisions, particularly on immigration reform, candidates had to possess a sense of rhetorical leadership. Candidates, writes Leroy Dorsey, "must actively engage in that process of investigation that will allow them to sift among available options for their audience, determine what might be best among these options and construct a message of some kind that would help the audience to align itself with that alternative."[39] If nothing else, the race for the GOP presidential nomination unveiled immigration reform as a central tenet; those candidates vying for frontrunner positioning had to embrace stances colloquially understood to be "tough." For Governor Perry, Gallup polling data revealed a once-prominent second place position (trailing Mitt Romney) from late July to mid-September 2011. As his rivals began to push Perry on immigration, his polling figures took a significant decline. He lost half of his base by early October, allowing Herman Cain to surge to a position just two points behind Governor Romney. Just prior to a

CNN Western Republican Leadership Conference in mid-October, Richard Dunham of the *Houston Chronicle* wrote, "There are signs of Perry's vulnerability in every new poll. A new CNN survey released Monday found Romney leading the GOP field with 26 percent, followed by former Godfather's Pizza CEO Herman Cain at 25 percent. Perry, at 13 percent, led the second tier."[40] Perry's failure to capture constituents' belief in his rhetorical leadership cost him support.

As campaign season progressed, so did attempts at jockeying for better polling positioning. Leading a newly charged strategy aimed at improving sagging poll numbers and filling the rhetorical void left by Governor Perry, Michelle Bachmann, the night before a campaign stop at the Hotel Pattee in Perry, Iowa, wrote on her Facebook page that she would make "an announcement that is sure to fire up this race." In the announcement, Bachmann introduced a pledge to voters, one that not only declared immigration to be her top priority, but also promised the completion of a fence along the U.S.-Mexico border by 2013. The use of federal agents to conduct raids for illegal immigrants was not ruled out as a possibility. Immigration reform, declared Bachmann, "will be job No.1 . . . and it will be every mile. It will be every yard. It will be every foot. It will be every inch of that border because that portion you fail to secure is the highway into the United States."[41] As the first presidential candidate in the campaign to sign a pledge offered by the political organization Americans for Securing the Border, Bachmann hoped her aggressive new stance on immigration reform would attract former Perry supporters and others who shared her newfound vision.

Bachmann was careful to dismiss charges of racism linked with her campaign pledge, aware as she was of a growing Latino constituency. Understanding both the timeliness of the issue and the potentially detrimental residual message her pledge could create, Bachmann argued, "It's okay to talk about this subject. Sometimes we're told it's not okay to talk about illegal immigration, that somehow that means we're prejudiced or we're bigoted or we're biased against Hispanics."[42] Bachmann quickly transitioned to depicting the southern border as a national security threat, stating, "Fifty-nine thousand this year came across the border . . . from Yemen, from Syria. These are nations that are state sponsors of terror. They're coming into our country."[43] (Yemen is not on the list of state sponsors of terror, according to the State Department.) Bachmann continued to illustrate her newly found discursive array of concerns over immigration reform. She now shifted to economics, using a litany of statistics to discuss the financial drain "illegal immigration" had on the nation and citing the controversial Federation for American Immigration Reform organization (FAIR) as the source of her economic data. Through Bachmann's eyes, "illegal immigrants" are more likely to be high-school dropouts; receive welfare; and cost local, state, and federal governments billions of dollars annually. The nonpartisan Congressional Budget Office questioned Bachmann's accuracy, declaring that there is no consensus on how to determine a national cost of "illegal immigrants."

None of the candidates, including the frontrunners, enjoyed their positions for very long. Governor Perry, for instance, led in Iowa polling at the time of his candidacy announcement, whereas a late November 2011 Rasmussen poll showed him tied for fifth place in Iowa. This downward spiral in the polls was no random occurrence—Governor Perry's perceived lack of rhetorical vision regarding immigration reform cost his campaign immensely. In a paid, automated telephone message to voters in Iowa, Mitt Romney accused Perry of contributing to the nation's immigration issue. Following the release of this message, Arizona Sheriff Paul Babeu observed:

> Rick Perry is part of the illegal immigration problem. . . . A lot of candidates agree we need a border fence. And almost all of them agree in-state tuition for illegal immigrants is wrong. However, Rick Perry disagrees. Rick Perry not only opposes a border fence. But he signed the bill to make Texas the first state in the nation to grant in-state tuition discounts to illegal immigrants.[44]

While Governor Perry's nationwide poll numbers hovered in the single digits, candidates continued to take aim at him over immigration, hoping to convert his followers to their respective camps.

Seizing the moment, both Michele Bachmann and Rick Perry had much ground to cover, yet Bachmann's immigration/border fence pledge caused some voters to give her a second glimpse. Former House Speaker Newt Gingrich, another candidate, enjoyed a generous surge in nationwide polling before coming under fire for his perceived malleable stance on immigration. (He later exited the race.) In Gingrich's words:

> If you've come here recently, you have no ties to this country, you ought to go home. If you've been here 25 years and you got three

kids and two grandkids, you've been paying taxes and obeying the law, you belong to a local church, I don't think we're going to separate you from your family, uproot you forcefully and kick you out.[45]

Immediately following the announcement of Gingrich's immigration platform, both Bachmann and Romney argued that such policy was akin to amnesty, with Bachmann calling for an end to "magnets," or policies that encourage wrongdoing instead of correcting the problem. Again, with frontrunner status and the benefits therein on the line, candidates continued to take new approaches to immigration reform, seeking to capture the imagination of a nation awaiting federal reform.

Like Gingrich, Governor Perry, feeling the immediacy of the moment, unveiled a new strategy of his own. In efforts to improve his image on immigration reform, Governor Perry secured the endorsement of "America's toughest sheriff," Joe Arpaio. The Maricopa County, Arizona, sheriff not only endorsed Governor Perry, but also campaigned with him in New Hampshire. Arpaio has since been the focus of a Department of Justice investigation that ultimately found him—and the law enforcement officers he directed—guilty of numerous illegal and unconstitutional violations. The Department of Justice found that Arpaio had been operating jails in a manner that discriminated against limited English proficient (LEP) Latino inmates. The DOJ also found reasonable evidence that the sheriff's office violated the First, Fourth, and Fourteenth Amendments along with Title 6 of the Civil Rights Act, including through discriminatory and retaliatory practices (such as unlawful profiling at traffic stops) against Latinos. Unfortunately for Perry, Arpaio's endorsement was a little too late—the Texas governor was unable to regain much of the political ground he lost.

The conversation surrounding immigration reform has seen increasing associations between "immigrant" and "terrorist," especially following the tragic events of September 11, 2001. With such a loose and thinly supported correlation come sweeping generalities and the establishment of widespread sentiments that place "terrorist" and "immigrant" on par with one another.

From Immigrants To Terrorists

The events of September 11 placed immigration policy and the security of the U.S.-Mexico border in a new rhetorical and political space. Now securing our borders was about stopping terrorists who were seeking to destroy not just the United States' hegemony, but all of western civilization. September 11 heightened our fears of borders lacking the necessary security to protect us from persons intent on doing us harm. It shifted the focus toward protection and enforcement. A secured border became necessary to protect the "homeland" from alien and foreign threats who opposed our worldview and civilization. Whereas previously, the purpose of a secure border was to control and limit the entry of undocumented immigrants, now it was meant to stop terrorists; the urgency to secure the border and to do so comprehensively was heightened proportionately.

Chris Newman, legal programs director at the National Day Laborer Organizing Network, believes that the events of September 11 increased our fear and suspicion of immigrants. According to Newman, "It's magnified the fear of the other and the fear of the newcomer, and the fear of people arriving on our shores," essentially poisoning the well over immigration in America.[46] Iowa Republican Senator Chuck Grassley, a member of the Senate Subcommittee on Immigration, Refugees, and Border Security, described how the events on September 11 "awoke everybody to the fact that it was awfully easy to get into the United States."[47] It also allowed immigration opponents to connect terrorism and undocumented immigrants with the need for increased border security. According to Grassley, "When you're talking about securing the border, you're talking about securing it for people who want to come here . . . for very peaceful reasons or even for very violent reasons. It doesn't matter whether they're disrespecting our laws on doing harm to Americans or disrespecting our laws on entering our country."[48]

Tying terrorism with immigration and border security is the new normal in immigration policy debates. Legislators now have no qualms publicly claiming—without any kind of proof—that there are terrorist training camps along the U.S.-Mexico border and that many terrorists have already crossed the border and set up training camps in the United States.[49] The 2003 absorption of the Immigration and Naturalization Service into the newly created Department of Homeland Security also deepened the connection between terrorism, immigrants, and border security. Now immigration matters are symbolically and institutionally homeland security matters, which means that immigration policy is now framed in terms of homeland security and must first satisfy the needs of homeland security. Indeed, after the events of September 11, immigration discourse, as Robert Koulish describes it, shifted radically "so that the problem was no longer about being poor, it was about being undocumented; anyone undocumented, unidentified, was now perceived as a potential terrorist."[50] Immigrants were cast as elusive perpetrators capable of slipping through our supposedly porous borders and getting past immigration controls. Framed this way, Koulish explains:

> Three things become evident: first, immigrants are elusive perpetrators; second, they place the nation at risk; and third, no expense is to be spared repairing the broken system. This prepares the way for punitive preemptive policies, overzealous enforcement and militarization of the border to be depicted as acts of patriotism, rather than inappropriate and illegal policies and practices.[51]

There are consequences that come with increasing border security that are often absent in policy discussions. Greater border security is responsible for many deaths on the U.S.-Mexico border as migrants seek to cross in increasingly desolate and dangerous places. According to Reverend Robin Hoover, founder of the Tucson-based group Humane Borders (which provides water stations for migrants along the Arizona side of the border), "What we've seen is that the death rate has gone up even though the number of people crossing has gone down, the direct result of more agents, more fencing and more equipment. The migrants are walking in more treacherous terrain for longer periods of time, and you should expect more deaths."[52] Moreover, Reverend Hoover is finding, by measuring where the bodies are being found, that death locations are generally farther away from roads than in previous years. "So they're going around the fences, the technology and where the agents are. And the farther you walk from a safe place, the more likely a broken ankle becomes a death sentence."[53] In fact, "In 2009, an analysis of bodies recovered in the deadliest section of the border found that the risk of dying was 1.5 times higher in 2009 than in 2004 and 17 times greater than in 1998."[54] In light of the increasing death toll of migrants on the border—now numbering over 5,000 in recent years, even though the number of migrants crossing the border has dropped significantly—a report titled "Humanitarian Crisis: Migrant Deaths at the U.S.-Mexico Border" concludes that U.S. "border security policies constitute the most obvious, the most acute, and the most systemic violation of human rights occurring on U.S. soil today."[55]

Whereas a nation needs fences and borders to define a territory that presumably makes for nationhood, capitalism thrives by eroding and diminishing fences and borders. Indeed, borders supposedly impede prosperity by encumbering the movement of services and resources and blocking the creation of new markets. This is why both the *Wall Street Journal* and the U.S. Chamber of Commerce oppose any immigration policy that promises to tighten border security. The *Wall Street Journal* wants the federal government to "recognize the economic realities that come with a long, porous border between an immensely rich country and a poor one," which begins with recognizing that tightening border security only makes our immigration problems "worse" by discouraging undocumented immigrants from returning to home nations.[56] The U.S. Chamber of Commerce's "Statement on Immigration Reform" contains no recommendations that make any mention of fences, borders, or border security. It also describes any attempt to remove the 10 to 12 million undocumented individuals in the United States as impractical. Like the *Wall Street Journal*, the USCC wants the government to find a way to either regularize or naturalize this population. According to a statement by the USCC, "Only by bringing undocumented workers out of the shadows can we protect them from unscrupulous employers who might exploit them, undermining the vast majority of employers who pay a fair wage."[57] In addition, the statement calls for recognition that the country will need immigrants, including those who do low-skilled jobs, in the future to continue to perform vital functions as the native population ages.

Underlying the *Wall Street Journal* and U.S. Chamber of Commerce position is a belief that the growth of capitalism will bring prosperity for both the United States and Mexico, making fencing the U.S.-Mexico border unnecessary. According to the *WSJ* and USCC, this is the case with the U.S.-Canada border, which is nearly 7,000 miles but yet never appears in immigration policy debates as a threat to national security. The contention is that prosperity makes for a natural security between nations, and that only capitalism can bring forth this kind of enduring prosperity by cultivating efficient markets. Efficient markets presumably make for efficient nations—as in, nations that will never waste valuable resources to build grand border fences that do nothing constructive. This is how Jason Riley recently articulated the argument at a book forum hosted by the Nelson A. Rockefeller Institute of Government:

What is the case for open borders? Very simply, the case for open borders is the case for allowing the free market to determine how many immigrants we need in this country. Letting the law of supply and demand work will do two things. It will reduce illegal immigration, first of all. These are economic migrants coming; they are coming to work. We have the jobs they need to work. Give them legal ways to come and fewer will come illegally. These folks have no desire to be in the country illegally. They would rather use the front door; let them use the front door and, thereby, reduce illegal immigration into the country. The second thing it will do . . . is make us a safer country from a homeland security standpoint. If we give people more legal ways to come and those people use those ways . . . our homeland security resources can focus on real threats, instead of trying to track down people coming here to burp our babies, or mow our lawns, or be short-order cooks or busboys.[58]

Riley highlights evidence that exposes popular myths about immigrants. In the case of undocumented immigrants engaging in criminal behavior, he reports:

The fact is that numerous studies by independent researchers and government commissions over the past 100 years repeatedly have found that immigrants are less likely to commit crimes or be behind bars than the native-born. In fact, among men between 18 and 39, who, of course, comprise the bulk of the prison population, the incarceration rate of natives is five times higher than the incarceration rate of immigrants.

In fact:

For every ethnic group, without exception, incarceration rates are lowest for immigrants. This holds true for the Mexicans, the Salvadoreans, and the Guatemalans who make up most of the illegal population in the U.S. Between 1994 and 2005, the illegal immigrant population in the U.S. is estimated to have doubled to around 12 million; yet, according to the Department of Justice, over that same period, the violent crime rate in the U.S. declined by a third; crimes against property declined by 26 percent. Crime rates have fallen in the cities with the largest immigrant populations—New York, Los Angeles, Miami, Chicago, and so forth, as well as in border cities experiencing the most illegal immigration, like San Diego and El

Paso. The bottom line is that crime in the U.S. is not caused or even aggravated by immigrants, regardless of their legal status.[59]

As for Latino immigration being a different kind from European immigration, Riley claims that "the rate of immigration from Europe in the nineteenth and early twentieth centuries far" exceeded "the rate of immigration from Mexico today." In the 1990s:

> Legal and illegal immigration from Mexico averaged an estimated 4.2 million, which works out to about 1.5 immigrants per 1,000 U.S. residents each year. By comparison, in the middle of the 19th century, the U.S. absorbed an average of 3.6 Irish immigrants per 1,000 residents. From 1840 to 1890, the rate of German immigration was greater in every decade than the current flow of Mexicans. And from 1901 to 1910, Russian, Italian, and Austro-Hungarian immigration each surpassed the current rate of Mexican immigration.[60]

Riley's point is that our perception of immigrants is different from the reality of immigrants. Policy-makers would do well to heed this fact.

Capitalism is always striving to become global, as efficient markets demand access to new services and resources. Without such access, capitalism collapses, threatening the prosperity that supposedly makes war impossible between nations politically and economically committed to capitalism. But easy access to markets also means easy access to markets that can afford cheap goods and services, and easy access to resources also means easy access to the cheap resources that are necessary for the provision of cheap goods and services. This, again, is why the *Wall Street Journal* and the U.S. Chamber of Commerce oppose any immigration policy that impedes access to resources, particularly human resources. So whereas immigration opponents argue that immigration suppresses the wages of natives, especially those of minority peoples, the *Wall Street Journal* and the USCC contend that immigrants make many goods and services affordable by cultivating efficient labor markets.

But efficient markets inevitably lead to surplus labor, as technology results in the need for less and less labor. The movement of manufacturing and service-oriented jobs—as a result of market pressures—to places that have the least expensive labor costs becomes a necessity.[61] With the loss of labor come the loss of incomes, the loss of taxes, the loss of houses, the loss of neighborhoods, the loss of businesses, and ultimately the loss of consumers. Simply put, the rise in surplus labor creates all manner of fear and anxiety as our prosperity becomes increasingly tenuous and out of our control. Unemployment and underemployment become the reality, and educational attainment loses its ability to control our fates against emerging market pressures that incessantly demand increasing levels of efficiency. The lack of border fences is presumably responsible for our current plight—it supposedly allows too many to pour into our country and drain our already-diminishing resources.

As much as capitalism aspires to flatten the world, to use Thomas Friedman's (2007) language, it also encourages the construction of border fences, as natives respond reactively to the fear and anxiety that come with the rise of global capitalism and its consequences, such as surplus labor. Nationalism and capitalism are at odds with each other. Capitalism's interests are global and universal. Nations, on the other hand, in seeking to protect the interests of the local customs, traditions, and institutions that supposedly make for nationhood (such as the preservation of local and national languages), undercut the globalism and universalism that capitalism needs to flourish. The result is that global capitalism has yet to produce its promised outcomes.[62] Instead of the promised peace and prosperity, global capitalism is creating increasing inequality, fermenting new kinds of hostility against immigrants, and encouraging the building of new border fences that reflect growing nationalist sentiments. In *World on Fire: How Exporting Free Markets Breeds Ethnic Hatred and Global Instability*, Amy Chua claims that globalization is only fueling strife and disintegration. She argues that, "far from making the world a better and safer place, democracy and capitalism—or at least in the raw, unrestrained form in which they are currently being exported—are intensifying ethnic resentment and global violence, with potentially catastrophic results."[63]

Conclusion

The border narrative that shapes and drives immigration policy in the United States and around the world makes various assumptions about what constitutes a good society. It assumes that homogeneity is vital for the making of nationhood, and secured borders are necessary for the achievement of this homogeneity. That is, without secured borders, without homogeneity, civilization becomes impossible. In protecting the integrity and stability of our traditions and institutions, secured borders presumably protect the integrity of the things that make our civilization possible. Thus secured borders are assumed to be particularly important in protecting a civilization that is already "great," "unsurpassed," and "extraordinary." If borders are understood to be necessary for any nation, secured borders are particularly necessary to protect the traditions and institutions (the supposed crown jewels) that are the hallmark of a "great" nation.

This border narrative assumes that great nations, and ultimately great civilizations, are born of great traditions and institutions, and secured borders are necessary to protect the integrity of such traditions and institutions. Simply put, how immigrants are accepted and absorbed into our society must be carefully orchestrated or else chaos and dysfunction will ensue. Secured borders presumably play a vital role in the administration of this assimilation process. Our own democracy in the United States is the supposed envy of western civilization—it is what makes us superior to others, and it is responsible for our unsurpassed social and material prosperity. According to Douglas Murray, a popular columnist and staunch opponent of immigration:

> Western values are not just another way to live, but the only way to live—the only system in human history in which the individual is genuinely free (in the immortal words of Thomas Jefferson) to 'pursue happiness.' Recognition of the superiority of our values is made with people's feet every day in the one-way human migration to the West. It is an admission which many make in private. But we seem to have become so comfortable with our rights that we no longer acknowledge their superiority, or the superiority of the values which gave them life.[64]

In *The Death of the West: How Dying Populations and Immigrant Invasions Imperil Our Country and Civilization*, Patrick Buchanan claims that "uncontrolled immigration threatens to deconstruct the nation we grew up in and convert America into a conglomeration of peoples with almost nothing in common—not history, heroes, language, culture, faith, or ancestors. Balkanization beckons."[65] According to Buchanan, "In half a lifetime, many Americans have seen their God dethroned, their heroes defiled, their culture polluted, their values assaulted, their country invaded, and themselves demonized as extremists and bigots for holding on to beliefs Americans have held for generations."⁶⁶ He claims, "The West is the most advanced civilization in history and America the most advanced nation—first in economics, science, technology, and military power."⁶⁷ Buchanan's thesis is that our lack of a secured-border immigration policy has allowed peoples from supposedly backward civilizations to overrun a superior civilization and defile the very traditions and institutions that made that civilization superior. Apparently, the fact that these supposedly backward peoples would rather destroy than adopt the traditions and institutions that could possibly lift them out of backwardness is final proof of their backwardness. Thus Buchanan writes ominously about what will become of the world as western civilization is "invaded," "polluted," and "defiled."

For opponents of immigration and those who claim to only have concerns about the quantity of immigrants, the fear is that most immigrants are coming from civilizations with traditions and customs that are hostile to our democracy, and they are reluctant to surrender those traditions and customs. According to this belief, most immigrants lack the temperament to deal with the rigors and challenges that our democracy requires. Foremost, our democracy presumably requires a capacity to engage and accommodate perspectives that are fundamentally different from our own; it requires a capacity for vigorous debate. It also necessitates the ability to be a minority—that is, to abide and respect the will of the majority. This includes obeying rules, decisions, and laws set by the majority through fair and regular elections.

In theory, our democracy cultivates the involvement of all citizens regardless of race, gender, creed, religion, or social status. No group or community gets special benefits or privileges, and all decisions and laws are equally binding for all citizens. In this way, our democracy presumably conflicts with many customs and traditions brought to America by immigrants. According to Francis Fukuyama:

> Some contemporary Muslim communities are making demands for group rights that simply cannot be squared with liberal principles of individual equality. These demands include special exemptions from the family law that applies to everyone else in the society, the right to set up special religious schools with state support, and the right to exclude non-Muslims from certain types of public events. In some more extreme cases, Muslim communities have

even expressed ambitions to challenge the secular character of the political order as a whole. Newspaper headlines also cast democracy and immigration (especially from outside the western world) as incompatible—e.g., "Why Muslim Immigration is a Threat to Western Democracy."[68]

We are to assume from immigration policy debates that most immigrants simply lack the temperament and willingness to do all the things our democracy requires, as well as the ability to recognize the many virtues that supposedly come with our democracy. As a result, the continuing mass migration of "alien" peoples to our lands—because of a lack of secured borders to stem that movement—presumably threatens the integrity and continuity of our most vital institutions.

Although the United States boasts of being a nation of immigrants, no other country has passed nearly as many immigration laws; the trend is in no way waning. According to the National Conference of State Legislators, U.S. legislators in 2006 were considering over 380 immigration bills and ordinances. In 2011, state lawmakers introduced more than 1,600 bills and resolutions relating to immigration and immigrants, up from about 1,400 in 2010. No doubt, fear of the many supposed threats that undocumented immigrants pose to cities and local municipalities is driving this legislative trend. Proponents of these new laws claim that the laws are responses to the federal government's unwillingness to enact a comprehensive immigration policy, which would begin with the building of a fence on the U.S.-Mexico border to stop undocumented immigrants from "pouring" into the United States. However, the population of undocumented immigrants in the United States has long been showing hardly any signs of growth, and the number of persons crossing the borders without documentation has long been declining, falling to 85,000 in 2011 from 600,000 in 2006.[69]

There is also no recognition in the debates surrounding the passage of these new laws that immigrants are "30 percent more likely to start new businesses than native-born Americans," and are also more likely to earn patents.[70] Moreover, there is no recognition that "almost all of the children of immigrants from Africa and Asia speak English and more than 90 percent of the children of Latin-American immigrants do."[71] Neither is there any recognition that immigrants, including undocumented immigrants, "are much less likely to wind up in prison or in mental hospitals than the native-born."[72] Or of the fact that nearly every study has found that immigrants, both legal and undocumented, pay more in taxes than they receive in benefits. In addition, Heidi Shierholz of the Economic Policy Institute reports that immigrants have no significant effect on the wages of most low-skilled workers. In fact, "Between 1994 and 2007 immigration increased overall American wages by a small amount ($3.68 per week)."[73] Finally, a pair of new reports by the Congressional Budget Office (CBO) and Joint Committee on Taxation (JCT) found that immigration reform could "result in net discretionary costs of $22 billion over the 2014–2023 period and $20 billion to $25 billion over the 2024–2033 period."[74] The CBO and JCT also found that immigration reform "would have no further net effect on budget deficits over the 2014–2023 period and would further reduce deficits (relative to the effects reported in the cost estimate) by about $300 billion over the 2024–2033 period."[75] The CBO and JCT expect "that new immigrants of working age would participate in the labor force at a higher rate, on average, than other people in that age range in the United States."[76] Both the CBO and JCT expect immigration reform to bring about a significant increase in average wages by 2025, raise capital investment, and boost "the productivity of labor and capital." Yet in the face of all this evidence that immigrants pose no threat to the prosperity or stability of the United States, immigration opponents remain obsessed with building new walls and fences on the U.S.-Mexico border. Evidently, immigration policy is again being shaped by fear rather than reason, restraint, and empathy.

No force is as corrosive, debilitative, and destructive as fear. Fear, writes Zygmunt Bauman, prompts "us to take defensive action." When taken, "defensive action gives immediacy and tangibility to fear."[77] Moreover, "our fears become self-perpetuating and self-reinforcing," acquiring "a momentum on their own—and [they] can go on growing by drawing exclusively on their own resources."[78] We are now, claims Bauman, saturated with fear, even "a surplus of fear." This surplus of fear produces "substitute targets" as we are unable "to slow the mind-boggling pace of change . . . [and] predict and control its direction."[79] These substitute targets represent the things we believe we can control, and, in so doing, limit the fast-moving change that is now threatening us. The most effective substitute targets are immigrants, as many fears can be neatly bundled into immigrants: fear of chaos as a result of language diversity, fear of losing our way of life, fear of our resources becoming depleted, fear of being criminally victimized, and so forth. Enacting new immigration laws, building higher and longer border fences, promoting English-only initiatives, and ending bilingual programs all have origins in a surplus of fear. This fear arises from many sources, such as a collapsing economy that is resulting in the loss of jobs and homes; the implosion of a worldview that promised so much in terms of security, stability, and prosperity; and an ever-widening gap between rich and poor that is emerging from the movement of wealth from the bottom to the top.

Historically, when resources begin to disappear, various groups become subject to persecution, expulsion, and even extermination. This is probably the most common narrative in human history. September 11 is merely pretext for another playing out of this narrative. Because our fear of terrorism is now so profound, any tying of immigrants to terrorists will set this narrative in motion. With all of this fear, facts become unnecessary. Perception is all that matters. Border security advocates appeal to our most primal instincts and impulses. Besides the fear of terrorism, there also exist within border security discourses the fears of a coming "invasion"; a loss of "our language and way of life"; a growing criminality and deviancy in border states as immigrants apparently "pour" over our borders; a "drain" on our dwindling natural and financial resources; and even the possible loss of California, New Mexico, Texas, and Arizona to Mexico.

Legislators know that building and maintaining a secure fence along the nearly 2,000-mile-long U.S.-Mexico border is financially and physically impossible.[80] Calls for the security and militarization of the border have nothing to do with the border. These calls assume that external forces are threatening the United States. We supposedly limit these external forces by securing the border. A secure border, by presumably protecting us from external threats, protects our prosperity. Calls for securing the border generally assume that our prosperity resides in the limitation of these external threats. This is why securing the border is now a national security matter. The future of our country and civilization is supposedly now at stake. The walls of our civilization are apparently now being breached. We must be ready to defend the border at any cost. To defend the border is to defend the homeland.

Eventually the many calls come laden with metaphors of pollution and contamination. Now every person running for elected office must publicly promise to do everything he or she can to defend the homeland, beginning with securing the border. Securing the border now functions as a litmus test for legislators. The external threats to our country and civilization are presumably terrorists and undocumented immigrants. One desires to destroy us and the other wants to drain our resources like parasites.

Calls to secure the border function as misdirection. In reality, the threats to our country and civilization are internal. Neither terrorists nor undocumented immigrants have anything to do with the increasing number of persons who are unemployed and underemployed, or the widening gap between rich and poor, or the unending ecological destruction, or the crushing amount of government debt, or the spreading of weapons of mass destruction, or the increasing dread and despair. Neither will securing the border do anything to alleviate these problems. Calls to secure the border keep us distracted. Such calls encourage us to believe that porous borders are the problem, and the solution is increased border security. The events on September 11 heightened this narrative by providing a menacing face to the external threat and visually capturing the murder and mayhem this threat is bent on inflicting upon penetrating the homeland.

Border security advocates contend that migrants are in no way being coerced to cross the border. As such, the United States is devoid of culpability for the deaths that occur in its deserts. In the end, every nation presumably has a right to secure borders because such borders are necessary and good. But this assumption about borders has no foundation in either history or theory. From a historical perspective, invention, innovation, and social evolution are associated with nations that had permeable borders. Indeed, this is the story of the United States. What would the prosperity of the United States be without immigrants arriving from all corners of the world? That is, what would have been the likelihood of the United States being "the greatest nation on earth," to use Patrick Buchanan's description, without an immigration policy that historically had little interest in border security?[81]

Indeed, the United States is genuinely a nation of immigrants. Immigrants bring new talents, new perspectives, and new resources. As Thomas J. Donohue, president and CEO of the U.S. Chamber of Commerce, points out, "Immigrants already represent one in four doctors, two in five biomedical scientists, and one in three computer software engineers."[82] Moreover, "More than half of the masters and doctoral students in high-tech disciplines at top U.S. universities are foreign."[83] By limiting and discouraging the movement of peoples, border fences also limit and thwart the movement of new talents, perspectives, and resources. Border security advocates claim that building a fence along the U.S.-Mexico border will do nothing to affect the entry of legal immigrants—that is, the good immigrants. But the notion of a "legal" immigrant is a political construct. The Naturalization Act of 1790, which restricted naturalization to "free white persons" of "good moral character," was legal. The Alien Friends Act of 1798, which authorized the president to deport any resident immigrant considered "dangerous to the peace and safety of the United States," was legal. The Page Act of 1875, which classified as "undesirable" any individual from Asia who was coming to the United States to be a contract laborer, was legal. The Chinese Exclusion Act of 1882, which sought to end Chinese immigration, was legal. The Emergency Quota Act of 1921, which established highly restrictive national immigration quotas, was legal. The Immigration Act of 1924, which sought to further limit the entry of Southern and Eastern Europeans, especially Jews, Italians, and Slavs, was legal. The Alien Land Act of 1913, which prohibited Japanese aliens from becoming naturalized and owning land and property, was legal. Who and what is legal is political, created by fears, interests, ambitions, and resources; legality is defined by those with the skills, power, and resources to impose what is so. Immigration policy is merely another playing out of this reality.

As a second line of defense against fraudulent entries and activities by immigrants in the United States, voter identification laws have quickly taken the nation by storm. In order to cease the so-called increasing number of fraudulent voters, many states have passed voter identification laws as a part of their overall reform measures. This will become more transparent in the chapter that follows.

Notes

1. Secure Fence Act of 2006 (Pub.L. 109-367).
2. Ibid.
3. Jonathan Weisman, "With Senate Vote, Congress Passes Border Fence Bill." *Washington Post*, September 30, 2006. Accessed June 12, 2003. http://www.washingtonpost.com/wp-dyn/content/article/2006/09/29/AR2006092901912.html.
4. Ibid.
5. Ben Daniel, *Neighbor: Christian Encounters with "Illegal" Immigration* (Louisville, KY: John Knox Press, 2010), 114.

6. "President Bush Signs Secure Fence Act," October 26, 2006. Accessed June 12, 2013. http://georgewbush-whitehouse.archives .gov/news/releases/2006/10/20061026.html.

7. Colin Hanna, "Border Fence Part of Larger Solution," *US News*, October 25, 2011. Accessed June 12, 2013. http://www.usnews.com/debate -club/should-the-united-states-build-a-fence-on-its-southern-border/ border-fence-part-of-larger-solution.

8. Ibid.

9. "Bipartisan Framework for Comprehensive Immigration Reform." Accessed June 12, 2013. http://s3.documentcloud.org/documents/ 562528/reform0128principlessenatefinal.pdf.

10. Ezra Klein, "The 5 Most Important Sentences in the Senate's Immigration Plan," *Washington Post*, January 28, 2013. Accessed June 12, 2013. http://www.washingtonpost.com/blogs/wonkblog/wp/2013/01/28/ the-5-most-important-sentences-in-the-senates-immigration-plan/.

11. Stephen Macedo, "The Moral Dilemma of U.S. Immigration Policy," Carol M. Swain, ed., *Debating Immigration* (New York: Cambridge University Press, 2007), 73.

12. Ibid.

13. Joseph Nevins, *Operation Gatekeeper and Beyond: The War on "Illegals" and the Remaking of the U.S.-Mexico Boundary* (New York: Routledge, 2002), 153.

14. Ibid., 8.

15. Ibid., 8.

16. Samuel Huntington, *Who Are We? The Challenges to America's National Identity* (New York: Simon & Schuster, 2004), xv–xvi.

17. Ibid., xvii.

18. Ibid., 11.

19. Patrick Buchanan, *Day of Reckoning: How Hubris, Ideology, and Greed are Tearing America Apart* (New York: St. Martin's Press, 2007), 5.

20. Ibid., 10.

21. Ibid., 9.

22. Ibid., 174.

23. Michael Huckabee, *A Simple Government* (New York: Sentinel, 2011), 134.

24. Ibid., 134.

25. Ibid., 139.

26. Ibid., 140.

27. Ibid., 142.

28. Ibid., 142.

29. James Edwards, "A Biblical Perspective on Immigration Policy," Carol M. Swain (ed.), *Debating Immigration* (New York: Cambridge University Press, 2007), 47.

30. Ibid., 47.

31. Ibid., 57.

32. Ibid., 59.

33. Eric Mandel, "Controversy Fails to Faze 'America's Toughest Sheriff,'" *Telegraph Herald*, September 17, 2011: 1.

34. The Angle ad is still available through many online campaign archives. To read more about the heated contest between Reid and Angle, see, Laura Myers, "Angle, Reid Play Endgame," *Las Vegas Review-Journal*, October 26, 2010, 1A.

35. Thomas Fitzgerald, "Perry Takes Heat in Debate Over His Immigration Policies," *Philadelphia Inquirer*, September 23, 2011, A08.

36. William March and Christian M. Wade, "Rivals Assail Perry in GOP Debate," *Tampa Tribune*, September 13, 2011, 1.

37. Ibid., 1.

38. No Author, "Perry Gets GOP Flak over Immigration," *The Dallas Morning News*, September 24, 2011, 1.

39. "Afterword: Rhetorical Leadership and Presidential Performance." *The Presidency and Rhetorical Leadership*. Ed. Leroy G. Dorsey. College Station: Texas A&M University Press, 2002, p. 242.

40. Richard Dunham, "Can Perry Cool Off Red-hot Issue?" *Houston Chronicle*, October 18, 2011, A3.

41. Seema Mehta, "Bachmann Draws Hard Line on U.S. Mexico Border," *Baltimore Sun*, October 16, 2011, 21A.

42. Ibid., 21.

43. Ibid., 21.

44. "Romney Automated Calls Assail Perry in Iowa," *The Capital*, November 5, 2011, A3.

45. Michael Finnegan and Maeve Reston, "GOP Spars Over Defense: Bachmann Calls Perry's Stance on Pakistan 'Naïve,'" *Baltimore Sun*, November 23, 2011, 8A.

46. Mallie Kim, "After 9/11, Immigration Became About Homeland Security," *US News*, September 8, 2011. Accessed June 13, 2013. http://www.usnews.com/news/articles/2011/09/08/after-911 -immigration-became-about-homeland-security-attacks-shifted-the -conversation-heavily-toward-terrorism-and-enforcement.

47. Ibid.

48. Ibid.

49. Sean Hannity, "Exclusive! Rep. John Culberson," *Fox News*, November 21, 2005. Accessed June 13, 2013. http://www.foxnews.com/on-air /hannity/2005/11/21/exclusive-rep-john-culberson#ixzz2V8i2jdYW.

50. Robert Koulish, *Immigration and American Democracy* (New York: Routledge, 2010), 15.

51. Ibid., 14.

52. "Death Toll Continues to Climb on US/Mexico Border," *Associated Press*, April 9, 2009. Accessed June 13, 2013. http://mexicomonitor .blogspot.com/2009/04/death-toll-continues-to-rise-on.html.

53. Ibid.

54. "Humanitarian Crisis: Migrant Deaths at the US/Mexico Border," *ACLU/Mexico's National Commission of Human Rights*, October 1, 2009. Accessed June 13, 2013. http://www.aclu.org/files/pdfs/ immigrants/humanitariancrisisreport.pdf.

55. Ibid., 14.

56. "The GOP's Immigration Fumble," *Wall Street Journal*, August 1, 2002, A.12.

57. "US Chamber of Commerce Statement on Immigration Reform." Accessed June 14, 2013. http://www.uschamber.com/issues/ immigration/us-chamber-commerce-statement-comprehensive -immigration-reform.

58. Jason Riley, *Let Them In: The Case for Open Borders*. A book forum by the Nelson A. Rockefeller Institute of Government. Accessed June

14, 2013. http://www.rockinst.org/pdf/public_policy_forums/2008
-06-23-public_policy_forum_let_them_in_the_case_for_open
_borders_a_book_forum_presented_by_jason_l_riley.pdf.

59. Ibid.

60. Ibid.

61. Jeremy Rifkin, *The End of Work* (New York: Tarcher/Putnam Books, 1995).

62. Joseph Stiglitz, *Free Fall: America, Free Markets, and the Sinking of the World Economy* (New York: W.W. Norton, 2010).

63. Amy Chua, *World on Fire: How Exporting Free Market Democracy Breeds Ethnic Hatred and Global Instability* (New York: Doubleday, 2003).

64. Douglas Murphy, "Western Values Are Better," *New English Review*. 2007. Accessed June 13, 2013. http://www.newenglishreview.org/blog_email.cfm/blog_id/10567.

65. Patrick Buchanan, *The Death of the West: How Dying Populations and Immigrant Invasions Imperil Our Country and Civilization* (New York: St. Martin's Press, 2002), 3.

66. Ibid., 5.

67. Ibid., 228.

68. Francis Fukuyama, "Identity and Migration," *Prospect Magazine* 131, no.1, February 25, 2007. Accessed June 13, 2013. http://www.prospectmagazine.co.uk/magazine/identity-migration-multiculturalism-francis-fukuyama/#.Ug0Gx6zDKzk.

69. Richard Stevenson, "Economic Nudge for an Immigration Overhaul," *New York Times*, January 30, 2013. Accessed June 14, 2013. http://thecaucus.blogs.nytimes.com/2013/01/30/immigration-shifts-could-provide-opening-for-compromise/?hp.

70. David Brooks, "The Easy Problem," *New York Times*, January 31, 2013. Accessed June 14, 2013. http://www.nytimes.com/2013/02/01/opinion/brooks-the-easy-problem.html.

71. Ibid.

72. Ibid.

73. Ibid.

74. "The Economic Impact of S. 744, the Border Security, Economic Opportunity, and Immigration Modernization Act," *Congressional Budget Office*, June 2013. Accessed June 14, 2013. http://cbo.gov/publication/44346.

75. Ibid.

76. Ibid.

77. Zygmunt Bauman, *Liquid Times: Living in an Age of Uncertainty* (New York: Polity, 2007), 9.

78. Ibid., 9.

79. Ibid., 11.

80. Mallie Kim, "After 9/11, Immigration Became About Homeland Security," *US News*, September 8, 2011. Accessed June 13, 2013. http://www.usnews.com/news/articles/2011/09/08/after-911-immigration-became-about-homeland-security-attacks-shifted-the-conversation-heavily-toward-terrorism-and-enforcement.

81. Peter Schrag, *Not Fit for Our Society: Nativism and Immigration* (Berkeley: University of California Press, 2010).

82. Thomas Donohue, "Immigrants Can Offset Declining Population, Boost Workforce," *Post-Standard,* June 9, 2013, E-4.

83. Ibid., E-4.

5

Immigration and Voting Rights

A cursory glance across the United States reveals disturbing trends in voter identification laws that challenge the existence of equal access to the polls. In 2003, new voter identification laws passed in Alabama, Colorado, Montana, North Dakota, and South Dakota. In 2005, Indiana, New Mexico, and Washington joined the ranks, while Georgia tightened an existing voter ID law to require photo identification. Voter ID laws passed in 2006 in Ohio and Missouri added photo identification requirements to extant laws. In 2009 and 2010, Utah, Idaho, and Oklahoma passed such laws. New laws passed in 2011 in Kansas, Mississippi, Rhode Island, and Wisconsin; Alabama, South Carolina, Tennessee, and Texas tightened existing laws to require photographic ID. (New laws in Texas, Mississippi, and South Carolina were rejected because they did not pass Department of Justice preclearance.)[1] In 2012, Minnesota, New Hampshire, Pennsylvania, and Virginia all passed new voter ID laws, although voters ultimately rejected Minnesota's law, which will not take effect. With the 2013 legislative calendar still underway as of the publication of this book, legislation is pending in 30 states. There are new voter ID law proposals in 12 states, proposals to strengthen existing photo ID laws in 7 states, and proposals to make other changes to existing photo ID laws in 11 states.

According to a recent study released by the nonpartisan Brennan Center for Justice at the New York University School of Law, about 11 percent of eligible voters lack the government-issued photo identification needed to comply with these new laws. More disturbing, nearly 500,000 eligible voters do not have access to a vehicle and live more than 10 miles from the nearest state ID-issuing office open more than two days a week. Moreover, many of these eligible voters live in rural areas with little or no public transportation.[2] With some projections showing that 25 percent of African Americans, 16 percent of Latinos, and 18 percent of Americans over age 65 do not have the forms of ID needed to comply with these new laws, voter identification laws become tantamount to a "test" or "device" restricting the opportunity to register and vote.[3] Data sets supplied to the Department of Justice by the states of Texas and South Carolina likewise illustrate that individuals in lower-income communities and those of color are substantially less likely to possess the kind of photo identification the proposed laws would require. While some states have offered to waive the costs associated with obtaining photo identification, this would not necessarily solve the problem. Such a waiver may appear to alleviate tensions to some, but critics argue that even if photo identification is "free," there still remains the cost of obtaining supporting documentation, like birth certificates.

The Lone Star Shootout: *Texas v. Holder*

As the legal battles unfold across the nation, the political stakes remain high, as the upcoming 2014 congressional and 2016 presidential elections have intensified efforts. In 2011, the Texas State Legislature passed Senate Bill 14, a measure requiring the presentation of certain, though not all, forms of photo identification to vote. Although initially introduced as an attempt to discourage "illegal immigrants" from voting, the state failed to provide any evidence of voter fraud; the 2011-2012 actions pertaining to the Texas Voter ID law continue to garner much attention and concern.

Texas's voter identification law is riddled with a fairly unusual history. Following the successful capturing of 26 seats in the State House, Texas Republicans sought to make a series of moves toward placing voter identification laws atop the state's list of priorities. Eager lawmakers introduced so many voter ID bills—at least 14—that a new "House Select Committee on Voter ID and Voter Fraud" was established to review the legislation. To help ensure that voter ID proposals would move through the legislative channel quickly, Texas Republican Governor Rick Perry used emergency powers to alter the usual legislative process, declaring voter ID an "emergency item." This declaration allowed legislators to begin deliberation on voter ID bills immediately, instead of waiting the customary 60-day period.

SB 14 would eviscerate the protections provided by existing voter identification requirements by generally barring voters from using their voter registration certificates and by mandating that they produce one of six forms of government-issued photo identification in order to vote in person. In the eyes of the law's dissenters, the details in the law—especially pertaining to what types of photo identification would be considered "valid" and "invalid"—were high on the list of concerns. For instance, Senate Bill 14 required the presentation of: a driver's license or personal identification card issued by the Department of Public Safety, which cannot have expired more than 60 days before the date of presentation; a U.S. military identification card; a U.S. citizenship certificate with the individual's photograph; a U.S. passport; a license to carry a concealed handgun; or a Texas-issued or -approved identification card with the individual's photograph.[4] These restrictions, claim dissenters, amount to nothing short of a thinly veiled attempt to invoke discriminatory actions against "minority" voters and those of lower socioeconomic standings. Without federal intervention, the Texas Voter ID law, claimed the Justice Department, could disenfranchise over one million otherwise eligible voters.[5] While proponents argued that SB 14 was only intended to preserve the "integrity" of voting, civil rights groups and other objectors agreed with Justice Department claims that SB 14 targeted racial minorities. Attorney General Eric Holder, in an address to the NAACP, "alluded to recent studies that found 8 percent of White voting-age U.S. citizens lack a government-issued photo ID, compared to 25% of black citizens." Holder sought to establish the discriminatory impact the proposed law would have.[6]

From the outset, Texas sought administrative preclearance shortly following the passage of SB 14, knowing that if preclearance were denied, federal law would prohibit the state from enacting the measure. Upon initial investigation and analysis of the law, particularly against the grander legal backdrop of the Voting Rights Act, the Department of Justice denied preclearance. Not pleased with the DOJ's decision, the state of Texas then sought judicial preclearance, which a three-judge district court denied in August 2012. Here, the court argued that SB 14 would disproportionately burden "indigent voters," who, in turn, are disproportionately racial minorities. Texas officials argued that the law was simply an attempt to require voters to produce valid photo identification at the polls, citing similar laws in states like Georgia and Indiana. But the Texas State Conference of the NAACP and the Mexican American Legislative Caucus of the Texas House of Representatives, along with the U.S. Justice Department, saw things differently.[7]

In 2012, the state of Texas and the Department of Justice met again in court, resulting in the Supreme Court case *State of Texas v. Holder*. The state of Texas requested that the Court strike down Congress's 2006 reauthorization of Section 5 or, at a minimum, either "discard" Section 5's prohibition on voting changes that will have a retrogressive effect on the position of racial minorities or bar its application to voting qualifications.[8] Section 5, a part of the larger Voting Rights Act of 1965, placed newly proposed election practices or procedures under review until they have been examined to ensure that such proposed changes have no disenfranchising impact. Essentially arguing that SB 14 violates Section 5, critics of the law refuted claims of the ease of obtaining certain photo identification, citing the 70 counties in Texas that do not have Department of Public Safety offices (the office charged with distributing drivers licenses). Proponents nonetheless sought the law's passage. Oddly enough, the passage of this 2011 law occurred after three previous failed attempts, in 2005, 2007, and 2009. Moreover, the bill's passage came amidst Governor Perry's GOP presidential bid, during which he famously told one Tea Party crowd that the state could secede from the union should "federal mandates" keep interfering with state business.

On trial in *Texas v. Holder* was effect/impact and not necessarily intent. The Department of Justice took aim at dismantling the argument that Section 5 was outmoded and no longer needed. The state of Texas maintained that Section 5 was no longer necessary because "[segregationist] judges have retired or died, [and] federal judges throughout the South can be trusted to faithfully enforce the Fifteenth Amendment and federal voting-rights laws," further contending that Section 5 was a response to a racist federal judiciary, instead of a response to pervasive state-sponsored racial discrimination (which persisted in the face of increasing federal voting rights protections and ongoing court-ordered relief).[9] During trial, the state of Texas presented extensive evidence to show that SB 14 would not have the effect of denying or abridging any citizen's right to vote on account of race or color, citing social-scientific studies as proof. This claim was later complemented by the results of "expert-administered surveys," in which those surveyed showed no disparity in photo identification possession among black, Latino, and "non-Hispanic" white voters.

With all their cards on the table, Texas lawmakers were confident that Senate Bill 14, as written, would survive federal preclearance—they were confident that no disparate impact existed pertaining to voter registration or turnout among communities of color. Not convinced that Texas satisfied its burden of proof, the Court issued its multitiered decision. First, the Court rejected Texas's claim that SB 14 would not have a retrogressive effect on voter turnout or participation, noting that despite the evidence presented by the state of Texas, "the effect of voter ID laws on turnout remains a matter of dispute among social scientists." The Court found that "all of Texas' evidence on retrogression is some combination of invalid, irrelevant, and unreliable."[10] In the eyes of the Court, the state of Texas also failed to meet its burden of demonstrating that SB 14 would not "lead to a retrogression in the position of racial minorities with respect to their effective exercise of the electoral franchise."[11]

Diving further into this claim, the Court highlighted three areas, or "three basic facts," that linked SB 14 with retrogression. First, it was:

Undisputed by Texas that a substantial subgroup of Texas voters, many of whom are African American or Hispanic, lack [the] photo ID required by SB 14. Second, the uncontested facts also showed that the burdens associated with obtaining ID will weigh most heavily on the poor. Third, undisputed U.S. Census data showed that racial minorities in Texas are disproportionately likely to live in poverty.[12]

Accordingly, SB 14 would also "lead to a retrogression in the position of racial minorities with respect to their effective exercise of the electoral franchise," so argued the Court, insisting that, "Simply put, many Hispanics and African Americans who voted in the last election will, because of the burdens imposed by SB 14, likely be unable to vote in the next election. This is retrogression."[13] The attempt by Texas lawmakers to implement disenfranchising voter laws was by no means an isolated incident. What remains most interesting throughout the pattern of these proposed laws is the occurrence of statistical shifts in the state's Latino population. Texas has long been predicted to become a Democratic-leaning state; there is already movement in some Texas counties to indicate that Texas may soon become a minority-majority state.[14] With the momentum still present to prevent certain communities of color from further impacting the political balance of power throughout the country—especially in the South.

The Court also rejected the argument that SB 14 was no different from two current laws in Indiana and Georgia, both of which Texas lawmakers drew upon when crafting their bill. The Court maintained, "The circumstances in Georgia and Indiana are significantly different from those in Texas," specifically noting that SB 14 was "far stricter" than the laws in Indiana and Georgia. A Texas birth certificate costs $22 (compared to $3 to $12 in Indiana), and roughly one-third of Texas's 254 counties do not have a Department of Public Safety office.

The long legal dispute over voter identification laws in Texas typifies both the breadth and depth of similar legal challenges. As Republican lawmakers continue to participate in this legislative movement, more controversy develops, as was the case in Arizona.

Arizona v. Inter Tribal Council of Arizona

No stranger to political controversy pertaining to race—whether that controversy relates to Senate Bill 1070,[15] the ban on teaching ethnic studies in public schools,[16] the 2012 court case *Escamilla v. Cuello*,[17] or otherwise—the state of Arizona often finds itself engulfed in debate over its comingling of race and politics. Following the November 2004 passage of Arizona Proposition 200, state law required prospective voters to present proof of citizenship when registering to vote and when casting a ballot in the state. Proposition 200 amended Arizona's voter registration procedure by (1) requiring the county recorder to reject any voter application that did not include valid proof of one's U.S. citizenship; and (2) requiring certain forms of identification when a voter attempted to cast a ballot. As a result of these changes, multiple parties sued the state of Arizona on the grounds that Congress had preempted the states in this area of election law with the National Voter Registration Act (1993, signed into law by President William Clinton). The NVRA does not require documentary evidence of citizenship and instead requires applicants to aver, under penalty of perjury, that they are citizens. Arizona law, despite that, allowed officials to "reject" any application for registration that was not accompanied by concrete evidence of citizenship. With many previously qualified voters now disenfranchised under the Arizona law, only the Supreme Court could decide whether Arizona's citizenship "test" was preempted by the National Voter Registration Act.

Before the case made its way to the Supreme Court, it engendered much legal tension. Proposition 200 drew much opposition, and in doing so, multiple plaintiffs filed separate suits. As a result, however, the United States District Court for the District of Arizona not only consolidated these cases, it unfortunately denied an injunction in favor of Jesus Gonzalez and the Inter Tribal Council of Arizona (ITCA). Upon appeal, ITCA's claim that Proposition 200 was akin to a poll tax was ultimately rejected, allowing the state to proceed with implementation. Although the Ninth Circuit denied the injunction, holding that the registration requirement was not an unconstitutional poll tax and was not made obsolete by the National Voter Registration Act, the legal dispute did not end there.

Upon appeal, Gonzalez challenged the District Court's decision that Proposition 200 was not a poll tax under the Fourteenth Amendment, was not in violation of the Voting Rights Act, and was not in violation of the Equal Protection Clause of the Fourteenth Amendment. All the Arizona lower courts arrived at the same outcome, but on October 15, 2012, the Supreme Court granted certiorari and decided to hear the case. As the rights of many voters faced various political obstacles, the Court was to determine the fates of many eager democratic participants. In the 2013 Supreme Court case *Arizona v. Inter Tribal Council of Arizona, Inc.*, tension rested in the context of interpretation, that is, how Arizona interpreted its right to invoke and enforce voter qualifications. Standing in the state's way was the National Voter Registration Act, which required state governments to allow qualifying voters to register when they applied for or renewed their driver's licenses or applied for social services.

The NVRA grants greater accessibility to voter registration and the polls by allowing voter registration by mail. Additionally, the NVRA permits prospective voters to register in elections for federal office by means of any of three methods: simultaneously with a driver's license application, in person, or by mail. Proposition 200 created confusion by requiring proof of citizenship when registering to vote and the presentation of identification when voting on Election Day. Furthermore, while the NVRA makes no mention of such requirements, the Arizona law required:

(1) proof of citizenship by means of: a photocopy of the applicant's passport or birth certificate; (2) a driver's license number, if the license states that the issuing authority verified the holder's U.S. citizenship; (3) evidence of naturalization; (4) tribal identification; or (5) "[o]ther documents or methods of proof . . . established pursuant to the Immigration Reform and Control Act of 1986.[18]

Regarding these major arguments, the plaintiffs maintained that constitutional authority was on their side. Specifically, if Arizona were allowed to set and enforce its new registration requirements, the entire federal-form registration would be in jeopardy. Furthermore, in the age of voter suppression, the argument could be made that if Proposition 200 had been validated by the Court, such a ruling would have undermined Congress's efforts to allow all citizens an equal opportunity to vote. On the other hand, supporters maintained that the Court should uphold Proposition 200 because requiring proof of citizenship supports congressional intent to protect the integrity of elections. Arizona contended that voter fraud is a problem in the state and that it poses a significant threat to the validity of elections there. Ironically akin to the *Texas* argument, Arizona too believed that additional requirements would not pose a substantial burden on potential voters attempting to register.

Mincing no words, the Court, in a 7-2 decision, found that Arizona erred in its interpretation and execution of federal law and authority, positing, "Arizona's reading is also difficult to reconcile with neighboring provisions of the NVRA."[19] Writing on behalf of the Court, Justice Antonin Scalia argued:

> Arizona's appeal to the presumption against pre-emption invoked in this Court's Supremacy Clause cases is inapposite. The power the Elections Clause confers is none other than the power to pre-empt. Because Congress, when it acts under this Clause, is always on notice that its legislation will displace some element of a pre-existing legal regime erected by the States, the reasonable assumption is that the text of Elections Clause legislation accurately communicates the scope of Congress's pre-emptive intent.[20]

As Arizona and other states throughout the nation continue to experience a shifting racial and political landscape, we encounter more and more policy efforts insistent upon requiring proof of citizenship. Attempts at altering state laws regarding voting are becoming increasingly commonplace. The issue of voter identification—particularly among a growing Latino population—weighs heavily on the mind of many Republican lawmakers who believe their party is on the verge of extinction.[21]

As one of the two dissenting justices in the case, Justice Samuel Alito offered his opinion that Arizona should be allowed to mandate the additional requirement. In his words:

> Exercising its right to set federal voter qualifications, Arizona, like every other state, permits only U.S. citizens to vote in federal

elections, and Arizona concluded that this requirement cannot be effectively enforced unless applicants for registration are required to provide proof of citizenship. . . . I would not require Arizona to seek approval for its registration requirements from the Federal Government, for, as I have shown, the Federal Government does not have the constitutional authority to withhold such approval.[22]

If Justice Alito's opinion had been that of the Court's majority, the case would have signaled a fairly interesting shift in legal direction. If states have the "right" to exercise their own federal voter qualifications, then a litany of obstacles and alterations to existing state laws could very well be introduced, potentially impacting whether millions of otherwise eligible people vote.

While states fight for their perceived authority to set their own voting sails, we continue to witness a rise in voting rights litigation. Like in the *Arizona* case, petitioner Shelby County, Alabama, believed that the federal government overstepped its legal boundaries. Shelby County contended that federal preclearance, under Section 5 of the Voting Rights Act, exceeded Congress's power and violated both the Fourteenth and Fifteenth Amendments. With the Voting Rights Act under legal challenge, *Shelby County v. Holder* represented the nation's latest pivotal case on Section 5 and voter identification laws.

Shelby County v. Holder

Ratified on July 9, 1868, as one of the Reconstruction Amendments, the Fourteenth Amendment affirms that, "No state shall make or enforce any law which shall abridge the privileges or immunities of citizens of the United States; nor shall any state deprive any person of life, liberty, or property, without due process of law; nor deny to any person within its jurisdiction the equal protection of the laws." The Fifteenth Amendment of the U.S. Constitution, ratified on February 3, 1870, as the third and final of the Reconstruction Amendments, prohibits federal and state governments from denying a citizen the right to vote based on that citizen's "race, color, or previous condition of servitude." Despite these supposed safeguards, many southern whites orchestrated discursive maneuvers to prolong African American disenfranchisement for years to follow.

Five anti-poll-tax bills were passed in the House of Representatives from 1942 to 1949, but either because of senatorial filibusters or simply because the legislation was denied a floor vote, all such measures failed. The passage of the Civil Rights Act of 1957 did little to enfranchise African Americans or increase voter turnout, as the law allowed a jury trial for those accused of having denied suffrage. Because the typically all-white juries selected for these and other related trials rarely, if ever, upheld the charges, the provision was nothing more than a mirage. After great efforts by Dr. Martin Luther King Jr., other civil rights activists, and politicians on both sides of the aisle, President Lyndon Johnson finally exercised deliberate speed to remedy a terrible situation.

Enacted by the 89th Congress and signed into law by President Johnson, the Voting Rights Act of 1965 was designed to eliminate rampant and widespread discriminatory voting practices, largely targeted at African Americans. Specifically, the VRA prohibits states from imposing any "voting qualification or prerequisite to voting, or standard, practice, or procedure . . . to deny or abridge the right of any citizen of the United States to vote on account of race or color." Or, as stated in *South Carolina v. Katzenbach*, South Carolina's 1966 challenge to Section 5, "The Voting Rights Act of 1965 was enacted to address entrenched racial discrimination in voting, an insidious and pervasive evil which had been perpetuated in certain parts of our country through unremitting and ingenious defiance of the Constitution."[23] The VRA was charged with the task of eliminating the many manifestations of voter suppression in place throughout the nation.

The VRA contains numerous safeguards aimed at preventing retrogression. Section 2 of the law bans any "standard, practice, or procedure" that "results in a denial or abridgement of the right of any citizen . . . to vote on account of race or color," and applies nationwide.[24] Section 4 provides the "coverage formula," basically defining the "covered jurisdictions" as states or political subdivisions that maintained tests or devices as prerequisites to voting, and that had low voter registration or turnout in the 1960s and early 1970s. As mentioned previously, Section 5 of the act indicates that no change in voting procedures can take effect in those covered jurisdictions until approved by specified federal authorities in Washington, D.C.

In 2006, Congress reauthorized, with unanimous consent, the Voting Rights Act for the next 25 years, not altering the coverage formula found under Section 4. Coverage still depended on whether a jurisdiction had a voting test and low voter registration or turnout in the 1960s or 1970s. Petitioner Shelby County, Alabama, a covered jurisdiction, asserted that federal preclearance exceeded Congress's power to enforce the Fourteenth and Fifteenth Amendments and violated the Tenth Amendment and Article IV of the U.S. Constitution. Continuing, Shelby County, in an argument similar to that in *Texas v. Holder*, maintained that current racial and political conditions no longer justified preclearance, and that the coverage formula was antiquated. Responding, Attorney General Eric Holder contended that preclearance remains a valid exercise of congressional power and that the formula, in combination with the VRA's "bailout" provision— which allows covered jurisdictions to seek a declaratory judgment from a three-judge panel in the U.S. District Court for the District of Columbia— is wholly constitutional.

Stemming from the lawsuit filed in the Federal District Court in Washington, D.C., Shelby County sought both a declaratory judgment that Sections 4(b) and 5 were facially unconstitutional, and a permanent injunction against their enforcement. Unfortunately for Shelby County, the district court upheld the act, finding that the evidence before Congress in 2006 was sufficient to justify reauthorizing §5 and continuing §4(b)'s coverage formula. After surveying the evidence in the record, the court accepted Congress's conclusion that §2 litigation remained inadequate in the covered jurisdictions to protect the rights of minority voters, §5 was therefore still necessary, and the coverage formula continued to pass constitutional muster.

Two questions stood at the center of the Supreme Court appeal: Did the renewal of Section 5 of the Voter Rights Act under the constraints of Section 4(b) exceed Congress's authority under the Fourteenth and Fifteenth Amendments? And did it therefore violate the Tenth Amendment and Article Four of the Constitution? The case was argued on February 27, 2013, and decided on June 25, 2013. Chief Justice John Roberts delivered the opinion of the Court. Joined in concurrence by Justices Scalia, Kennedy, Thomas, and Alito, with Justices Ginsburg, Breyer, Sotomayor, and Kagan in dissension, Chief Justice Roberts argued that Section 4 was unconstitutional in light of current conditions. Beginning his initial dismantling of Section 4, Roberts declared:

Nearly 50 years later, things have changed dramatically. Largely because of the Voting Rights Act, [v]oter turnout and registration rates in covered jurisdictions now approach parity. Blatantly discriminatory evasions of federal decrees are rare. And minority candidates hold office at unprecedented levels. The tests and devices that blocked ballot access have been forbidden nationwide for over 40 years yet the Act has not eased §5's restrictions or narrowed the scope of §4's coverage formula along the way. Instead those extraordinary and unprecedented features have been reauthorized as if nothing has changed, and they have grown even stronger. . . . In 1966, the coverage formula was rational in both practice and theory. . . . Coverage today is based on decades-old data and eradicated practices. . . . Today the Nation is no longer divided along those lines, yet the Voting Rights Act continues to treat it as if it were.[25]

In a rather interesting view of race relations, among other variables, Chief Justice Roberts found fault with the Department of Justice's rationale for the continual use of the Section 4 formula and Congress's handling of the Voting Rights reauthorization in 2006. While it is correct, at least to some degree, that the "tests and devices that blocked ballot access have been forbidden nationwide for over 40 years," this does not fully address the grander context pertaining to voter suppression. "Tests" and "devices" like literacy exams and poll taxes are largely antiquated procedures, but changes to voter identification laws, as successfully argued by the Department of Justice in the *Texas* case, can have much of the same outcome. If Chief Justice Roberts sought to gauge racial tensions in the United States, he left much to be desired.

Sensing the urgency to provide proof that racial tensions have calmed and that Section 4 is no longer justified, Chief Justice Roberts offered a rather unique defense. In his words:

During the "Freedom Summer" of 1964, in Philadelphia, Mississippi, three men were murdered while working in the area to register African-American voters. On Bloody Sunday in 1965, in Selma, Alabama, police beat and used tear gas against hundreds marching in support of African American enfranchisement. Today, both of those towns are governed by African American mayors.[26]

In perhaps one of the most ill-supported claims that the United States is making great strides toward racial equality, Chief Justice Roberts was convinced that these mayors represented the high watermark for inclusion and political equity. Missing, of course, from his examples was the fact that Philadelphia, Mississippi, has just fewer than 10 percent more

African Americans than the state's overall average. Or that in Selma, Alabama, African Americans comprise just over 80 percent of the population, nearly 60 percent higher than the state's overall average. Throughout his defense of invalidating Section 4, Chief Justice Roberts avoided making any remarks about existing tensions regarding Latinos, as his focus was solely dedicated to African Americans and the 1950–1960s.

Also missing from Chief Justice's argument over the state of our racial betterment was thoroughness. Nowhere in the Court's majority opinion did we encounter any grappling with gerrymandering or other political mechanisms traditionally used to dilute minority votes and/or districts. Nowhere in the Court's majority opinion did we encounter any grappling with the linkage between voter identification laws and disparate retrogression for the poor and communities of color. And nowhere in the Court's majority opinion did we encounter any grappling with the fact that, despite the Chief Justice's claim of racial betterment to the extent that Section 4 was outmoded, America's hate groups, as reported by the Southern Poverty Law Center, are on the rise. Instead, the Court offered a tepid reading of the nation's race relations by describing the success of two African American mayors in the South.

Deviating from his conversation on the state of race and politics in America, Chief Justice Roberts explained why Section 4 infringes upon "equal sovereignty" among the states. Citing the Court's previous grappling with Section 4 in the 2008 case *Northwest Austin Municipal v. Holder*,[27] Chief Justice Roberts argued:

> And despite the tradition of equal sovereignty, the Act applies to only nine States (and several additional counties). While one State waits months or years and expends funds to implement a validly enacted law, its neighbor can typically put the same law into effect immediately, through the normal legislative process. Even if a non-covered jurisdiction is sued, there are important differences between those proceedings and preclearance proceedings; the preclearance proceeding not only switches the burden of proof to the supplicant jurisdiction, but also applies substantive standards quite different from those governing the rest of the nation.[28]

In an opinion that appeared to turn a slightly blind eye and deaf ear to the various state-guided manifestations of discrimination, as Justice Ruth

Bader Ginsburg addressed next, Chief Justice Roberts found solace in equal sovereignty. While he acknowledged past acts of disenfranchisement and even recognized that some states and regions were worse offenders than others, those acts and actions were in the past, whereas today our concern should be centered on ensuring equality in legislative procedure in all states. Given the grander context surrounding both past and present attempts and lawsuits against the VRA, we are not necessarily convinced that the "equal sovereignty" argument is most effective in a case that contains so many moving parts.

We, like most others, welcome the day when preclearance and other federal safeguards are no longer needed. Justice Ginsburg and the three other dissenting justices argued that the Court's majority left much to be desired on many fronts. In Justice Ginsburg's eyes, all safeguards ensured under the VRA are still needed; she believes the Court overlooked many indications that we are not as all-inclusive of a democracy as some justices contend. As Justice Ginsburg explained:

> Second-generation barriers come in various forms. One of the blockages is racial gerrymandering, the redrawing of legislative districts in an effort to segregate the races for purposes of voting. Another is adoption of a system of at-large voting in lieu of district-by-district voting in a city with a sizable black minority. By switching to at-large voting, the overall majority could control the election of each city council member, effectively eliminating the potency of the minority's votes. A similar effect could be achieved if the city engaged in discriminatory annexation by incorporating majority white areas into city limits, thereby decreasing the effect of VRA-occasioned increases in black voting. Whatever the device employed, this Court has long recognized that vote dilution, when adopted with a discriminatory purpose, cuts down the right to vote as certainly as denial of access to the ballot.[29]

In grave departure from Chief Justice Robert's rationale, Justice Ginsburg approached the case from a perspective that took into account the larger backdrop of past and present developments in voter suppression. Citing a litany of individual cases of gerrymandering and other voter suppression tactics from across the country, Justice Ginsburg was far from convinced that the Court acted in the best interests of the historically disenfranchised. Even when signing the 2006 reauthorization of the VRA, President George W. Bush confirmed the need for "further work . . . in the fight against injustice."[30] Congress came to much of the same conclusion that year as well, noting, "Intentional racial discrimination in voting remains so serious and widespread in covered jurisdictions that Section 5 preclearance is still needed."[31] If, in the years following this reauthorization, we abscond from these behaviors, then Chief Justice Roberts will be proven correct. However, little, if any evidence, supports this progressive transformation.

With the Court's 5-4 decision, Section 4 of the Voting Rights Act is now deemed unconstitutional. While the VRA has recently been used to block a voter ID law in Texas and delay the implementation of another in South Carolina,[32] under the direction of the Court, both states are no longer subject to the preclearance requirement. Most troubling about this decision is the underlying belief that race no longer guides or exists as a premeditated political variable amid debates over voting rights. Harkening back to Dr. Martin Luther King Jr.'s May 17, 1957, speech, "Give Us the Ballot"; to Dr. King, Congressman John Lewis and other civil rights activists' march from Selma to Montgomery, Alabama, on Bloody Sunday in 1965; and to other battles against voter suppression, the fight continues. As expressed by Justice Ginsburg in her dissent, "Just as buildings in California have a greater need to be earthquakeproofed, places where there is greater racial polarization in voting have a greater need for prophylactic measures to prevent purposeful race discrimination."[33]

Because the judiciary's main weakness pertains to enforcing its own rulings, the onus is on Congress to thoughtfully engage in legislative process. Whether Congress is ready or able to debate and craft a new Section 4 formula remains to be seen, as immigration reform continues to encounter various delays and complications from congressional Republicans, particularly in the House of Representatives.

Conclusion

Voter identification laws, akin to what essentially amount to "tests" or "devices," have reignited debate throughout the nation. Many otherwise qualified voters remain in jeopardy at the hands of sweeping voter identification laws—their retention of the right to vote and register to vote is at risk. A June 2012 example involving Pennsylvania Republican House Majority

Leader Mike Turzai only muddied the waters. Referring to Pennsylvania's efforts to secure its photo identification provision, Turzai remarked that such a change would "allow Governor Romney to win the state."[34] Debates circulate over intent (which it is often unnecessary to argue about), with some citing a partisan voting war being waged by Republicans against lower-income communities and those of color, many of whose members overwhelmingly vote Democratic. But intent does not trump effect, as has been proven by photo identification laws.

As seen throughout these legislative and legal battles, intent has occupied a major presence in the arguments both upholding and dissenting against new alterations to voting rights. In Tennessee, for example, a 2013 attempt at securing a voter identification law met legal challenge, in an episode that essentially mirrored the failed effort in Texas to require certain, but not all, forms of photo identification. The city of Memphis argued in a federal lawsuit that the law in question, which would require voters to present photo identification before casting a ballot, was unconstitutional. In court, the city of Memphis tried to convince a federal judge that photo IDs issued by the Memphis Public Library system should be accepted as valid forms of identification, but two days before the August 2 primary election, it was ruled that library cards could not be used as such. The ruling declared that such a law violates the state's constitution and possesses the effect of disenfranchising just under 400,000 voters. To date, the decision awaits ruling from the Tennessee Supreme Court.[35]

In March 2013, Arkansas Governor Mike Beebe vetoed SB 2, which would have amended that state's voter ID law to make it of the strictest photo-identification variety. The General Assembly only needed a simple majority to override the veto; the Arkansas House voted to override Governor Beebe's veto, as did the Arkansas Senate. In Virginia, Governor Bob McDonnell has signed Senate Bill 1256, eliminating all non-photo IDs, thus placing Virginia in the strict-photo-identification column. The law also requires the State Board of Elections to provide free photo IDs for voting purposes. This new law becomes effective on July 1, 2014.

As a result of the *Shelby County* decision, the future trajectory of voter identification laws, along with other changes in related procedure, remains in the hands of Congress. Congress is now charged with writing the next chapter in American history pertaining to the rights of potential and already-registered voters, and with determining the fate of comprehensive immigration reform.

Notes

1. Matthew Streb, ed., *Law and Election Politics: The Rules of the Game* (New York: Routledge, 2013).

2. Keesha Gaskins and Sundeep Iyer, "The Challenge of Obtaining Voter Identification," Brenan Center for Justice at New York University School of Law, 2012. Accessed June 15, 2013. http://www.brennancenter.org/sites/default/files/legacy/Democracy/VRE/Challenge_of_Obtaining_Voter_ID.pdf.

3. Ibid.

4. Texas Senate Bill 14, 2011.

5. Gary Martin, "Voter ID Law; Foes Say Bill Was Rushed by GOP," *San Antonio Express News*, July 11, 2012, p. 1A.

6. Joe Holley, "NAACP Convention; Holder Likens Voter ID Law to Poll Tax," *Houston Chronicle*, July 11, 2012, p. 1.

7. Richard Hasen, *The Fraudulent Fraud Squad: Understanding the Battle over Voter ID: A Sneak Preview from the Voting Wars, from Florida 2000 to the Next Election Meltdown* (New Haven, CT: Yale University Press, 2012).

8. Texas v. Holder, No. 12-cv-128, 2012 WL 3743676, (D.D.C. Aug. 30, 2012).

9. Ibid.

10. Ibid.

11. Ibid.

12. Ibid.

13. Ibid.

14. Gail Collins, *As Texas Goes . . . : How the Lone Star State Hijacked the American Agenda* (New York: W.W. Norton & Company, 2012).

15. Donathan L. Brown, "An Invitation to Profile: *Arizona v. United States*," *International Journal of Discrimination and the Law* 12, no. 2 (2012): 117–127.

16. Jeff Biggers, *State Out of the Union: Arizona and the Final Showdown Over the American Dream* (New York: Nation Books, 2012).

17. Donathan L. Brown, "When English is Not Enough: *Cabrera v. Cuello*," *Harvard Journal of Hispanic Policy* 25, no.1 (2013): 49–68.

18. Ariz. Rev. Stat. Ann. §16-166(F).

19. *Arizona v. Inter Tribal Council of Arizona, Inc*, 133 S.Ct. 476 (2012).

20. Ibid.

21. Theda Skocpol, and Lawrence Jacobs. eds., *Reaching for a New Deal: Ambitious Governance, Economic Meltdown, and Polarized Politics in Obama's First Two Years* (New York: Russell Sage, 2011).

22. *Arizona v. Inter Tribal Council of Arizona, Inc*, 133 S.Ct. 476 (2012).

23. *South Carolina v. Katzenbach*, 383 U.S. 301, 309 (1966).

24. 42 U.S.C. §1973.

25. *Shelby County v. Holder*, 570 U.S. (2013).

26. Ibid.

27. *Northwest Austin Municipal Utility District No. 1 v. Holder*, No. 08-322 (2009).

28. *Shelby County v. Holder*, 570 U.S. (2013).

29. Ibid.

30. 152 Cong. Rec. S8781.

31. 679 F. 3d, at 866.

32. Ellen Katz, "South Carolina's Evolutionary Process," *Columbia Law Review* 113, no. 1 (2013): 55–65.

33. *Shelby County v. Holder*, 570 U.S. (2013).

34. Arlene Ash and John Lamperti, "Elections 2012: Suppressing Fraud or Suppressing the Vote?" *Statistics, Politics and Policy* 4, no.1 (2013): 14–28.

35. Gary May, *Toward Justice: The Voting Rights Act and the Transformation of American Democracy* (New York: Basic Books, 2013).

6

Recommendations and Conclusion

The state of immigration reform in America is extremely multifaceted and contains issues and debates pertaining only to the border between the United States and Mexico. Considering the discursive political history surrounding immigration policy in America, we know all too well that lawmakers at all levels of government continue to seek the passage of various laws housed under the grander umbrella of "immigration reform." As constituents, we believe that it is in the best interest of the nation to "take our country back" by executing the tasks Congress has struggled to complete. Our collective impulses inform us that any office-holder or -seeker who aspires to represent us at the state, local, or federal level must share our belief that immigration reform is just as much of a local concern as a congressional one, and they must articulate best practices toward implementing policies in our best interest.

Our chief goal in this book was to identify and analyze how political and legal debates over immigration reform not only produce policies that maliciously target Latinos, regardless of legal status, but also illustrate the expansive nature that immigration reform embodies. With attention to policy formations at all levels of government, our efforts have exposed the contemporary continuation and expansion of historically rooted actions. For instance, rarely do we consider and analyze the central role bilingual education and official language laws have played against the larger backdrop of immigration reform. We know that bilingual education and official language laws were instrumental in setting school curricula pertaining to the study of foreign languages, at least when such courses were permissible under law. Furthermore, we know that linguistic policies allowed for the persistence of old antagonistic tactics into new discriminatory policies, ultimately leading to the legal protection of those defined as "national origin minorities," among other developments. We know that the legal battle over the state of bilingual education has resulted in many lawsuits alleging physical and verbal altercations and even participatory exclusion of many limited English proficient students.

With respect to official language laws, much of the same legal and political fallout exists, as immigration opponents believe that one of the best ways to expedite immigrant assimilation is through the declaration of such laws. Despite lacking any empirical evidence or other proof to support the belief that official language laws assist or encourage the learning of English, these laws have become a staple of the immigration reform movement. As seen in the first two chapters, both bilingual education and official language legislation play a great role in how many lawmakers envision immigration reform.

Debates and laws pertaining to the spatial aspects of immigration reform are perhaps the most popularly known. In this respect, we placed our attention on two manifestations: the growth in local housing ordinances and the notion of borders as a rhetorical phenomenon. Regarding the expansion of local housing ordinances, we not only illustrated how these laws seek to limit the inflow of immigrants into various townships, but more specifically, we paid careful attention to how proponents of these laws rhetorically reconfigure the legal concept of dwelling and housing rights for the purposes of immigration legislation. Our attention to how "border security" debates appear solely in reference to the southern border serves dual purposes. Only 2 percent of the U.S.-Canada border is "secured," according to the Department of Homeland Security, and convicted terrorists, including those involved in the September 11 tragedy, have entered the United States from Canada; we attended to this incongruence along with its peculiar racial dimensions. While "border security" represents an attempt to control the absorption and incorporation of those who seek to the enter the United States, new waves of voter identification laws, according to their proponents, are a second line of defense against unlawful and fraudulent activities. Statistics provided by states with voter identification laws bespeak previously held beliefs pertaining to the number of fraudulent voters. Voter identification laws exist as perhaps the fastest growing and most widely controversial aspect of immigration reform.

To provide updates on the latest developments on this front, we dedicate the epilogue to a brief overview of the recent Supreme Court case *Shelby County v. Holder*.

In order for any book pertaining to the correlation between race and immigration reform to be successful, it must account for the multifaceted state of our latest attempts at immigration policy. As the debates continue over how best to fix a broken system, state, local, and federal officeholders are approaching and advocating policies that only cause more problems than they claim to resolve. Our attention turns to these "resolutions" next.

The Continual Shortcomings in Immigration Reform

In fiscal year 2012, the United States spent approximately $18 billion on immigration and border enforcement, more than all other federal law enforcement efforts combined. Our analyses reveal that immigration debates and the policies they produce contain three fundamental problems: 1) an unwillingness of immigration opponents to come to terms with the facts and reality of immigration; 2) a misunderstanding of the history of immigration in the United States, in which immigrants are viewed as a threat despite having assimilated, thrived, and contributed significantly to the country's prosperity; and 3) a refusal to observe all the implications and consequences that will result from different kinds of immigration policy. Immigrants are by no means the only group adversely affected by immigration policy. For example, with respect to overarching claims that America is "flooding" with immigrants from Mexico who refuse to adopt our customs and values and obey our laws, a March 2013 report from the Manhattan Institute for Policy Research reveals a different reality. The findings of the report, "Measuring Immigrant Assimilation in Post-Recession America," run counter to the arguments waged by immigration reform advocates. It states, "The immigrant population has shifted dramatically since the recession, whereas migration rates from Mexico have been very slow for the past five years, while rates from other parts of the world—notably Asia—have quickened." In 2011, the total number of Mexican immigrants and the total number of immigrants from all Asian countries were roughly equal.[1] Oddly enough, these facts about immigration patterns and figures go largely unmentioned in contemporary debates.

Among other elements of these debates that ignore the facts, the so-called concerns pertaining to immigrant assimilation appear to be nothing more than a mirage. According to the same report, immigrants are now more assimilated, on average, than at any point since the 1980s. The rise in assimilation has been most apparent along cultural and civic dimensions: "In a stark reversal of this historical pattern, post-recession immigrants are more culturally and economically similar to natives than immigrants arriving as much as a decade earlier."[2] The findings of the report are damning to immigration opponents, as they essentially demonstrate that the supposed cultural and economic differences between immigrants and natives are now less noticeable than they have been in a generation. In fact, second-generation Americans—the 20 million adult U.S.-born children of immigrants—are substantially better off than immigrants themselves on key measures of socioeconomic attainment, according to a new Pew Research Center analysis of U.S. Census Bureau data. Here, again, we are continuously misled by speeches and declarations that cause us to believe in the existence of a mythical drain on economic resources. Shockingly, at least to some, "the Pew Research surveys also find that second-generation Hispanics and Asian Americans place more importance than does the general public on hard work and career success," debunking the mythic correlation between immigrants and vagabonds.[3] With respect to language, the fraudulent claims from official language proponents continue. As Pew reveals, "about nine-in-ten second-generation Hispanic and Asian-American immigrants are proficient English speakers, substantially more than the immigrant generations of these groups," inviting much doubt of claims that argue otherwise.

The shortcomings associated with much of the debate over immigration reform rest on many misguided claims. One popular rhetorical pairing that is the object of great misuse is that of law and social order pertaining to new immigrants. Reform opponents consistently claim that immigrants promote deviancy and criminality, despite the fact that research indicates otherwise. According to Walter Ewing of the Immigration Policy Center, "Between 1990 and 2010, the foreign-born share of the U.S. population grew from 7.9 percent to 12.9 percent and the number of unauthorized immigrants tripled from 3.5 million to 11.2 million." However, "During the same period, FBI data indicates that the violent crime rate declined 45 percent and the property crime rate fell 42 percent. The decline in crime rates was not just national, but also occurred in cities with large immigrant populations such as San Diego, El Paso, Los Angeles, New York, Chicago, and Miami."[4] Claims of increased criminality, whether they relate to immigrant-caused beheadings in the Arizona deserts or otherwise, lack any serious foundation in reality. Our debates are led by such claims, which have neither permanency nor accountability to facts, but which contain enough fear and paranoia to cause kneejerk approval of various forms of legislation.

In discussions of the so-called economic threat that immigrants are said to unleash upon the nation, we continuously find one common argument: the claim that "immigrants are taking our jobs." In 2012 in California (the nation's largest farm state), the Western Growers Association, a group consisting of farmers and others in the agriculture business, famously reported a nearly 20 percent drop in laborers. The WGA cited stronger border control and issues related to the current guest worker program as causes for the decline, arguing that not enough workers were being provided to meet their needs. The California Farm Bureau Federation insisted that worker shortages would lead to less available produce, thus possibly causing higher prices for consumers. The story did not end here. Responding to the claim that immigrants were "taking" jobs from American workers, the United Farm Workers launched its "take our jobs" campaign, encouraging American citizens to apply for these vacant positions.[5] As reported by *CNN Money*, "Most applicants quickly lose interest once the reality sinks in that these are back-breaking jobs in triple-digit temperatures that pay minimum wage, usually without benefits, according to the union. Some small farms are not required to pay minimum wage and in 15 states farms aren't required to offer workers' compensation."[6] Even when provided with encouragement to "take immigrant jobs," few Americans are willing to engage in the physical labor. The labor shortfall thus remains unresolved.

Immigrants are by no means the only group adversely affected by immigration policy. Designing such policy out of spite and ignorance affects many Americans. We constantly witness calls for closed borders and mass deportations as solutions to our immigration problems. Many of us are under the impression that building and extending a fence along the southern border will alleviate the multifaceted tensions we face. But as we continue to see, there are more to these propositions than what initially meets the eye. As reported by the Immigration Policy Center:

The high costs of an enforcement-only response to unauthorized immigration have been estimated by Peter Dixon and Maureen

Rimmer, as well as by Raúl Hinojosa-Ojeda, who found that a mass deportation and zero-immigration policy would decrease U.S. GDP by $2.6 trillion over 10 years. Dixon and Rimmer have also modeled the effects of various enforcement strategies (including border and workplace enforcement), finding reduced GDP effects, while Hinojosa projects soaring costs per apprehension.[7]

The Obama administration deported more immigrants during Obama's first term in office than former President George W. Bush deported in both terms, earning the United States the unflattering nickname "Deportation Nation." According to Joanna Dreby from the Center for American Progress, nearly "400,000 people deported each year since 2009 represents more than twice the 189,000 deported in 2001."[8] We have yet to give serious consideration to easing these tensions through new resolutions.

The conversation in both chambers of Congress over "best practices" for reforming immigration law receives ample news coverage. House Resolution 6429, introduced by Texas Republican Congressman Lamar Smith, sought to amend the 2011 Immigration and Nationality Act to "promote innovation, investment, and research in the United States, to eliminate the diversity immigrant program, and for other purposes."[9] This 2011 bill, touting 68 cosponsors (67 of whom were Republicans), was met with great controversy, which perhaps explains why the bill died in committee. First, H.R. 6429 sought numerical limitation from any single foreign state. Second, and perhaps most controversial, it offered "preference allocation for employment-based immigrants." The bill recommended preference to:

Aliens holding doctorate degrees from U.S. doctoral institutions of higher education in science, technology, engineering, or mathematics (A) In General- Visas shall be made available, in a number not to exceed the number specified in section 201(d)(2)(D)(ii), to qualified immigrants who— (i) hold a doctorate degree in a field of science, technology, engineering, or mathematics from a United States doctoral institution of higher education; and (ii) have taken all doctoral courses in a field of science, technology, engineering, or mathematics, including all courses taken by correspondence (including courses offered by telecommunications) or by distance education, while physically present in the United States. In general- Any visas not required for the class specified in paragraph (6) shall be made available to the class of aliens who— (i) hold a master's degree in a field of science, technology, engineering, or mathematics from a United States doctoral institution of higher education that was either part of a master's program that required at least 2 years of enrollment or part of a 5-year combined baccalaureate-master's degree program in such field; (ii) have taken all master's degree courses in a field of science, technology, engineering, or mathematics, including all courses taken by correspondence (including courses offered by telecommunications) or by distance education, while physically present in the United States; and (iii) hold a baccalaureate degree in a field of science, technology, engineering, or mathematics or in a field included in the Department of Education's Classification of Instructional Programs taxonomy within the summary group of biological and biomedical sciences.[10]

Dissenters quickly highlighted what some lawmakers, like Illinois Democratic Congressman Luis Gutiérrez, called "picking and choosing" which immigrants we want and which we do not. Recalling earlier times in American political history, the bill insisted on certain qualities making for a "better" immigrant. For instance, according to H.R. 6429, each country must be awarded no more than 7 percent of the total number of green cards being offered, meaning the wait time for those from countries like Mexico and China, which have a high number of applicants, would be much longer. While it is correct that thousands of immigrants with master's and doctorate degrees face the prospect of being forced to leave the United States every year, the bill duly proposed to eliminate an equal number of visas in the diversity visa lottery program, a program that awards visas to a mix of low- and high-skilled workers. H.R. 6429 would have created 55,000 green card visas granting permanent residence to immigrants with advanced degrees, but would have eliminated an equal number from the lottery program.

The House of Representative has been most active in its attempts to produce immigration reform legislation, but it continues to only address part of the problem—and even then, we see nothing more than a repetition of circular talking points. April 2013 saw the introduction of House Resolution 1417 by Texas Republican Congressman Michael McCaul. This bill, dubbed the Border Security Results Act of 2013, contained discursive strategies for achieving "situational awareness and operational control of the border." In what amounts to an overhaul of standard operating procedures for securing the border, the bill noted:

> Not later than 180 days after the date of the enactment of this Act, the Secretary of Homeland Security shall submit to the appropriate congressional committees a comprehensive strategy for gaining and maintaining situational awareness, and operational control of high traffic areas, by the date that is not later than two years after the date of the submission of the implementation plan required under subsection (c), and operational control along the southwest border of the United States by the date that is not later than five years after such date of submission [including] . . . an assessment of principal border security threats, including threats relating to the smuggling and trafficking of humans, weapons, and illicit drugs . . . [the] use of manned aircraft and unmanned aerial systems, including camera and sensor technology deployed on such assets [and]. . . efforts to detect and prevent terrorists and instruments of terrorism from entering the United States.[11]

From the outset, it is difficult to understand the mission of the bill against the grander backdrop of homeland security and immigration reform. It does not take careful reading to notice that while thwarting terrorists from entering the country and eliminating human, drug, and weapons smuggling are worthy goals, the bill's attention is only given to the *least* porous border. All Department of Homeland Security facts and figures confirm that although the border between the United States and Mexico is the most patrolled and militarized, crime and fraudulent crossings have declined. According to the Department of Homeland Security, "Apprehensions have dropped by 53 percent since 2008, indicating that fewer people are attempting to illegally cross the border; while the Border Patrol is better staffed than at any time in its history with more than 21,000 border agents—most of these agents at the Southwest border."[12] Moreover, "The Border Patrol is better staffed today than at any time in its 88-year history. Along the Southwest border, DHS has increased the number of boots on the ground from approximately 9,100 border patrol agents in 2001 to more than 18,500 today." Now, 100 percent of southbound rail shipments are screened for illegal weapons, drugs, and cash. The Unmanned Aircraft System (UAS) has been expanded to cover the entire southwest border, and 651 miles of fencing have been completed. Oddly enough, these facts and statistics never find their way into the stump speeches and other saber rattlings used during immigration policy advocacy.

If our attention were to shift just slightly, we would discover serious inequities in funding and resources for our *most porous* border, that being the one between the United States and Canada. While there are 18,500 border agents along the southern border, there are only 2,200 along the northern border. More alarming is that "950 miles along the Northern border from Washington to Minnesota are currently covered by unmanned aircraft, in addition to approximately 200 miles along the northern border in New York and Lake Ontario—none of which were covered prior to the creation of DHS."[13] Despite this reality, House Resolution 1417 focused its attention on the southern border, defying its stated purpose of developing "a comprehensive strategy to gain and maintain operational control of the international borders of the United States." By no means should such a measure come as any surprise. Not only did it fail to become law, but its misguided singular border focus only reaffirmed the many dimensions entangled in attempts at comprehensive immigration reform.

Just one month following this failed attempt, Texas Republican congressman Lamar Smith introduced House Resolution 1901, a bill "to amend the Immigration and Nationality Act to provide for extensions of detention of certain aliens ordered removed, and for other purposes." The bill, dubbed the Keep Our Communities Safe Act of 2013, advocated a belief that extending the detention period for those charged with fraudulent border crossing would keep our communities safe. In order to better understand the backdrop of this law, it is imperative to note the 2001 decision of *Zadvydas v. Davis* and the 2005 decision of *Clark v. Martinez*. In the *Zadvydas* case, the Supreme Court entertained the question, "Does the post-removal-period statute authorize the Attorney General to detain a removable immigrant indefinitely beyond the 90-day removal period?" In a 5-4 decision, the Court ruled that no, the post-removal statute does not "permit indefinite detention." Immigrants could be detained for deportation for more than 90 days, but for no longer than was reasonably necessary. Nonetheless, there still existed legal ambiguity pertaining to "inadmissible immigrants," that is, those who fail health screenings for communicable diseases of public health significance, have convictions of certain crimes, or have been or are currently illicit traffickers, among other factors. Given this ambiguity, *Clark v. Martinez* presented the question of whether or not "inadmissible immigrants" were protected under the *Zadvydas* decision. In a 7-2 decision, the Court ordered that immigrants, both admissible and inadmissible, cannot be detained longer than reasonably necessary for deportation. House Resolution 1901 sought to counter these rulings by legislating that the Secretary of Homeland Security "may continue to detain an alien for 90 days beyond the removal period." The underlying belief, as indicated by the bill's title, was that extending the three-month detention period to an unspecified amount of time served as a good policy toward reducing crime, despite facts and figures that belie surges in crime caused by immigrants.

As the national call for immigration reform gathers momentum, there are increasingly more problems than proposed solutions. Offered by Louisiana Republican Senator David Vitter, Senate Joint Resolution 4 was a 2013 bill aimed at amending the U.S. Constitution's definition of citizenship. The bill stated:

A person born in the United States shall not be a citizen of the United States unless—(1) at the time of the person's birth, one parent of the person is—(A) a citizen of the United States; (B) an alien lawfully admitted for permanent residence in the United States who resides in the United States; or (C) an alien performing active service in the Armed Forces of the United States; or (2) the person is naturalized in accordance with the laws of the United States.[14]

Vitter's obvious attempt to alter, or in this case end, the notion of birthright citizenship did not secure any cosponsors. House Resolution 326, a similar bill introduced in August 2013 by Georgia Republican Congressman Paul Broun Jr., touted itself as "expressing the sense of the House of Representatives that any immigration reform proposal adopted by Congress should not legalize, grant amnesty for, or confer any other legal status condoning the otherwise unlawful entry or presence in the United States of any individual."[15] These two bills represent a growing domain within immigration reform policy that seeks to alter the legal definitions and obtainment of citizenship and the rights therein.

Oddly enough, as we continue to witness discursive attempts to redefine citizenship, further militarize the southern border, extend the detention period for "inadmissible" immigrants, insert preferences for which immigrants we want and denials of those we do not, insist upon official language legislation, pass voter identification laws, and so forth, immigration reform remains a policy failure. Within this constant stream of legislation, many peculiarities exist. In light of the aforementioned policies, one House Resolution (2377), of 2013, sought to "authorize the enlistment in the Armed Forces of certain aliens who are unlawfully present in the United States and were younger than 15 years of age when they initially entered the United States, but who are otherwise qualified for enlistment . . . by reason of their honorable service [they] . . . may be lawfully admitted to the United States for permanent residence."[16] One can read this bill as being an attempt to boost enlistment numbers in the wake of declining military enrollment. Yet even so, the bill strikes an odd tone in the immigration policy debate.

Despite legislative attempts at all levels of government to enact comprehensive immigration reform, no meaningful change has yet to reach the public, perhaps because of the continual failure of Congress or the ill-advised shortcomings of many of the state-orchestrated laws. In late September 2013, the "gang of seven" legislators from the House of Representatives who took up the charge to chart out an immigration overhaul hit a snag. In a shocking announcement, two Texas Republican members (congressmen Sam Johnson and John Carter) publically resigned, citing a lack of confidence in President Obama's leadership when it came to upholding new laws while enforcing existing ones.

If we are to move forward with this debate and produce policy that actually solves existing problems, collaboration and compromise are essential. First, we must cease to promote official language laws as steps toward immigration reform, as there exists no evidence to suggest that newcomers to America do not already understand the pivotal role English plays in our society. In fact, all polling data reveals quite the opposite. Even more important is a matter of practicality. No official language policies seek to provide resources for those seeking to learn English, leaving one to question their actual purpose. Next, housing ordinances do very little, if anything, to reform immigration laws. Revisions to local ordinances that require prospective tenants to provide documentation verifying their immigration status invite racial profiling, as the Supreme Court warned would happen in its landmark ruling on Arizona's Senate Bill 10, *Arizona v. United States*. From there, voter identification laws, while argued to provide an added layer of protection against fraudulent voters, only disenfranchise the poor. Upon examination of state-provided evidence, we see that these efforts have a net success rate of 2 percent or less. These tensions represent just some of the troubles involved in implementing comprehensive immigration reform. Our next section provides emerging policy recommendations that seek to move beyond our current state of affairs.

Policy Recommendations

As the political saga over immigration reform continues, we constantly forget the many social, cultural, and economic benefits immigrants bring to our country. Often, our debates are beholden to demonizing and contestable claims; as a result, our collective perceptions of reality become blurred amidst a quickly flowing stream of inaccuracies. Comprehensive immigration reform must acknowledge and apply a multidimensional approach that is accountable to facts, not paranoia. Said best by former President George W. Bush, our current approach to immigration reform simply does not work. In his words:

> America can be a lawful society and a welcoming society at the same time. We can uphold our traditions of assimilating immigrants and honoring our heritage as a nation built on the rule of law. But we have a problem. The laws governing the immigration system aren't working. The system is broken. We're now in an important debate in reforming those laws. And that's good. I don't intend to get involved in the politics or the specifics of policy. But I do hope there is a positive resolution to the debate, and I hope during the debate that we keep a benevolent spirit in mind and we understand the contributions that immigrants make to our country.[17]

While President Bush was unable to enact comprehensive immigration reform during his eight years in office, his observation about current trends in state and local laws provides sound advice for lawmakers on both sides of the aisle, especially Republican lawmakers who need to win the votes of Latino constituents in order to sustain their political viability. If nothing else, the observations made by President Bush are beholden to no partisan ideology. His concerns are more practical than political.

Because immigration reform exceeds just issues pertaining to the southern border, a comprehensive approach must have several features. These include but are not limited to: (1) a method that reflects actual statistics on crime, border crossings, and worker exploitation; (2) a path to citizenship that understands that forcibly removing all 12 million undocumented immigrants is logistically impossible; and (3) a stronger border patrol presence between the United States and Canada. There exist many policy recommendations from lawmakers, pundits, think tanks, and other organizations. Here we offer our own series of possible solutions.

Recommendation One: Restore Integrity to Our Borders

Our current patchwork state of border control is inadequate and impractical. Any border security attempt that does not seek to strengthen our U.S. and Canada crossing points is ultimately flawed. We must understand the differences in terrain between our northern and southern borders. Restoring integrity to our borders must comprise of installing new security measures and technologies in specified locations along the border, including specific numbers of surveillance towers, camera systems, ground sensors, radiation detectors, mobile surveillance systems, airborne radar systems, helicopters, and ships. While some recommendations have called for roughly doubling the number of border patrol agents stationed along the U.S.-Mexico border, we have found no evidence to support this so-called need.

Recommendation Two: Resolve the Undocumented Problem

As mentioned previously, with an estimated 12 million undocumented people in the United States, it is unrealistic on multiple levels to advocate mass deportation, as it is logistically and economically unfeasible. A pathway to citizenship is more realistic. Given the multiplicity of options, we recommend a combination of available possibilities from both Democrats and Republicans. Specifically, we support the following elements in a pathway to citizenship:

(1) Immigrants who do not have a felony conviction or three or more misdemeanors are eligible for citizenship.

(2) Immigrants who have been deported for noncriminal reasons can apply to reenter on provisional status if they have a spouse or child who is a U.S. citizen or permanent resident, or if they were brought to the United States as a child.

(3) People brought to the country as youths can get green cards in five years and citizenship immediately thereafter.

(4) Immigrants pay a $500 fine during the first five years when seeking citizenship.

(5) Resources for learning English, should they be needed, are provided.

(6) Immigrants in provisional legal status can work and travel in the United States and can only become eligible for federal and public benefits if employed.

(7) After five years in provisional status, immigrants can seek a green card and lawful permanent resident status if they are current on their taxes, pay a $1,000 fine, have maintained continuous physical presence in the United States, meet work requirements, and demonstrate a command of English.

Recommendation Three: Manual Labor Workers

Many debates and falsehoods circulate around "low-skilled" workers, particularly those who ensure the availability of various crops and other agricultural commodities for mass consumption. Regardless of whether these discussions pertain to California or upstate New York, labor continues to be a controversial issue. To begin resolving this multilayered issue, we believe the recommendations from the U.S. Senate's version of immigration reform are most fitting. Specifically, the introduction of a new W visa would allow up to 200,000 low-skilled workers a year in the country for jobs in construction, long-term care, hospitality, and other industries. Additionally, a new agricultural worker visa program would be established to replace the existing program. Undocumented agriculture workers who have worked in the industry for at least two years could qualify in another five years for green cards if they stay in the industry.

Recommendation Four: "High-Skilled" Workers

As previously discussed, any immigration reform bill pertaining to the demands of the U.S. labor force that does not address both "high-" and "low-" skilled workers is incomplete. Specifically, we believe that the cap on the H-1B visa program for high-skilled workers should be immediately raised from 65,000 visas a year to 110,000 a year, with 25,000 more set aside for people with advanced degrees in science, technology, engineering, or math from U.S. schools. The cap could go as high as 180,000 a year, depending on demand. New protections would crack down on companies that use H-1B visas to train workers in the United States only to send them back overseas. A new merit visa, for a maximum of 250,000 people a year, would award points to prospective immigrants based on their education, employment, length of residence in the United States, and other considerations. Those with the most points would earn visas. To strategically streamline this progress with U.S. interests in mind, we advise eliminating the government's Diversity Visa Lottery Program, which randomly awards 55,000 visas to immigrants from countries with historically low rates of immigration to the United States. Without this program, more visas could be awarded for employment and merit ties.

Recommendation Five: Employment Verification

In order to close loopholes and correct past problems related to employment, we believe that within four years of implementation, all employers should use E-Verify, a program to verify electronically workers' legal status. As part of that, noncitizens would be required to show photo ID that must match a photo in the E-Verify system.

Concluding Thoughts

We took an expansive view of immigration policy in this book. Any serious conversation pertaining to comprehensive immigration reform must account for and acknowledge the widening reach of immigration policies. According to the Center for American Progress, "The U.S. Border Patrol's annual budget has increased by more than 700 percent since 1992, and the number of border patrol agents has increased nearly 400 percent. . . . The number of undocumented immigrants in the United States has tripled to approximately 12 million during that same time period."[18] Militarizing the southern border has obviously failed as a singular immigration control strategy. Despite this reality, we remain in disarray when it comes to implementing meaningful policy. Throughout this book, we sought to illustrate the discursive array that immigration reform has embodied. Of particular interest to us were policy actions occurring at the state, local, and federal levels, as those most accurately reflect the nationwide debate over the absorption and incorporation of our nation's newcomers.

With gridlocks in both chambers of Congress, we expect the trend of state-mandated efforts to continue. Unfortunately, as the previous chapters have discussed, many of the proposed laws solve absolutely nothing, and instead only produce debates that are guided by fear rather than facts. As seen throughout American history, immigration reform does not materialize overnight. In our attempt to shed light on these debates and the policy shortcomings they produce, we welcome meaningful reform that rejects the diminishment of our understanding of the issues in an "us" vs. "them" dichotomy and instead embraces a more holistic approach.

Notes

1. Jacob Vigdor. "Measuring Immigrant Assimilation in Post-Recession America," Manhattan Institute for Policy Research, March 2013. Accessed June 12, 2013. http://www.manhattan-institute.org/html/cr_76.htm#.UjR-JKXBPGB.

2. Ibid.

3. "Second-Generation Americans: A Portrait of the Adult Children of Immigrants," Pew Research, February 7, 2013. Accessed September 15, 2013. http://www.pewsocialtrends.org/2013/02/07/second-generation-americans/.

4. Jason Riley, "Immigrants and Crime," *Wall Street Journal*, July 26, 2013. Accessed September 15, 2013. http://online.wsj.com/article/SB10001424127887324564704578629804202239328.html.

5. "Take Our Jobs!" United Farm Workers. Accessed September 15, 2013. http://www.ufw.org/toj_play/TOJNEW_12_JAL.html.

6. Aaron Smith, "Farm Workers: Take Our Jobs, Please!" *CNN Money*, July 7, 2010. Accessed September 15, 2013. http://money.cnn.com/2010/07/07/news/economy/farm_worker_jobs/index.htm.

7. Raul Hinojosa Ojeda and Sherman Robinson, "Adding It Up: Accurately Gauging the Economic Impact of Immigration Reform," Immigration Policy Center, May 2013. Accessed June 14, 2013. http://www.immigrationpolicy.org/just-facts/adding-it-accurately-gauging-economic-impact-immigration-reform.

8. Joanna Dreby, "How Today's Immigration Enforcement Policies Impact Children, Families, and Communities: A View from the Ground," Center for American Progress, August 2012. Accessed September 16, 2013. http://www.americanprogress.org/wp-content/uploads/2012/08/DrebyImmigrationFamiliesFINAL.pdf.

9. House Resolution 6429, 112th Congress, 2012.

10. Ibid.

11. House Resolution 1417, 113th Congress, 2013.

12. "Border Security Overview," Department of Homeland Security. Accessed June 14, 2013. http://www.dhs.gov/border-security-overview.

13. "Border Security Results," Department of Homeland Security. Accessed June 14, 2013. http://www.dhs.gov/border-security-results

14. Senate Joint Resolution 4, 113th Congress, 2013.

15. House Resolution 326, 113th Congress, 2013.

16. Ibid.

17. Peter Baker, "Obama and Bush Promote Benefits of Immigration," *New York Times,* July 10, 2013. Accessed September 16, 2013. http://thecaucus.blogs.nytimes.com/2013/07/10/obama-and-bush-promote-benefits-of-immigration/?_r=2.

18. Marshall Fitz and Angela Kelley, "Principles for Immigration Reform: Guidelines for Fixing Our Broken Immigration System." Center for American Progress, December 2009. Accessed September 25, 2013. http://www.americanprogress.org/wp-content/uploads/issues/2009/12/pdf/immigrationreform.pdf.

Epilogue:
Since *Shelby County v. Holder*

Just hours after the landmark 5-4 ruling invalidating Section 4 of the Voting Rights Act, controversy was already taking place. While individuals and news outlets dedicated incalculable amounts of chatter to the landmark decision, lawmakers in some states were preparing to introduce what previously would have been unconstitutional measures. Within two hours of the Supreme Court's decision, Greg Abbott, attorney general for the state of Texas, announced that the voter identification law that had been blocked in 2012 by the Justice Department would go into effect immediately. Additionally, the state's once-invalidated redistricting map, which the Court famously argued was a result of "substantial surgery" (and noted that its gerrymandering was done to predominantly black districts, cutting off representatives' offices from their strongest fundraising bases), was to become law immediately.

In North Carolina, voter identification legislation is back in play, a key General Assembly leader remarked after the *Shelby* decision. A bill requiring voters to present one of several forms of state-issued photo identification, starting in 2016, cleared the North Carolina House earlier in 2013, although it has since been sitting in the Senate Rules Committee awaiting a ruling in the *Shelby* case. At least as of right now, North Carolina and other states can enact such laws because the formula previously used to determine preclearance is no longer constitutional. With this green light from the Court, what once were invalidated voter identification measures are being born anew.

In Jackson, Mississippi, voters could be required to present photo identification at the polls as early as the June 2014 federal primaries.

Secretary of State Delbert Hosemann remarked after the U.S. Supreme Court ruling that certain state and local governments no longer need federal approval to change their election laws or procedures. As such legislative moments gain traction, there still remains hope for dissenters of the *Shelby* decision. Section 3 of the Voting Rights Act provides a mechanism by which jurisdictions could be brought back under preclearance. Under Section 3, a federal court may place a jurisdiction under preclearance if, during the course of a Voting Rights Act lawsuit, it determines that "violations of the fourteenth or fifteenth amendment justifying equitable relief have occurred within the territory of such State or political subdivision." However, Section 3's language is quite vague, essentially explaining that if an uncovered jurisdiction is found to be a "pocket" of discrimination, it may be required to seek preclearance. Again, unfortunately for dissenters, Section 3 was not used prior to 1975. Since then, it has bailed out two states, six counties, and one city; for this very reason, there exist very few precedents governing its use.

Bibliography

Books

Alba, Richard and Victor Nee. *Remaking the American Mainstream: Assimilation and Contemporary Immigration.* Cambridge, MA: Harvard University Press, 2003.

Baron, Dennis. *The English-Only Question: An Official Language for Americans?* New Haven, CT: Yale University Press, 1990.

Bauman, Zygmunt. *Liquid Times: Living in an Age of Uncertainty.* New York: Polity, 2007.

Berman, David. *Arizona Politics and Government: The Quest for Autonomy, Democracy and Development.* Lincoln: University of Nebraska Press, 1998.

Biggers, Jeff. *State Out of the Union: Arizona and the Final Showdown Over the American Dream.* New York: Nation Books, 2012.

Bohm, David. *Thought As A System.* New York: Routledge, 1994.

Borman, Ernest. *Force of Fantasy: Restoring the American Dream.* Carbondale: Southern Illinois University Press, 2001.

Buchanan, Patrick. *Day of Reckoning: How Hubris, Ideology, and Greed are Tearing America Apart.* New York: St. Martin's Press, 2007.

Buchanan, Patrick. *The Death of the West: How Dying Populations and Immigrant Invasions Imperil Our Country and Civilization.* New York: St. Martin's Press, 2002.

Chavez, Leo. *The Latino Threat: Constructing Immigrants, Citizens, and the Nation.* Redwood City, CA: Stanford University Press, 2008.

Chua, Amy. *World on Fire: How Exporting Free Market Democracy Breeds Ethnic Hatred and Global Instability.* New York: Doubleday, 2003.

Collins, Gail. *As Texas Goes . . . : How the Lone Star State Hijacked the American Agenda.* New York: W.W. Norton & Company, 2012.

Crawford, James. *Bilingual Education: History, Politics, Theory, and Practice.* Los Angeles: Bilingual Education Services, Inc., 1995.

Daniel, Ben. *Neighbor: Christian Encounters With "Illegal" Immigration.* Louisville, KY: John Knox Press, 2010.

Dolan, Julie and David Rosenbloom. *Representative Bureaucracy: Classical Readings and Continuing Controversies.* Amonk, NY: ME Sharpe, 2003.

Drinnon, Richard. *Facing West: The Metaphysics of Indian-Hating and Empire-Building.* Minneapolis: University of Minnesota Press, 1980.

Edelman, Murray. *Constructing the Political Spectacle.* Chicago: University of Chicago Press, 1988.

Hasen, Richard. *The Fraudulent Fraud Squad: Understanding the Battle over Voter ID: A Sneak Preview from the Voting Wars, from Florida 2000 to the Next Election Meltdown.* New Haven, CT: Yale University Press, 2012.

Hofstadter, Richard. *The Paranoid Style in American Politics and Other Essays.* Cambridge: Harvard University Press, 1965.

Huckabee, Michael. *A Simple Government.* New York: Sentinel, 2011.

Huntington, Samuel. *Who Are We? The Challenges to America's National Identity.* New York: Simon & Schuster, 2004.

Kanellos, Nicolas and Helvetia Martell. *Hispanic Periodicals in the United States, Origins to 1960: A Brief History and Comprehensive Bibliography.* Houston: Arte Publico Press, 2000.

Kinney, James. *Amalgamation! Race, Sex and Rhetoric in the Nineteenth-Century American Novel.* Westport, CT: Greenwood Press, 1985.

Koulish, Robert. *Immigration and American Democracy.* New York: Routledge, 2010.

Lemire, Elise. *Miscegenation: Making Race in America.* Philadelphia: University of Pennsylvania Press, 2002.

Lieberman, Robert. *Shaping Race Policy: The United States in Comparative Perspective.* Princeton, NJ: Princeton University Press, 2005.

Lovejoy, Arthur. *The Great Chain of Being: A Study of the History of an Idea.* New York: Harper & Brothers, 1936.

Macedo, Donaldo. *Literacies of Power: What Americans Are Not Allowed to Know.* Boulder, CO: Westview Press, 1994.

MacNeil, Robert and William Cran. *Do You Speak American?* New York: Random House, 2007.

Marshall, David and Gerda Bikales, *The Question of an Official Language: Language Rights and the English Language Amendment.* Ann Arbor: University of Michigan Press, 1986.

May, Gary. *Toward Justice: The Voting Rights Act and the Transformation of American Democracy.* New York: Basic Books, 2013.

Meier, Kenneth J. and Joseph Stewart. *The Politics of Hispanic Education: Un Paso Pa'lante y Dos Pa 'Tras.* Albany: State University of New York Press, 1991.

Mosher, Frederick. *Democracy and the Public Service.* New York: Oxford University Press, 1968.

Nevins, Joseph. *Operation Gatekeeper: The Rise of the "Illegal Alien" and the Making of the U.S.-Mexico Boundary.* New York: Routledge, 2002.

Palmer, Vernon Valentine, ed. *Mixed Jurisdictions Worldwide: The Third Legal Family.* Cambridge: Cambridge University Press, 2012.

Piatt, Bill. *Only English? Law & Language Policy in the United States.* Albuquerque: University of New Mexico Press, 1990.

Peterson, Paul. *No Child Left Behind? The Politics and Practice of Accountability.* Washington, D.C.: Brookings Institute Press, 2003.

Rifkin, Jeremy. *The End of Work.* New York: Tarcher/Putnam Books, 1995.

Rodriguez, Amardo. *Diversity: Mestizos, Latinos and the Promise of Possibilities.* Mountain View, CA: Floricanto Press, 2007.

Rodriguez, Amardo. *Revisioning Diversity in Communication Studies.* Leicester, UK: Troubador Publishing, 2010.

Roosevelt, Theodore. *Works, vol. XXIV.* New York: Charles Scribner's Sons, 1926. San Miguel Jr., Guadalupe. *Contested Policy: The Rise and Fall of Federal Bilingual Education in the United States, 1960-2001.* Denton: University of North Texas, 2004.

Santa Ana, Otto and Celeste González de Bustamante, eds. *Arizona Firestorm: Global Immigration Realities, National Media, and Provincial Politics.* Lanham, MD: Rowman and Littlefield Publishers, 2012.

Schiappa, Edward. *Defining Reality: Definitions and the Politics of Meaning.* Carbondale: Southern Illinois University Press, 2003.

Schrag, Peter. *Not Fit for our Society: Nativism and Immigration.* Berkeley: University of California Press, 2010.

Skocpol, Theda and Lawrence Jacobs. eds. *Reaching for a New Deal: Ambitious Governance, Economic Meltdown, and Polarized Politics in Obama's First Two Years.* New York: Russell Sage, 2011.

Sollors, Werner. *Interracialism: Black and White Intermarriage in American History, Literature and Law*. Oxford, UK: Oxford University Press, 2000.

Stiglitz, Joseph. *Free Fall: America, Free Markets, and the Sinking of the World Economy*. New York: W.W. Norton, 2010.

Streb, Matthew, ed. *Law and Election Politics: The Rules of the Game*. New York: Routledge, 2013.

Sunstein, Cass. *Going to Extremes: How Like Minds Unite and Divide*. New York: Oxford University Press, 2009.

Vicino, Thomas. *Suburban Crossroads: The Fight for Local Control of Immigration Policy*. Lanham, MD: Rowman and Littlefield, 2012.

Wilkins, David and Heidi Stark. *American Indian Politics and the American Political System*. Lanham, MD: Rowman and Littlefield, 2010.

Zarefsky, David. *President Johnson's War On Poverty: Rhetoric and History*. Tuscaloosa: University of Alabama Press, 2005.

Articles and Chapters

Alvins, Alfred. "Anti-Miscegenation Laws and the Fourteenth Amendment: The Original Intent." *Virginia Law Review* 52, no. 7 (1966): 1224–1255.

Ash, Arlene and John Lamperti. "Elections 2012: Suppressing Fraud or Suppressing the Vote?" *Statistics, Politics and Policy* 4, no. 1 (2013): 14–28.

Barreto, Matt, Sylvia Manzano, Ricardo Ramirez, and Kathy Rim. "Mobilization, Participation, and Solidaridad: Latino Participation in the 2006 Immigration Protest Rallies." *Urban Affairs Review* 44, no. 5 (2009): 736–764.

Brown, Donathan L. "Legislating Language In the Name of National Unity: An Oklahoma Story." *International Journal of Discrimination and the Law* 12, no. 3 (2013): 4–17.

Brown, Donathan L. "When English is not Enough: *Escamilla v. Cuello*." *Harvard Journal of Hispanic Policy* 25, no. 1 (2013): 49–68.

Brown, Donathan L. "An Invitation to Profile: *Arizona v. United States*." *International Journal of Discrimination and the Law* 12, no. 2 (2012): 117–127.

Brown, Donathan L. "In Defense of Unity & English-Only: On the Early Political Battles to 'Unite' the Nation." *Communication Law Review* 11, no. 1 (2011):15–28.

Cisneros, David. "Contaminated Communities: The Metaphor of Immigrant as Pollutant in Media Representations of Immigration." *Rhetoric & Public Affairs* 11, no. 4 (2008): 569–602.

Edwards, James. "A Biblical Perspective on Immigration Policy." In *Debating Immigration,* edited by Carol M. Swain, 46–64. New York: Cambridge University Press, 2007.

González, Josué M. and Ha Lam, "The *Lau v. Nichols* Supreme Court Decision." In *Latino Education in the U.S.,* edited by Lourdes Diaz Soto, 283–295. Lanham, MD: Rowman & Littlefield Education, 2007.

Guzman, Daniel. "There is No Shelter Here: Anti-Immigration Ordinances and Comprehensive Reform." *Cornell Journal of Law and Public Policy.* 20 (2010): 399–439.

Hochschild, Jennifer. "You Win Some, You Lose Some: Explaining the Pattern of Success and Failure in the Second Reconstruction." In *Taking Stock: American Government in the Twentieth Century*, edited by Morton Keller and R. Shep Melnick, 219–258. New York: Cambridge University Press, 1999.

Huddy, Leonie. "From Social to Political Identity: A Critical Examination of Social Identity Theory." *Political Psychology* 22, no. 1 (2001): 127–156.

Katz, Ellen. "South Carolina's Evolutionary Process." *Columbia Law Review* 113, no. 1 (2013). 55–65.

King, Desmond and Rogers Smith. "Strange Bedfellows? Polarized Politics? The Quest for Racial Equity in Contemporary America." *Political Research Quarterly* 61, no. 4 (2008): 686–703.

Macedo, Stephen. "The Moral Dilemma of U.S. Immigration Policy." In *Debating Immigration* edited by Carol M. Swain, 63–80. New York: Cambridge University Press, 2007.

Meier, Kenneth J. "Latinos and Representative Bureaucracy: Testing the Thompson and Henderson Hypotheses." *Journal of Public Administration Research and Theory* 3, no. 4 (1993): 393–414.

Meier, Kenneth J. "Representative Bureaucracy: A Theoretical and Empirical Exposition." In *Research in Public Administration, Volume II*, edited by James Perry, 1–36. San Francisco: Jossey-Bass, 1993.

Meier, Kenneth J. and Daniel P. Hawes. "Ethnic Conflict in France: A Case of Representative Bureaucracy?" *American Review of Public Administration* 4 (2008): 1–26.

Moran, Rachel. "Bilingual Education as a Status Conflict." *California Law Review* 75 (1987): 321–362.

Myers, Laura. "Angle, Reid Play Endgame." *Las Vegas Review-Journal*, October 26, 2010.

Ovanda, Carlos. "Bilingual Education in the United States: Historical Development and Current Issues." *Bilingual Research Journal* 27, no.1 (2003): 1–24.

Petonito, Gina. "Racial Discourse and Enemy Construction: Justifying the Internment 'Solution' to the 'Japanese Problem' During World War II." In *Social Conflicts and Collective Identities*, edited by P. Coy and L. Woehrle, eds, 19–40. Latham, MD: Rowman & Littlefield, 2000.

Reibach, Amy. "The Power Behind the Promise: Enforcing No Child Left Behind to Improve Education." *Boston College Law Review* 45 (2004): 667–704.

Ross, William. "A Judicial Janus: *Meyer v. Nebraska* in Historical Perspective." *University of Cincinnati Law Review* 57 (1988): 1–25.

Tran, Van. "English Gain vs. Social Loss? Language Assimilation among Second-Generation Latinos in Young Adulthood." *Social Forces* 89, no. 1 (2010): 257–284.

Court Cases

Arizona v. Inter Tribal Council of Arizona, Inc, 133 S.Ct. 476 (2012).

Cacho et al v. Gusman, 2:11-cv-00225 (2011).

Escamilla v. Cuello, CV-12-0039 (2012).

Frye v. United States, 293 F. 1013, 1014 (App. D.C. Dec. 03, 1923).

Galarza v. Szalczyk et al., 5:10-cv-06815 (2012).

Lau v. Nichols, 414 U.S. 563 (1974).

Lozano v City of Hazleton, No. 07-3531 (2010).

Northwest Austin Municipal Utility District No. 1 v. Holder, No. 08-322 (2009).

Quezada v. Mink, No. 10-0879 (2010).

Shelby County v. Holder, 570 U.S. (2013).

South Carolina v. Katzenbach, 383 U. S. 301, 309 (1966).

Texas v. Holder, No. 12-cv-128, 2012 WL 3743676, (D.D.C. Aug. 30, 2012).

United States Ex. Rel. Negron v. State of New York, 434 F.2d 386 (1970).

Newspapers

Dinan, Stephen. "GOP Votes to Lift Deportation Limits; Signals Trouble for Broader Reform Bill." *Washington Times* (June 7, 2013): 3.

Dinan, Stephen and Jerry Seper. [No Title.] *Washington Times* (November 3, 2007): A01.

Donohue, Thomas. "Immigrants Can Offset Declining Population, Boost Workforce." *Post-Standard* (June 9, 2013): E-4.

Dunham, Richard. "Can Perry Cool Off Red-Hot Issue?" *Houston Chronicle* (October 18, 2011).

Finnegan, Michael and Maeve Reston. "GOP Spars Over Defense: Bachmann Calls Perry's Stance on Pakistan 'Naïve.'" *Baltimore Sun* (November 23, 2011).

Fitzgerald, Thomas. "Perry Takes Heat in Debate Over His Immigration Policies." *Philadelphia Inquirer* (September 23, 2011).

"The GOP's Immigration Fumble." *Wall Street Journal* (August 1, 2002).

Hoebrock, Bruce. "English on the Ballot as the State's Official Language." *Tulsa World* (September 19, 2010): A19.

Holley, Joe. "NAACP Convention; Holder Likens Voter ID Law to Poll Tax." *Houston Chronicle* (July 11, 2012): 1.

Mandel, Eric. "Controversy Fails to Faze 'America's Toughest Sheriff.'" *Telegraph Herald* (September 17, 2011).

March, William and Christian M. Wade. "Rivals Assail Perry in GOP Debate." *Tampa Tribune* (September 13, 2011).

Martin, Gary. "Voter ID Law; Foes Say Bill Was Rushed by GOP." *San Antonio Express News* (July 11, 2012): 1A.

Mehta, Seema. "Bachmann Draws Hard Line on U.S. Mexico Border." *Baltimore Sun* (October 16, 2011).

McNutt, Michael. "Two Language Measures Move Forward in the House." *The Oklahoman* (February 19, 2009): 12A.

"Perry gets GOP flak over Immigration." *The Dallas Morning News* (September 24, 2011).

"Romney Automated Calls Assail Perry in Iowa." *The Capital* (November 5, 2011).

Shear, Michael. "Seeing Citizenship Path Near, Activists Push Obama to Slow Deportations." *New York Times* (February 23, 2013): 12.

State, Local and Federal Laws

14th Amendment, United States Constitution, 1787.

42 U. S. C. §1973.

107 Neb. 657 (1919).

152 Cong. Rec. S8781.

262 U.S. 390 (1923).

679 F. 3d, at 866.

Ariz. Rev. Stat. Ann. §16-166(F).

Arizona House Bill 2283, 2013.

Arizona Senate Bill 1070 (2010).

Article 28, Section I, Arizona Constitution.

Beason-Hammon Alabama Taxpayer & Citizen Protection Act (Act 2011-535).

Carroll County, Maryland Ordinance 2013-01, 2013.

Equal Educational Opportunity Act, 20 USC Sec. 1703.

House Resolution 6429 (2012).

House Resolution 326 (2013).

House Resolution 1417 (2013).

House Resolution 2377 (2013).

House Resolution 5855 (2013).

Illegal Immigration Relief Act of San Bernardino, CA, 2006.

New York Senate Bill 1902, 2013.

Oklahoma House Bill 1804. (2007).

Oklahoma State Question 751, the English is the Official Language of Oklahoma Act, (2010).

Ordinance No. 2006-38 R.

Pennsylvania House Bill 361. (2011).

Secure Fence Act of 2006 (Pub.L. 109-367).

Senate Joint Resolution 4 (2013).

Texas Senate Bill 14, 2011.

United States Congress, Border Protection, Antiterrorism, and Illegal Immigration Control Act of 2005. 109TH Congress, 1st Session, December 6, 2005.

United States Congress, Comprehensive Immigration Reform Act of 2006, 109th Congress, 1st Session, April 7, 2006.

United States Congress, Elementary and Secondary Education Amendments of 1967 Public Law 90-247; 81 Stat. 783 [H.R. 7819], 90th Congress, 1st Session (January 2, 1968).

United States Congress, English Language Acquisition, Language Enhancement, and Academic Achievement Act. Public Law 107-110, 107th Congress, 1st Session, January 8, 2002.

United States Congress, The Hawkins/Stafford Elementary and Secondary School Improvement Amendments. Public Law 100-297 [H.R. 1755], 96th Congress, 1st Session, April 28, 1988.

Government Documents

Bilingual Education Programs: Hearings Before the General Subcommittee on Education 90-1 on H.R. 9840, H.R. 10224 (June 28, 29 1967).

"English Use Among Hispanics in the United States." Pew Hispanic Center, 2007.

Taylor, Paul, Mark Hugo Lopez, Jessica Hamar Martinez and Gabriel Velasco, "When Labels Don't Fit: Hispanics and Their Views of Identity." Pew Hispanic Center, 2012.

U.S. Congress, Senate, Congressional Record, 61st Cong., 2d Sess. (1910), p. 109.

United States Department of Health, Education, and Welfare, DHEW Memo Regarding Language Minority Children (Washington, D.C.: Federal Registry).

Online Publications

Archibold, Randal. "On Border Violence, Truth Pales Compared to Ideas." *New York Times,* June 19, 2010. Accessed June 2, 2013. http://www.nytimes.com/2010/06/20/us/20crime.html?pagewanted=all&_r=0.

Baker, Peter. "Obama and Bush Promote Benefits of Immigration." *New York Times,* July 10, 2013. Accessed September 16, 2013. http://thecaucus.blogs.nytimes.com/2013/07/10/obama-and-bush-promote-benefits-of-immigration/?_r=2.

"Bipartisan Framework for Comprehensive Immigration Reform." Accessed June 12, 2013. http://s3.documentcloud.org/documents/562528/reform0128principlessenatefinal.pdf.

Brewer, Janice K. "Statement by Governor Jan Brewer." April 23, 2010. Accessed June 2, 2013. http://azgovernor.gov/dms/upload/PR_042310_StatementByGovernorOnSB1070.pdf.

Brooks, David. "The Easy Problem." *New York Times*, January 31, 2013. Accessed June 14, 2013. http://www.nytimes.com/2013/02/01/opinion/brooks-the-easy-problem.html.

"Death Toll Continues to Climb On US/Mexico Border." *Associated Press*, April 9, 2009. Accessed June 13, 2013. http://mexicomonitor.blogspot.com/2009/04/death-toll-continues-to-rise-on.html.

Dreby, Joanna. "How Today's Immigration Enforcement Policies Impact Children, Families, and Communities: A View from the Ground." Center for American Progress, August 2012. Accessed September 16, 2013.

http://www.americanprogress.org/wp-content/uploads/2012/08/Dreby
ImmigrationFamiliesFINAL.pdf.

"The Economic Impact of S. 744, the Border Security, Economic Opportunity, and Immigration Modernization Act." Congressional Budget Office, June 18, 2013. Accessed June 14, 2013. http://cbo.gov/
publication/44346.

Esbenshade, Jill. "Division and Dislocation: Regulating Immigration
Through Local Housing Ordinances." Immigration Policy Center
(2007). Accessed March 2, 2012. http://www.immigrationpolicy.org/
special-reports/division-and-dislocation-regulating-immigration
-through-local-housing-ordinances.

Fitz, Marshall and Angela Kelley, "Principles for Immigration Reform:
Guidelines for Fixing Our Broken Immigration System." Center for
American Progress (2009). Accessed September 25, 2013. http://
www.americanprogress.org/wp-content/uploads/issues/2009/12/pdf/
immigrationreform.pdf.

Fukuyama, Francis. "Identity and Migration." *Prospect Magazine*
Vol. 131, No.1, February 25, 2007. Accessed June 13, 2013. http://
www.prospectmagazine.co.uk/magazine/identity-migration-multi
culturalism-francis-fukuyama/#.Ug0Gx6zDKzk.

Gaskins, Keesha and Sundeep Iyer, "The Challenge of Obtaining Voter
Identification." Brenan Center for Justice at New York University
School of Law (2012). Accessed June 15, 2013. http://www.brennan
center.org/sites/default/files/legacy/Democracy/VRE/Challenge
_of_Obtaining_Voter_ID.pdf.

Hanna, Colin. "Border Fence Part of Larger Solution." *US News*, October
25, 2011. Accessed June 12, 2013. http://www.usnews.com/debate
-club/should-the-united-states-build-a-fence-on-its-southern-border/
border-fence-part-of-larger-solution.

Hannity, Sean. "Exclusive! Rep. John Culberson." *Fox News*, November
21, 2005. Accessed June 13, 2013. http://www.foxnews.com/on-air/
hannity/2005/11/21/exclusive-rep-john-culberson#ixzz2V8i2jdYW.

Hazleton, P.A. "Anti-Immigrant Law Is Unconstitutional, Federal Appeals
Court Rules." American Civil Liberties Union, September 9, 2010.
Accessed June 4, 2013. http://www.aclu.org/immigrants-rights/hazleton
-pa-anti-immigrant-law-unconstitutional-federal-appeals-court-rules.

"Humanitarian Crisis: Migrant Deaths at the US/Mexico Border." *ACLU/
Mexico's National Commission of Human Rights*, October 1, 2009.

Accessed June 13, 2013. http://www.aclu.org/files/pdfs/immigrants/ humanitariancrisisreport.pdf.

Jackson, Kent. "Court Tosses Ruling Against Hazleton Immigration Law." *Citizens Voice*, June 7, 2011. Accessed June 2, 2013. http://citizens voice.com/news/court-tosses-ruling-gainst-hazleton-immigration-law -1.1158009.

Kim, Mallie. "After 9/11, Immigration Became About Homeland Security." *US News*, September 8, 2011. Accessed June 13, 2013. http:// www.usnews.com/news/articles/2011/09/08/after-911-immigration -became-about-homeland-security-attacks-shifted-the-conversation -heavily-toward-terrorism-and-enforcement.

Klein, Ezra. "The 5 Most Important Sentences in the Senate's Immigration Plan." *Washington Post*, January 28, 2013. Accessed June 12, 2013. http://www.washingtonpost.com/blogs/wonkblog/wp/2013/01/28/ the-5-most-important-sentences-in-the-senates-immigration-plan/.

Lakoff, George and Sam Ferguson. "The Framing of Immigration." Rockridge Institute (2006). Accessed June 14, 2013. http://economicrefugee .wordpress.com/what-does-economic-refugee-mean.

"Legislative Update: Texas House Passes Sanctuary Cities Bill." Republican Party of Texas. Accessed June 12, 2013. http://www.texasgop.org/ posts/153-legislative-update-texas-house-passes-sanctuary-cities-bill.

Lopez, Ricardo. "Arizona Supreme Court Bars Candidate With Limited English." *Los Angeles Times*, February 8, 2012. Accessed April 14, 2012. http://articles.latimes.com/2012/feb/08/nation/la-na-san-luis -english-20120208.

McKinley, Jesse. "Immigration Protection Rules Draw Fire." *New York Times*, November 12, 2006. Accessed June 11, 2013. http://www .nytimes.com/2006/11/12/us/12sanctuary.html?_r=0.

Mora, Edwin. "House Bill Seeks to Deny 'Sanctuary Cities' Immigration Enforcement Funds." *CNS News*, May 14, 2012. Accessed June 10, 2013. http://cnsnews.com/news/article/house-bill-seeks-deny -sanctuary-cities-immigration-enforcement-funds#sthash.TTWsp KZY.dpuf.

Murphy, Douglas. "Western Values Are Better." *New English Review* (2007). Accessed June 13, 2013. http://www.newenglishreview.org/ blog_email.cfm/blog_id/10567.

Office of Chief of Police Special Order No. 40. Accessed June 14, 2013. http://keepstuff.homestead.com/Spec40orig.html.

"President Bush Signs Secure Fence Act." Accessed June 12, 2013. http://georgewbush-whitehouse.archives.gov/news/releases/2006/10/20061026.html.

Raffles, Hugh. "What To Do About Invasive Species." *New York Times*, April 9, 2011. Accessed June 12, 2013. http://www.nytimes.com/2011/04/10/opinion/l10species.html.

Riley, Jason. *Let Them In: The Case For Open Borders*. A book forum by the Nelson A. Rockefeller Institute of Government. Accessed June 14, 2013. http://www.rockinst.org/pdf/public_policy_forums/2008-06-23-public_policy_forum_let_them_in_the_case_for_open_borders_a_book_forum_presented_by_jason_l_riley.pdf.

Riley, Jason. "Immigrants and Crime." *Wall Street Journal*, July 26, 2013. Accessed September 15, 2013. http://online.wsj.com/article/SB10001424127887324564704578629804202239328.html.

Robbins, Ted. "The Man Behind Arizona's Toughest Immigrant Laws." National Public Radio, March 12, 2008. Accessed June, 2, 2013. http://www.npr.org/templates/story/story.php?storyId=88125098.

"Second-Generation Americans: A Portrait of the Adult Children of Immigrants." Pew Research, February 7, 2013. Accessed September 15, 2013. http://www.pewsocialtrends.org/2013/02/07/second-generation-americans/.

Smith, Aaron. "Farm Workers: Take Our Jobs, Please!" *CNN Money*, July 7, 2010. Accessed September 15, 2013. http://money.cnn.com/2010/07/07/news/economy/farm_worker_jobs/index.htm.

Stevenson, Richard. "Economic Nudge For An Immigration Overhaul." *New York Times*, January 30, 2013. Accessed June 14, 2013. http://thecaucus.blogs.nytimes.com/2013/01/30/immigration-shifts-could-provide-opening-for-compromise/?hp.

"Take Our Jobs!" United Farm Workers. Accessed September 15, 2013. http://www.ufw.org/toj_play/TOJNEW_12_JAL.html.

Tramonte, Lynn. "Debunking the Myth of 'Sanctuary Cities': Community Policing Policies Protect Americans." Immigration Policy Center, April 2011. Accessed June 10, 2013. http://www.immigrationpolicy.org/sites/default/files/docs/Community_Policing_Policies_Protect_American_042611_update.pdf.

Trowbridge, Alexander and Mackenzie Weinger. "Alabama Immigration Law is Working, Rep. Mo Brooks Says." *Politico*, October 6,

2011. Accessed June 9, 2013. http://www.politico.com/news/stories/1011/65351.html.

United States Census Bureau, Oklahoma Quick Facts. Accessed June 11, 2013. http://quickfacts.census.gov/qfd/states/40000.html.

"US Chamber of Commerce Statement on Immigration Reform." Accessed June 14, 2013. http://www.uschamber.com/issues/immigration/us-chamber-commerce-statement-comprehensive-immigration-reform.

Vaughan, Jessica. "A Cost-Effective Strategy to Shrink the Illegal Population." Center for Immigration Studies, April 2006. Accessed June 2, 2013. http://www.cis.org/Enforcement-IllegalPopulation.

Vigdor, Jacob. "Measuring Immigrant Assimilation in Post-Recession America." Manhattan Institute for Policy Research, March 2013. Accessed September 15, 2013. http://www.manhattan-institute.org/html/cr_76.htm#.UjiNUtKsiSq.

Weisman, Jonathan. "With Senate Vote, Congress Passes Border Fence Bill." *Washington Post*, September 30, 2006. Accessed June 12, 2003. http://www.washingtonpost.com/wp-dyn/content/article/2006/09/29/AR2006092901912.html.

Index

About the Authors

Dr. Donathan Brown is Assistant Professor in the Department of Communication Studies at Ithaca College and Editor of the *Journal of Race and Policy*. Dr. Brown conducts research at the intersection of race, rhetoric, and public policy, particularly pertaining to African Americans and Latinos. His research has appeared in the *Harvard Journal of Hispanic Policy;* the *International Journal of Discrimination and the Law;* the *Journal of Latino and Latin American Studies;* the *Journal of Race and Policy; Counterterrorism: From the Cold War to the War on Terror (Praeger); Studies In Ethnicity and Nationalism; The Routledge Companion to Race and Ethnicity; Communication Law Review; Anti-Immigration in the United States: A Historical Encyclopedia* (Greenwood): the *Widener Journal of Law, Economics & Race; Racism, Slavery and Literature* (Peter Lang); and *Domestic Policy Discourse in the New World Order* (Cambridge Scholars Publishing).

Dr. Amardo Rodriguez is the Laura J. and L. Douglas Meredith Professor in the Department of Communication and Rhetorical Studies at Syracuse University and Book Review Editor for the *Journal of Race and Policy*. Dr. Rodriguez is the author of nine books, many book chapters, and dozens of articles that have appeared in journals spanning Sociology, Communication Studies, Psychology, Higher Education, Religion, Cultural Studies, and Latino Studies.